THE CHOSEN NATION HAGGADAH

הגדה עם הנבחר

הגדה עם הנבחר

THE AUTHOR WISHES TO EXPRESS HIS GRATITUDE TO

PATRICE AND GARY FRAGIN

FOR THEIR GENEROUS HELP IN ENABLING THE

PUBLICATION OF THIS HAGGADAH.

The author wishes to express his gratitude to Patrice and Gary Fragin for their generous help in enabling the publication of this Haggadah.

THE CHOSEN NATION HAGGADAH

RABBI AVROHOM DOV KAHN

CfR PUBLICATIONS
85-35 117TH ST, JAMAICA, NY 11418

Copyright © 1994 by Avrohom Dov Kahn

Published by CFR Publications

85-35 117th Street, Jamaica, NY 11418

(718) 849-6787   Fax (718) 847-8669

The author will be happy to receive comments about this work at the above address.

All rights reserved.

No part of this book may be reproduced in any form or by any means without the prior written permission of the Publisher.

First Edition March, 1994

ISBN:
(soft cover) 0-9640293-0-8
(hard cover) 0-9640293-1-6

Design by: M. Kahn
Typography: Star Composition
Cover design: Carl S. Gluck
Printed by: Gross Bros.
Illustrated by: Jeremy Rosenstein

TABLE OF CONTENTS

ישיבה שער התורה־גרודנה
Yeshiva Shaar Hatorah-Grodno

בס"ד

Rabbi Zelik Epstein
Rosh Hayeshiva

אהרן זליג הלוי עפשטיין
ראש הישיבה

ח' חנוכה ה'תש[...]

לכבוד ידי"נ הרב ר' אברהם דב הכהן קויפמן שליט"א
לבית עולה וכל טוב.

[...]

ACKNOWLEDGEMENTS

Anyone who writes a book soon takes on the status of a debtor. The following are my creditors:

For the **initial idea** I must thank *Ed Burnbaum*, with whom, while learning the *Haggadah*, I developed many of the insights presented in my commentary, and *Dr. Ralph Silverman*, who first suggested that these insights should assume published form.

For the **writing**, a special thanks to *Dr. Abbott Katz*, through whose deft literary hand every page of this *Haggadah* passed, and thereby flourished. Thanks also go to *Shlomo Zalman Satanovsky, Rabbi Akiva Schutz*, and *Rabbi Shmuel Steinhart* zt"l.

Many are the perceptive eyes that **reviewed** the various drafts of this *Haggadah*. They include *Rabbi Sholom Spitz, Rabbi Akiva Weiner, Mrs. Ellen Wasserman, Rabbi Dr. Noam Gordon, Dr. Arnold Eisenman, Dr. Avi Greenfield, Rabbi Gidon Goldberg, Rabbi Yisroel I. Z. Herczeg, Dr. Thomas Schick, Dovid Libman, Aharon Dovid Lebovics, Elie Markin, Zevi Reichman, Shai Solomon, Zvi Weinman* and *Rabbi Uri Deblinger*.

No book can be published without the **"prodders"**, the people who cajole and harangue the faltering author until his work achieves completion. My beneficent taskmasters - the *Roshei Yeshiva* and *talmidim* of *Yeshiva Shaar HaTorah* - inspired me with their enthusiasm and collective push to see this project through. May their aspirations for this *Haggadah* be fulfilled.

It was a pleasure working with *Jeremy Rosenstein*, whose original **artwork** adorns this volume.

There are no shortage of authors who extoll the patience and encouragement of their wives, but their obligation to do so pales compared to mine. My wife *Miriam* **typeset** and **designed** the layout for the entire manuscript. In truth, she is a full partner in the creation of this work.

My heartfelt thanks go to one of the true Gedolim of our times, *HaRav HaGaon, Rav Zelik Epstein*, shlita, for his **approbation** and continuous support. May the Rosh HaYeshiva be blessed with good health and many more years of Torah leadership to *K'lal Yisroel*.

Nearly a decade ago, God granted me the good fortune to meet *Gary* and *Patrice Fragin.* Since that first encounter, our friendship has grown and brought us ever closer.

After reading the *Haggadah*, the Fragins were excited about its potential impact on the hearts and minds of English-speaking Jewry. They generously offered to help bring this Haggadah, and its message, to fruition.

May they be blessed with only good and may the bonds between us strengthen and deepen.

Writing this commentary on the *Haggadah* has been a humbling experience. This project, originally intended to be completed in a few weeks, stretched to several months and then wore on for almost two years. We *toil* but only the Almighty **accomplishes**.

I am indeed fortunate the Almighty allowed me to complete this commentary. May all who read and study its message come closer to Him Who chose the nation Israel.

Avrohom Dov Kahn

Shevat, 5754

January, 1994

PUBLISHER'S PREFACE

Why Is A New Haggadah Commentary Needed?

The Passover Seder has endured for 3300 years, distinguishing it as humanity's most ancient and continuous religious communal observance.

Jews of every religious inclination participate in this annual celebration. The *Haggadah* is the Seder's guidebook; consequently, it is the Jewish text with which Jews are most acquainted. Myriad commentaries on this work have been produced.

Despite this pervasive familiarity and the vast amount of commentaries, it appears to many as an outdated, mostly irrelevant collection of unrelated passages. The response to this misconception has been the recent publication of new *Haggadahs* which have forsaken the traditional text for a more "modern" approach, emphasizing a current set of political or social ideologies in an attempt to heighten its relevance. These efforts reflect a tragic failure to understand and appreciate the *Haggadah's* true meaning and eternal relevance.

While completely loyal to the traditional text, our *Haggadah* commentary brings to the modern-day Jew a clear unambiguous theme, which speaks to us with as powerful a relevance as that felt by our ancestors.

What Distinguishes This Haggadah Commentary From All Others?

Our commentary demonstrates decisively that the *Haggadah* intends to transmit the idea that we Jews are God's chosen nation.

This concept is the single thread that weaves its way throughout the entire text, bringing together every fiber in its rich tapestry. Classical approaches have focused on "micro-commentary", brilliantly expounding each section independently. This *Haggadah* offers a "macro-commentary", establishing a connection between each of the sections to create a unified, interrelated whole. In addition to providing a global understanding of the *Haggadah*, this unique approach answers questions posed by the classical commentators, viewing them in the light of our central theme - "chosenness".

Who Should Use This Hagaddah?

Optimally, this *Haggadah* will be used by a relatively knowledgeable person who plans to conduct a Seder for less learned guests. It is particularly apt for such an assemblage because it provides a unified thematic guide to the *Haggadah*. The Seder leader should familiarize himself with our commentary in advance to most fruitfully convey its message.

This commentary's emphasis of a single message throughout the entire *Haggadah* makes it a perfect guide for those with limited background in Judaism, communicating powerfully the basic, yet profound message: the Jewish nation is bound up in a special relationship with God. The commentary is not, however, mere homiletic exposition; even the erudite will find our approach quite helpful in uncovering new and deeper insights.

How Should This Haggadah Be Used?

After having briefed himself with the commentary's central idea, the leader can then commence the Seder by orally presenting the commentary's motif as well as directly quoting from the text. The leader should go on to urge the gathering to anticipate how the theme will illuminate each ensuing section. After allowing for a round of useful speculation, the leader or one of the other participants may then read aloud from the commentary to learn how the author has continued to weave his theme.

In order to promote this use, we have chosen brevity as our guiding principle, allowing easy access to the author's integration of the central theme in each section.

It goes without saying that a full appreciation of this work is possible only if the user first reads through the *Haggadah's* Hebrew text or its English translation and then refers to our commentary. Without doing so a great deal of our commentary's basic substance and nuance will be lost on the uninitiated.

What Special Features Are Contained In This Haggadah?

Besides our unique approach in connecting the entire *Maggid* section of the *Haggadah* with one unifying theme, the several appendices offer the reader a rich background in Jewish law and history. These include: *A **Time Line** schematic of the Jewish nation's Egyptian experience, a full listing of the **Biblical commandments** of Passover, and a **Glossary of Hebrew terms**.*

The appendices are constructed so as to be beneficial to the beginner, intermediate and advanced reader.

AUTHOR'S PREFACE

In the spring of the year 2448 from Creation (1313 B.C.E.), God worked great miracles and brought out a nation from slavery to freedom. God gave this nation a set of laws called the *Torah* and therein commanded its people to retell the story of their deliverance. That nation was Israel, and we use this book, the Passover *Haggadah*, to fulfill God's commandment. Indeed, the word "*haggadah*" means the act of retelling or declaring (see *Deuteronomy XXVI:3*).

Traditionally, we begin the Passover night festivities by singing a short song whose lyrics comprise the fourteen parts of the "Seder" (order) about to unfold. All the components of the evening must be performed in precise sequence; hence the term "*Seder night*" (night of order). The *Haggadah* was so arranged to serve as a guidebook for us to best accomplish all the *mitzvos* of this night (see Appendix). "*Maggid*" names the fifth section in this order, and is a cousin to the word *Haggadah*, sharing the same Hebrew root. It is in *Maggid* that we retell the Exodus saga for which the *Haggadah* is named.

The *Haggadah* text we have before us today was painstakingly composed by the greatest minds in Jewry. It was shaped, ordered and sealed over an eighteen-hundred year period, from Moses through the later sages of the *Talmud*. Though Biblical law does not quite bind us to use the standard *Haggadah* in all its particulars, it is at the same time the work that best facilitates our Seder, because all the basic components necessary to fulfill our Biblical obligations are addressed. The rabbis helped the average person by presenting a uniform text and procedure so that everyone, learned or not, could be sure to fulfill all the commandments incumbent on Seder night.

No other Jewish book, including the Bible itself, has invited as many commentaries as the Passover *Haggadah*. Why is this so? The answer lies in the very injunction to retell the story of the Exodus.

The *Haggadah* instructs us: "In each generation, a Jew is obligated to see himself as having gone out of Egypt, as it says, 'You should tell your son on that day saying, "because of this did God do for **me** when **I** went out of Egypt." ' "

The *Hagaddah*, quoting the source verse of the commandment to retell the story of the Exodus, speaks of a parent, his child, and the message the one imparts to the other. But as the *Haggadah* points out, the verse discussing the substance of the message says nothing about the historical epic of the Exodus itself, only that it happened to "me", i.e., the parent. The *Haggadah* deduces that this is in fact the critical substance of the message to be transmitted: **It happened to me**.

The *Haggadah* derives from the above *Torah* verse that a fulfillment of the Biblical injunction to retell the story of the Exodus to the next generation is accomplished only by an autobiographical account; if the substance of the transmission is "It happened to me" it can only be imparted through a personalized recounting. Indeed, it must be so for the message to have any meaning. The events of the Exodus are historical trivia and meaningless to the child without a Jew internalizing and reliving that very event. Only when a parent says "My child, it happened to me", does it assume a life-directing character.

But how is it possible for someone at the Seder who is living hundreds or thousands of years after the Exodus to say, "when **I** left Egypt," much less believe it?

The answer comes with an understanding of the message of the Exodus. True, the miracles the message recounts are historical, having occurred in the year 2448. *However, in each generation, our obligation at the Seder is much more than mere remembrance. Every Jew must recognize that when God took us out of Egypt with great miracles, He chose us as His special nation.* This "chosenness" was bestowed upon the Jewish nation as a whole and devolved upon each Jew for all time. In that sense Jews in every generation can truly say, "***I was 'chosen' at the Exodus***."

The importance of the Exodus and the reason why we are instructed to recount its events to ourselves and to our children lies not in its history but in its modern and eternal relevance to the Jewish people: we were chosen to be God's nation through the Exodus and we therefore continue to be His chosen today and for all eternity.

This personal interaction with the Exodus is critical to *Maggid*. Without this feeling on the part of the parent, a Jewish child will never accept the message of his "chosenness". Logically, a Jewish child reasons, "If my parents were not chosen at the Exodus, why should I be so endowed?"

Now we can also understand the reason for the plethora of commentaries found on the *Haggadah*, as each expounder, from the greatest *Talmudic* sage to the once-a-year improviser, injects his own insights into the story of the Exodus. Though Biblical and rabbinic parameters encode the transmission, its soul is entrusted to each individual, who relates it through his own insights and understanding. **After all, it is an autobiographical account for each and every Jew.**

Bearing this in mind, I too feel the need to comment. I have always been bothered by the seeming lack of order in the *Maggid* portion of the *Haggadah*. Anyone reading through it is immediately struck by an apparently haphazard arrangement of its paragraphs. Nowhere is there any indication of a thematic scheme that would unify this section. It seems ironic that the very night known as "Seder night" is on the surface devoid of the essential quality of orderliness inherent in its name.

I have come across many beautiful interpretations of specific passages in the course of my studies. At the same time, however, I long yearned for a unified approach to the *Haggadah* that would explain the sequencing of its various components and the strange omission of some, and paradoxical inclusion of other, personages and Biblical passages. I searched for an analytical power tool, as it were, that would fashion a base for the *Haggadah* superstructure.

At the same time, colleagues, friends and acquaintances have often asked me to advise them how best to conduct a Seder for guests with little or no background. The Seder night serves as a golden opportunity for those who were blessed with a good Jewish education to share their *Torah* knowledge with less erudite fellow Jews who come to hear the *Haggadah's* message. This eager group, in its widest geographic sense, numbers in the tens of thousands. A golden opportunity indeed for Jewish outreach and education!

After many years of studying and lecturing on the *Haggadah*, I have, with God's help, formulated a unified approach explaining what the *Haggadah* wants to accomplish and how it goes about doing so. Thus our *Haggadah* is perhaps unique in that a single thread is woven throughout to bring together every fiber in the text's rich tapestry.

Optimally, this *Haggadah* will be used by a relatively knowledgeable person who plans to conduct a Seder for less learned guests.

This commentary's emphasis of a single message throughout the entire *Haggadah* makes it a perfect guide for those with limited background in Judaism, communicating powerfully the basic, yet profound message: the Jewish nation is bound up in a special relationship with God. The commentary is not, however, mere homiletic exposition; even the erudite will find our approach quite helpful in uncovering new and deeper insights.

My sole intent in the publication of this *Haggadah* is to benefit Jews who do not yet know how great and special they are. It is therefore my hope that this *Haggadah* will bring to the reader an insight not only into the Passover Seder night observance, but more importantly, a heightened appreciation of our very identity as Jews, which should inspirit us every moment of our lives.

The Premise

A Unified Approach To Understanding The Haggadah

Declaring the Birth of the Chosen Nation

The Jew's guidebook for all of life is the holy *Torah*: the written text and its oral tradition. Given by God Himself, it maps out His will for both the physical universe with all its vastness and all humanity, but most importantly it speaks to His chosen nation - the Jews - about how they should serve Him. The *Torah* and its commandments are neither opinion nor option, but the directives of God and binding on all existence.

There are 613 *mitzvos*, or commandments, in the *Torah* which we, the Jewish people, observe. One of those *mitzvos* is to retell the story of the Exodus.

The broad elements of how to accomplish this "retelling" are outlined in the oral tradition. The *Haggadah* is the standard text produced over many centuries by our nation's greatest scholars, and best satisfies each narrative element the *Torah* requires.

Reviewing the *Haggadah* even casually, it becomes undeniably clear that the "retelling" is not a historical narrative of the Exodus; critical dates, places and personages are omitted entirely!

It is this commentary's contention that the commandment to retell the Exodus saga is really an obligation to declare through the events of the Israelites' redemption that God elected the Jewish people to be His chosen nation that Passover night 3300 years ago.

Through the questions and answers in the next several pages we hope to prove this thesis conclusively.

ולקחתי אתכם לי לעם...

"And I will take you to Me for a nation, and I will be to you a God; and you shall know that I am the Lord your God, Who brings you out from under the burdens of Egypt."' *(Exodus VI:7)*

אתכם לקח ה'...

"But you [Israel] the Almighty has taken and brought you out of the iron crucible, from Egypt, so that you would be **His heritage nation**, as you are this day." *(Deuteronomy IV:20)*

ותחת כי אהב את אבתיך...

"And because He loved your fathers, and **chose** their seed after them, and brought you out before Him, with His great powers, from Egypt." *(Deuteronomy IV:37)*

כי עם קדוש אתה...

"For you are a holy nation to the Almighty your God: the Almighty your God has **chosen you to be to Him a beloved nation**, from all the nations that are upon the face of the earth." *(Deuteronomy VII:6)*

(The verse continues and says, through which act did the Almighty choose you as His beloved nation?)

הוציא ה' אתכם...

"... the Almighty has brought you out with a mighty hand, and redeemed you out of the house of bondage, from the hand of Pharaoh king of Egypt." *(Deuteronomy VII:8)*

Four Questions To Ask
Before Asking
The Four Questions.

Moses, our great leader, is not mentioned in the *Haggadah*. Didn't God Himself deem it necessary to enlist Moses as His agent to redeem the Jewish people? Was it not Moses who went to Pharaoh to convey God's demand, "Let My people go"? Was it not Moses who (together with his brother Aaron) unleashed the plagues upon the Egyptian slave masters?

If the purpose of the Haggadah is to tell the story of the Exodus, how can Moses possibly be omitted?

QUESTION ONE:

The great *Tanaaim* (sages of the *Mishnaic* era, circa 150 B.C.E. - 200 C.E.) were adamant that children remain awake during the Seder so that they should be able to ask, "Why is this night different?", and thereupon be told the story of the Exodus (see Tractate *Pesachim*, 109a). All this was done to fulfill the Biblical verses which bid the father to transmit to his children the saga of our forebears' Exodus from Egypt.

QUESTION TWO:

*Why is it so critical to tell the children **this** story? Why not tell the children the stories of: the patriarchs and matriarchs, the twelve sons of Jacob, Moses, Aaron, the receiving of the Torah at Mount Sinai, the Judges and Kings of Israel, the building of the Holy Temple, its destruction or the entire history of the diaspora?*

No other historical event is so privileged by Jewish law. Why are we required to recount, with such detail, only the events of our deliverance from Egypt, transmitting them to the next generation? What distinguishes the Exodus from all other events in Jewish history?

For instance: Wouldn't it be similarly appropriate to tell our children about *Succos*? After all, the *Torah* states about the *mitzvah* of *Succos*: "During these seven days you must live in thatched huts. Everyone in Israel must live in thatched huts. This is so that future generations will know that I had the Israelites live in huts when I brought them out of Egypt, I am God your Lord." (*Leviticus XXIII:42-43*) Yet, nowhere do we find a law to prompt the children to ask why we change our dwelling from inside the house to the succah for seven days (eight in the diaspora), nor are we instructed to tell them why.

In short, what is so unique about the story of the Exodus that it is the lone historical message we are instructed to transmit to the next generation of Jews?

QUESTION THREE: *Why have Jews always referred to the holiday as "Passover"?* After all, the *Torah* refers to the festival as חג המצות "*Chag HaMatzohs*", the Holiday of *Matzohs* (*Exodus XXIII:15, XXXIV:18*). If our intention is to commemorate our redemption from slavery, which the miracles of the Exodus accomplished, we should refer to the holiday as זמן חרותנו "*Z'man Cheiruseinu*" the time of our redemption (as it is referred to in the prayer service).

Of all the miracles of the Exodus and their historic results, why does God's passing over the Jewish homes in Egypt capture the essence of the holiday for all generations?

QUESTION FOUR: The bulk of the *Maggid* section of the *Haggadah* is a *midrashic* elaboration of four verses in Deuteronomy XXVI:5-8. These verses describe the declaration made by a Jewish farmer who comes to Jerusalem and offers the first fruits of his field in the Holy Temple. The *Talmud* specifically instructs us to use these verses Passover night. (*Pesachim* 116a)

Why are these four verses more central to our Egyptian experience than the 13 chapters in the book of Exodus which detail the story of the Israelites' enslavement, Moses' mission, the ten plagues, and the actual Exodus?

We have posed four questions that prefigure those asked at the Seder and will now attempt to convey one, unifying answer to them all.

SOME BACKGROUND FIRST

A Historical Perspective:
The Covenant With Abraham

As believing Jews we know that there are no accidents in history.

Jacob went down to Egypt together with his family in the year 2238 from creation (1523 B.C.E.), to join his son Joseph. Joseph had become Egypt's viceroy after the unfolding of an intricate set of divinely orchestrated circumstances. **The Israelites were to be in Egypt; it had to be so.**

In fact, the inevitability of the Egyptian experience was foretold by God Himself in the **"Covenant Between The Halves"** exactly two hundred and twenty years before Jacob and his Israelite clan set foot in Egypt.

To understand the *Haggadah*, it is necessary to analyze the prophetic vision of the Covenant Between the Halves in its entirety. (*Genesis XV: verses 1 -21*)

Being childless, Abraham feared his servant Eliezer would inherit him. God assured Abraham that the heir to both his spiritual legacy and personal fortune would be his own flesh and blood, and that his descendants would be as numerous as the stars in the sky. Abraham had absolute trust in this assurance (*verses 1 - 6*).

God then tells Abraham that He took him out of his native land, Ur Casdim, to give the land of Israel to both him and his descendants (*verse 7*).

With regard to **this** promise, Abraham, the paragon of faith, nevertheless demands of God: "Through what can I be assured that it will be an inheritance?" (*verse 8*).

God immediately tells Abraham, "Take for me three calves, goats and rams, a dove and a young pigeon." Abraham sets up all these species in the ancient manner of those about to enter a covenant (*verses 9 - 11*).

Following this, Abraham goes into a deep sleep and receives a prophetic vision:

"Know for sure that your descendants will be foreigners in a land that is not theirs for 400 years. They will be enslaved and oppressed. But I will finally bring judgment against the nation that enslaves them and they will then leave with great wealth. The fourth generation will return here since the Amorites' sin will not have run its course until then.

The sun set and it became very dark. A smoking furnace and a flaming torch passed between the halves of the animals. On that day God made a covenant with Abraham saying, 'To your descendants I have given this land, from the Egyptian river as far as the great river, the Euphrates. [This area includes the lands of] the Kenites, the Kenizites, the Kadmonites, the Hittites, the Perezites, the Rephaim, the Amorites, the Canaanites, the Girgashites and the Yebusites.' " (*verses 12 - 21*)

We are immediately struck by a number of questions:

1.   Why did Abraham request a sign about his prospective inheritance of the land, but not his imminent fatherhood? After all, Abraham was elderly and childless; his wish for a son was surely preeminent in his mind.

2.   Why does Abraham, the great pillar of faith in God, request a sign? Doesn't such a petition suggest a lack of faith?

3.   Why does God tell Abraham about Egypt and our servitude in that country? It seems irrelevant to the question concerning inheriting the land of Israel. Would it not have been sufficient just to state the covenant as in verse 18, "To your descendants I have given this land..."?

Understanding Abraham's Request:
To Be The Chosen Nation

Let us begin by stating a premise: The Covenant Between the Halves was of cosmic import for the very nature of the Jewish people for all time and not just a promise of some real estate to Abraham's descendants.

Abraham understood that the promise of the land of Israel would culminate the process of choosing the Jewish nation as God's people, because it is there that God's earthly presence resides. The divinely-appointed site of the Holy Temple is in the very midst of that land, and there His chosen are to live side-by-side with Him. Therefore, the promise of the land which Abraham received was tantamount to an endowment of "chosenness" for his progeny.

But Abraham worried. Perhaps only the saintly of his lineage would secure the legacy of "chosenness"; he sought assurance that "chosenness" would devolve upon the entire nation of Israel.

A chosen "nation" is what Abraham requested of God; not just an elite progeny but a nation. And once that nation was to be brought into being, Abraham asked that its members secure absolute spiritual citizenship as an unimpeachable birthright. He sought this status even for sinners shunning repentance, along with all their children after them (provided they were born of a Jewish mother). Abraham desired that the Jewish nation remain indivisible. Thus is Abraham's concern - "How do I know it will be an *inheritance?*" - to be understood; an inheritance implies that it will always revert to the inheritor without prejudice to the inheritor's individual merit.

God's Reply:

The Necessity of the Egyptian Experience

God's reply to Abraham's petition can thus be understood: Were you to be a father of a uniformly saintly people, all that would be required would be the holy spiritual gene pool of the three patriarchs and four matriarchs. To create the "chosen nation" however, that alone will not suffice; an "iron crucible" is needed to fashion that nation.

That "iron crucible" was the Egyptian experience.

The Bible itself speaks in these terms: "But you [Israel], God Himself took, and He brought you out of the iron crucible that was Egypt, so that you would be His heritage nation, as you are today." (*Deuteronomy IV:20*)

Subjugated in a foreign land, surrounded by an idol-worshipping and immoral culture, enslaved and oppressed, yet all the while adhering to the traits that give the Jews their national identity - this was the crucible that shaped and molded the nation Israel.

At the precise moment that God knew the forging process was complete He proclaimed to the world through the miraculous medium of the Exodus, "... you shall be My special treasure among all nations, even though all the world is Mine. You will be a kingdom of priests and a holy nation to Me." (*Exodus XIX:5-6*) That moment occurred 400 years after the birth of Isaac, Abraham's son. It had taken 400 years for Abraham's descendants to become a nation. God's promise had been kept.

That Israel become a nation at the time of the Exodus is clearly expressed in the "The Way of God", authored by the saintly Rabbi Moshe Chaim Luzzato, known by the acronym *Ramchal* (b. 1707 Italy - d. 1746 Israel), Part II, Chapter IV, Subsection 5:

> One must know: just as the descendants of Adam are divided into primary "trees" [of lineage] and their "branches", so too each individual primary tree has, as part of it, distinguishable branches from which emanate all the particular parts.
>
> The distinguishable branches in Abraham's tree total 600,000, representing the number of Jews who came out of Egypt. ***They became the nation of Israel***, and to them was the land of Israel given.
>
> All their descendants are considered offshoots of the primary branches. And to these primary branches the *Torah* was given.
>
> When this occurred, the tree was said to have attained maturity.

Later, in Part IV, Chapter 4, Subsection 9, the Ramchal *adds with great clarity:*

> ... Even though our patriarch Abraham was chosen so that he and his progeny would be set apart from all nations to be God's people, still there was not yet the opportunity for them to be established as a nation...
>
> Therefore, they needed to be exiled to Egypt and enslaved there. In that great enslavement they were refined like gold in a smelter and thus purified.
>
> When the proper time came, God lifted them from their degraded state up to Him. They were thus permanently redeemed from evil and from that time onward they were **established as a nation**, attached to God and crowned by Him.

Four Questions, One Answer

We are now prepared to answer the four questions posed above.

On Passover night we are not merely obligated to retell the story of our enslavement and deliverance from Egypt as an end unto itself. The *Haggadah* text makes this very obvious. The omission of Moses and our neglect of the Biblical narrative in the Book of Exodus defy any such position.

Our Biblical obligation is rather, to declare and transmit, to ourselves and the next generation, that the great miracles God wrought during the Exodus were to demonstrate to the entire world God's choice of the Jewish nation, from all the nations of the world, to be His.

With this premise, our four questions dissolve.

1.   By definition, becoming God's chosen could only be accomplished through His personal intercession, as expressed clearly in the *Haggadah's* exposition of the Biblical verse *(Exodus XXII:12)*: "I will pass through the land of Egypt on that night [the 15th of *Nissan*], I and no angel; I will slay all the firstborn in the land of Egypt - I and no *seraph*. And upon all the gods of Egypt will I execute judgments - I and no messenger; I, Hashem - it is I and no other..."

This explains why Moses is not mentioned in the *Haggadah*. While he was the divinely-appointed agent for all the events leading up to the Exodus, he played no part in the actual redemption of the Jews on the night and morning of the 15th of *Nissan*. The defining moment, at which God chose the nation Israel, had to be effected by God Himself. **God's chosen had to be chosen by God - none other!**

The obligation to retell the events of the Exodus refers to those specific events through which the nation of Israel was chosen. Those events began with God's inflicting the tenth and last plague, the killing of the firstborn. Thus the mention of Moses is irrelevant because he played no role in the killing of the firstborn, serving only as the agent for the first nine plagues, which had no direct bearing on the "chosenness" of the nation Israel. This answers the first of our four questions.

2.   We now can also understand why the Exodus is the sole historical episode which we are commanded to transmit to the next generation of Jews.

The greatest gift a Jewish parent can give his child is a sense of inheritance - his entitlement to a share in the chosen nation. This is the gift we are commanded to give our children on Passover night - teaching them the lesson of our "chosenness". If this sense is missing from the heart and mind of the child, how can he possibly understand his unique position in the world? What imperative is there for him to adhere to the *Torah* and all its laws if they are meaningless to him? Why should he strive to be different and unique?

We must show our children how much we identify with the nation Israel from its very inception, sharing in its entire national experience. We have to feel ourselves bound to the chosen nation Israel, and make certain that our children understand and internalize their chosen national status. The entire commandment to relate the story of the Exodus to our children can only be understood within this context. Every generation of Jews must affirm its "chosenness", thus explaining why the Exodus saga is the only one which the *Torah* insists must be transmitted from father to son. **Knowledge of our "chosenness" is the surest means for perpetuating the Jewish nation.** This answers the second of our four questions.

3. Question three asks why the *Torah* speaks of the חג המצות - "Festival of *Matzohs*" - while the Jewish nation has always referred to the holiday as פסח "Passover".

The answer is: The Exodus was the historical event through which God chose the Jewish people. The "choosing" was accomplished through God's selection of the Jewish homes, to "pass over", while wreaking retribution on the homes of their Egyptian oppressors. In affirmation of God's choice of Israel we designate the name of the holiday by its defining message - "chosenness". **Passover, is the name that most clearly expresses our election to "chosenness".**

This idea is perhaps best expressed by the *Sh'La HaKadosh* (b. Prague 1560 - d. Tiberias, Israel 1630), who kabbalistically explains the etymology of פסח "*Pesach*", the Hebrew word for Passover, as coming from two other words פה "peh" and סח "sach" which translate as "mouth" and "speech". We are commanded to affirm the message of the Exodus by speaking about God's choice of Israel as His nation. This is what we do in the *Haggadah*. To signify how important this commandment is, the Jewish nation has designated the name of the holiday "*Pesach*" (Passover).

4. Question four asks why the *Haggadah* attaches such great impor-

tance to the several verses in Deuteronomy (XXVI:5-8) pronounced by a Jewish farmer when bringing his first fruits to the Holy Temple.

Since our "retelling" is really a declaration that God chose us on that Passover night 3300 years ago, the *Haggadah* seeks the clearest, most emphatic pronouncement of that declaration. The *Haggadah* finds it in the words of the Jewish farmer.

The farmer, whose acquaintance with the land is most intimate, declares how fortunate he is to have been chosen by God in Egypt and to have merited His sacred proximity. True, the Exodus *initiated* the choosing of Israel, but the process was not completed until the Jews settled the "Promised Land". **The ultimate *proof* of our "chosenness" is the fact that we live, work and derive sustenance from the same land where God's presence is most apparent**.

Being chosen means we merit a special closeness to God. Only in the land of Israel do the Jews achieve this closeness. When we find ourselves in the land of Israel, with Jerusalem and the Holy Temple resonating to God's earthly presence, our chosenness is indeed consummated.

Our thesis clarifies two additional points of Jewish law.

Many are perplexed why **women**, who are generally exempt from *mitzvos* which must be performed within a bounded time frame, are nevertheless obligated in *Maggid* (See *Sefer HaChinuch*, 13th Century Spain and the associated commentary of the *Minchas Chinuch*). After all, *Maggid* must be accomplished on Passover night only; so why indeed should women be obligated? The answer becomes clear in the context of our thesis: They are obviously a primary and integral part of the chosen nation. God's choice of Israel was all-inclusive. By necessity, then, women must commemorate this anniversary no less compulsorily than men.

Circumcision and the Pascal lamb are the only two positive commandments whose transgression incurs the severe punishment of *"Kareis"*; our thematic explains why. Both of these commandments are the emblem of a Jew and a sign denoting membership in the chosen nation. Anyone who spurns the King's commission is guilty of *"lese majeste"*, high treason against the Almighty King.

Having set forth our thesis, we are now prepared to proceed to the *Maggid* portion of the *Haggadah*, analyzing it paragraph by paragraph.

The Seder

Seder Plate

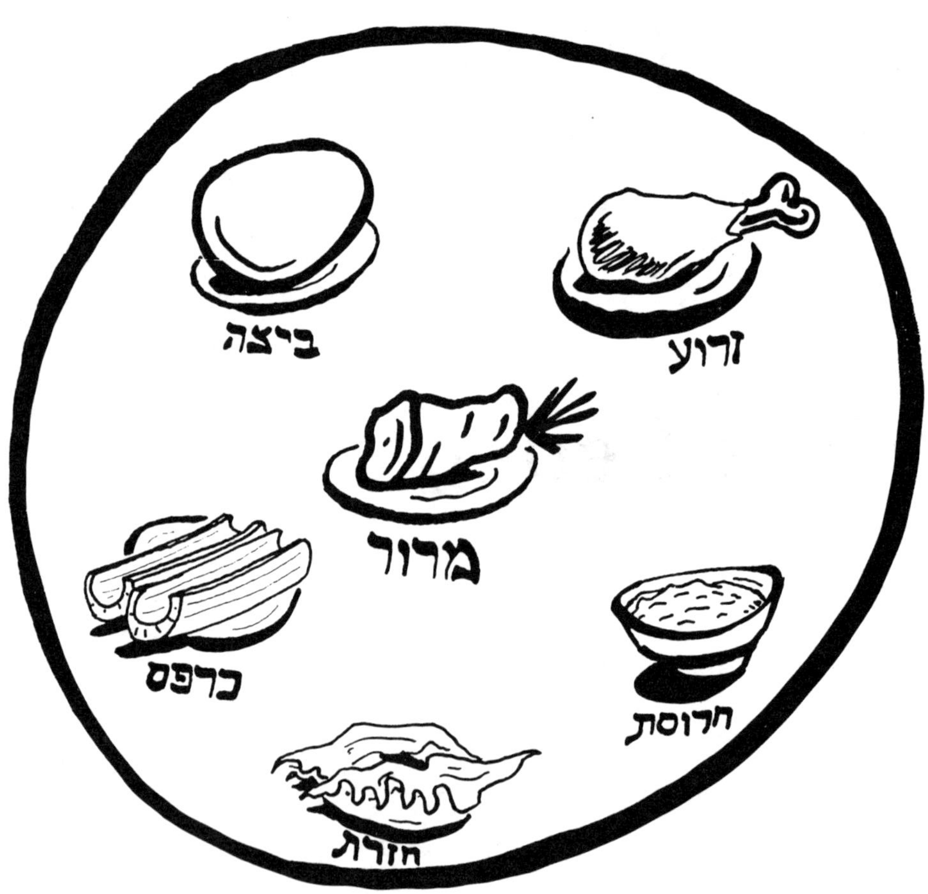

סדר

The "Seder" and Its Sections

The word "*Seder*" means order, and each of the words in the mnemonic displayed below stands for one of the Seder events about to unfold.

This arrangement is ascribed to *Rashi* (Rabbi Shlomo Yitzchoki, b. Troyes, France, 1040 - d. Troyes, 1105), the greatest commentator on both the oral and written portions of the *Torah*. Surely this giant of *Torah* planned more for this listing than a mere aid to recollection; doubtless he meant to vest it with precise halachic intent.

We must assume that all of the elements in this list necessarily fulfill or relate to some commandment unique to Seder night. We will thus explicate each of the Seder stages signified in the mnemonic in their respective introductions, and point to their relevance to Passover and the retelling of the Exodus saga.

קדש	ורחץ
כרפס	יחץ
מגיד	רחצה
מוציא מצה	מרור
כורך	שלחן עורך
צפון	ברך
הלל	נרצה

KADESH

Kiddush - Sanctification Over Wine

Why do we make *Kiddush*?

"Remember the Sabbath day to keep it holy." (*Exodus XX:8*) This, the fourth of the Ten Commandments, is the source for the recitation of *Kiddush* on the Sabbath. Although the verse says "Remember", which could be taken to mean merely a mental awareness, the Oral Sinaitic Law defines the remembrance as a verbal testimony. (*Toras Cohanim*, introduction to *Parshas B'chukosai*). It should be pointed out that men and women are equally obligated in *Kiddush*. (*Mishnah Berurah*, 271:2)

The Rabbis further decreed: although not Biblically required, one should make *Kiddush* on the Holidays (*Yomim Tovim*) as well, with all the attendant laws that apply to *Kiddush* on the Sabbath.

On Passover night, the **text** of the *Kiddush* blessing at once accomplishes two ends: (1) the sanctification of the Passover holiday, and (2) the blessing for the retelling of the Exodus saga, as maintained by *Rabeinu Yerucham* (b. Provence, France 1280 - d. Todelo, Spain 1350), in his *Sefer Adom* (*Nesiv 5* part 4) and developed at length in our commentary on the "*Asher G'alanu*" blessing.

Why is wine necessary for *Kiddush*?

Wine amplifies and heightens the sanctifying role of *Kiddush*.

Although, as already stated, *Kiddush* itself has a Biblical source, there is a dispute among the great medieval *Talmudists* whether the use of wine in the ritual is a Biblical, or only a rabbinic, mandate. (*Aruch HaShulchan*, 271:1-4)

On Passover night, the *Kiddush* **wine** serves a dual function: (1) It heightens the sanctification ritual, and (2) it serves as the first of the "four cups" of wine required at the Seder.

What is the proper time for *Kiddush*?

Although on the Sabbath and *Yom Tov*, *Kiddush* may precede nightfall, Seder night is an exception. The reason is as follows: through Biblical sources we learn the fulfillment of all *Seder* commandments can only be accomplished after nightfall. (Even the Rabbinic commandments of the *Seder* follow this time constraint.) *Kiddush*, acting as both the blessing over *Maggid* (see above) and the first of the evening's obligatory "four cups", must therefore take place after nightfall.

"Nightfall" is defined as that point in the evening when three medium-size stars become visible.

Who recites *Kiddush*?

For all other *Kiddushim* throughout the year it is preferable for one of the assembled (usually the head of the family) to make *Kiddush* on behalf of the entire gathering (*Chaye Odom*, 5:17) but at the Seder the custom is not so. The practice here is for each male present to recite his own *Kiddush*. This is so because *Kiddush* is the first of the "four cups", and each participant must partake of his own cup; for all other *Kiddushim* there is no such obligation. By convention, even on Passover night, the head of the household makes *Kiddush* on behalf of the women present; nevertheless women must drink their own cup.

Is there an obligation to recline while drinking the *Kiddush* wine?

Yes! If one forgot to recline, see *Magen Avraham*, (Rabbi Avraham Gombiner b. Gombin, Poland, 1634 - d. Kalish, Poland, 1682), *Shulchan Orach, O. C.* 472:7.

כִּי בָנוּ בָחַרְתָּ וְאוֹתָנוּ קִדַּשְׁתָּ מִכָּל הָעַמִּים

Kiddush should be recited and the Seder begun as soon after synagogue services as possible - however, not before nightfall. (Orech Chaim 472:1) Each participant's cup should be poured by someone else to symbolize the majesty of the evening, as though everyone present had a personal valet. (Ramah, O.C. 473:1)

(On the Sabbath begin here and include all passages in parentheses)

(AND THERE WAS EVENING AND THERE WAS MORNING THE SIXTH DAY. NOW THE HEAVEN AND THE EARTH WERE FINISHED AND ALL THEIR HOST. AND ON THE SEVENTH DAY THE ALMIGHTY FINISHED HIS WORK WHICH HE HAD DONE: AND HE RESTED ON THE SEVENTH DAY FROM ALL HIS WORK WHICH HE HAD DONE. AND THE ALMIGHTY BLESSED THE SEVENTH DAY AND MADE IT HOLY, FOR ON THAT DAY HE RESTED FROM ALL HIS WORK WHICH HE HAD CREATED AND MADE.)

(Genesis II:1-3)

(וַיְהִי עֶרֶב וַיְהִי בוֹקֶר יוֹם הַשִּׁשִּׁי, וַיְכֻלּוּ הַשָּׁמַיִם וְהָאָרֶץ וְכָל צְבָאָם: וַיְכַל אֱלֹהִים בַּיּוֹם הַשְּׁבִיעִי מְלַאכְתּוֹ אֲשֶׁר עָשָׂה, וַיִּשְׁבּוֹת בַּיּוֹם הַשְּׁבִיעִי מִכָּל מְלַאכְתּוֹ אֲשֶׁר עָשָׂה: וַיְבָרֶךְ אֱלֹהִים אֶת יוֹם הַשְּׁבִיעִי וַיְקַדֵּשׁ אֹתוֹ, כִּי בוֹ שָׁבַת מִכָּל מְלַאכְתּוֹ אֲשֶׁר בָּרָא אֱלֹהִים לַעֲשׂוֹת:)

BLESSED ARE YOU ALMIGHTY, OUR GOD, KING OF THE UNIVERSE, WHO CREATES THE FRUIT OF THE VINE.

סַבְרִי מָרָנָן וְרַבָּנָן וְרַבּוֹתַי:

בָּרוּךְ אַתָּה יהוה, אֱלֹהֵינוּ מֶלֶךְ הָעוֹלָם, בּוֹרֵא פְּרִי הַגָּפֶן.

BLESSED ARE YOU ALMIGHTY, OUR GOD, KING OF THE UNIVERSE, WHO HAS

בָּרוּךְ אַתָּה יהוה, אֱלֹהֵינוּ מֶלֶךְ הָעוֹלָם, אֲשֶׁר בָּחַר בָּנוּ מִכָּל עָם וְרוֹמְמָנוּ מִכָּל

CHOSEN US FROM ALL NATIONS AND HAS RAISED US ABOVE ALL TONGUES AND HAS MADE US HOLY BY HIS COMMANDMENTS. YOU, ALMIGHTY GOD, HAVE GIVEN US IN LOVE (THE SABBATH FOR REST), APPOINTED TIMES FOR GLADNESS, FESTIVALS AND SEASONS FOR REJOICING; THIS DAY (SABBATH AND) FESTIVAL OF MATZOHS, WHICH IS THE SEASON OF OUR FREEDOM (IN LOVE) AS A HOLY CONVOCATION IN MEMORY OF THE EXODUS FROM EGYPT. FOR YOU HAVE CHOSEN US, AND SANCTIFIED US ABOVE ALL NATIONS, (AND THE SABBATH) AND YOUR HOLY FESTIVALS (IN LOVE AND FAVOR) IN GLADNESS AND JOY, YOU GRANTED US AS A HERITAGE. BLESSED ARE YOU, ALMIGHTY, WHO SANCTIFIES (THE SABBATH) ISRAEL AND THE FESTIVE SEASONS.

לָשׁוֹן וְקִדְּשָׁנוּ בְּמִצְוֹתָיו, וַתִּתֶּן לָנוּ יהוה אֱלֹהֵינוּ בְּאַהֲבָה (שַׁבָּתוֹת לִמְנוּחָה וּ) מוֹעֲדִים לְשִׂמְחָה, חַגִּים וּזְמַנִּים לְשָׂשׂוֹן, (אֶת יוֹם הַשַּׁבָּת הַזֶּה וְ) אֶת יוֹם חַג הַמַּצּוֹת הַזֶּה, זְמַן חֵרוּתֵנוּ, (בְּאַהֲבָה) מִקְרָא קֹדֶשׁ, זֵכֶר לִיצִיאַת מִצְרָיִם. כִּי בָנוּ בָחַרְתָּ וְאוֹתָנוּ קִדַּשְׁתָּ מִכָּל הָעַמִּים, (וְשַׁבָּת) וּמוֹעֲדֵי קָדְשֶׁךָ (בְּאַהֲבָה וּבְרָצוֹן) בְּשִׂמְחָה וּבְשָׂשׂוֹן הִנְחַלְתָּנוּ. בָּרוּךְ אַתָּה יהוה, מְקַדֵּשׁ (הַשַּׁבָּת וְ) יִשְׂרָאֵל וְהַזְּמַנִּים.

(On Saturday night, add all passages in brackets)

[BLESSED ARE YOU ALMIGHTY, OUR GOD, KING OF THE UNIVERSE, WHO CREATES THE ILLUMINATION OF THE FIRE.]

[בָּרוּךְ אַתָּה יהוה, אֱלֹהֵינוּ מֶלֶךְ הָעוֹלָם, בּוֹרֵא מְאוֹרֵי הָאֵשׁ:]

[BLESSED ARE YOU ALMIGHTY, OUR GOD, KING OF THE UNIVERSE, WHO DISTINGUISHES BETWEEN THE HOLY AND PROFANE, BETWEEN LIGHT AND DARKNESS, BETWEEN ISRAEL AND THE NATIONS, BETWEEN THE SEVENTH DAY AND THE SIX WORKING DAYS. YOU HAVE MADE A DISTINCTION BETWEEN THE HOLINESS OF THE SABBATH AND THE HOLINESS OF THE FESTIVAL, AND SANCTIFIED THE SEVENTH DAY, SETTING IT ABOVE THE SIX WORKING DAYS. YOU HAVE DISTINGUISHED AND SANCTIFIED YOUR NATION ISRAEL WITH YOUR HOLINESS. BLESSED ARE YOU, ALMIGHTY, WHO HAS MADE A DISTINCTION BETWEEN HOLY AND HOLY.]

[בָּרוּךְ אַתָּה יהוה, אֱלֹהֵינוּ מֶלֶךְ הָעוֹלָם, הַמַּבְדִּיל בֵּין קֹדֶשׁ לְחוֹל, בֵּין אוֹר לְחשֶׁךְ, בֵּין יִשְׂרָאֵל לָעַמִּים, בֵּין יוֹם הַשְּׁבִיעִי לְשֵׁשֶׁת יְמֵי הַמַּעֲשֶׂה. בֵּין קְדֻשַּׁת שַׁבָּת לִקְדֻשַּׁת יוֹם טוֹב הִבְדַּלְתָּ. וְאֶת יוֹם הַשְּׁבִיעִי מִשֵּׁשֶׁת יְמֵי הַמַּעֲשֶׂה קִדַּשְׁתָּ. הִבְדַּלְתָּ וְקִדַּשְׁתָּ אֶת עַמְּךָ יִשְׂרָאֵל בִּקְדֻשָּׁתֶךָ: בָּרוּךְ אַתָּה יהוה, הַמַּבְדִּיל בֵּין קֹדֶשׁ לְקֹדֶשׁ:]

BLESSED ARE YOU ALMIGHTY, OUR GOD, KING OF THE UNIVERSE, WHO HAS KEPT US ALIVE AND SUSTAINED US, AND ENABLED US TO REACH THIS SEASON.

בָּרוּךְ אַתָּה יהוה, אֱלֹהֵינוּ מֶלֶךְ הָעוֹלָם, שֶׁהֶחֱיָנוּ וְקִיְּמָנוּ וְהִגִּיעָנוּ לַזְּמַן הַזֶּה:

One must drink the wine while leaning to the left. (O.C. 473:2) *The minimum halachic requirement is to drink a majority of the cup; it is preferable to drink the entire cup.* (O.C. 472:9 with the gloss of Mishnah Berurah)

וּרְחַץ

U'RECHATZ

Ritual Washing of the Hands

Why do we wash?

The *Talmud* in Tractate *Pesachim* 115a states "All [foods] dipped in liquid require a ritual washing of the hands." Since *karpas* (the next item on the Seder's agenda) is a vegetable dipped in salt water, a ritual washing is necessary.

A thorough understanding of this Rabbinic decree involves extensive knowledge of the laws of "*Tumah* and *Tahara*" (ritual purity) and is beyond the scope of this commentary (see *Mishnah Zavim*, 5:12; *Mishnah Chagiga*, 2:5; Tractate *Chagiga*, 18b; Tractate *Chullin*, 106a with *Tosafos* - "*Mitzva Lishmoa*"; Tractate *Berachos*, 53b - end of folio page; *Shulchan Aruch*, O.C. 158:4; *Aruch HaShulchan*, O.C. 158:1-2, 4-12).

Halachic complications notwithstanding, there is, however, a strong question which is readily intelligible to all. Addressing the above statement about foods dipped in liquid, *Tosafos* (one of the preeminent *Talmudic* commentaries composed by various scholarly schools of Germany and France in the 12th through 14th centuries), comments: Since the majority of laws dealing with ritual purity apply only at the time of the Holy Temple, ritual washing for foods dipped in liquid does not apply nowadays. *Tosafos* concludes that anyone who does wash for such foods and makes a blessing errs. (*Tosafos* distinguishes between this washing and the Rabbinic decree to wash for bread, which certainly applies today.)

Although the *Gaon* of Vilna (Rabbi Eliyahu, b. 1720 - d. 1797) and the *Taz* before him (Rabbi David HaLevi, b. 1586 - d. 1667) strongly argue with *Tosafos*, *Tosafos*' view has in effect been accepted by virtually all of Jewry.

Nevertheless, it is clear from *Tosafos* that although one doesn't ritually wash for foods dipped in liquid throughout the rest of the year,

וּרְחַץ

on Passover night, however, we do wash for *karpas*, albeit without a blessing. Quoting Rabbi Meir of Rottenberg (b. 1215 - d. 1293), the *Tur* (Rabbi Yaakov ben Asher, b. Germany, 1275 - d. Toledo, Spain, 1340), states this clearly: One does not wash for foods dipped in liquid, **except on Passover night**.

Tosafos' demand that we wash prior to eating *karpas* on Seder night is perplexing. If ritual washing is unnecessary for foods dampened by liquid throughout the year, why institute an exception for the Seder?

Suggesting that this ritual washing, unique to Passover night, was designed merely to prompt the children to ask "Why is this night different?" (an objective which in fact motivates several of our actions at the seder), cannot resolve our quandary. Being sacrosanct, *halacha* cannot be refashioned merely to provoke a child's question. The perplexity remains.

We are forced to conclude that Passover night demands a higher level of spiritual purity than that exacted by the rest of the year, and *Tosafos'* insistence on washing for *karpas* necessarily follows. Passover night demands this higher level because, as the *Haggadah* instructs us, "In each generation, a Jew is obligated to view himself as having gone out of Egypt, as it says in the verse: 'You shall tell your son on that day, "Because of this did the Almighty do for *me* when *I* went out of Egypt." ' " When leaving Egypt the Jews had to scale the highest level of spiritual purity, in order to partake of the Pascal lamb, a holy sacrificial repast. We who are this evening "reliving" the Exodus must do so as well. Anyone about to eat the Pascal lamb would certainly wash for *karpas*, even according to *Tosafos!*

לגאולה

ורחץ

משעבוד

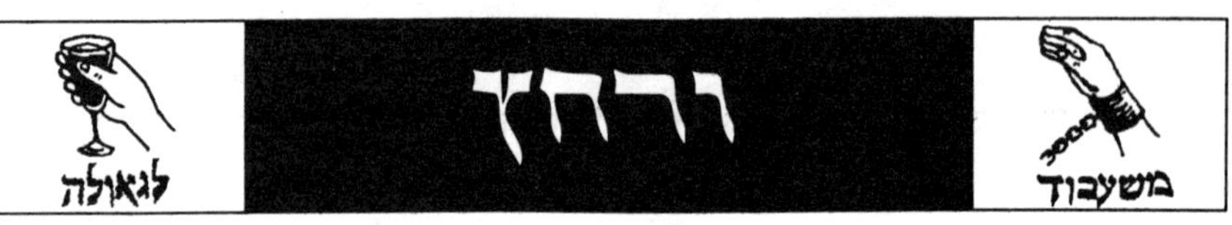

All present ritually wash their hands *without* ***making a blessing.*** *(O.C. 473:6)*

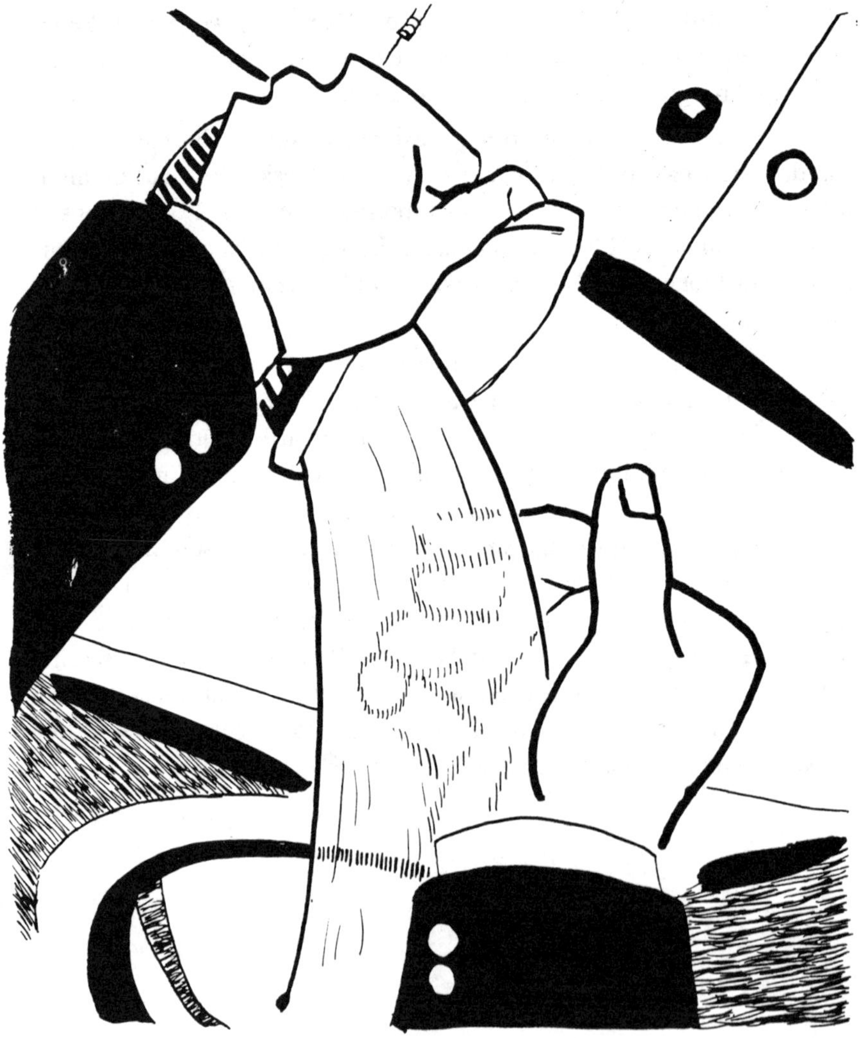

KARPAS

The Eating of a Vegetable Dipped in Salt Water

Why do we eat *Karpas*?

The *Talmud* in Tractate *Pesachim* 114b tells us the reason we eat vegetables before the meal - something highly unusual (they would typically be eaten during the meal proper) - is so the children will wonder why and ask. By so doing, they will remain awake, alert to the evening's message: We are the nation God chose to be His by bringing us out of Egypt.

What does the word *Karpas* mean?

Karpas is the Hebrew word for celery, and is found in the *Mishnah* (*Sh'viis* 9:1) and the *Talmud* (*Succah* 39b). But why was this particular vegetable singled out by the *Haggadah* as the generic term for "a vegetable dipped in liquid." Why not use the term "*yerek*", the Hebrew word for vegetable?

The *Maharil* (Rabbi Yaakov Moelin, b. Mainz, Germany 1365 - d. Worms, Germany 1427) explains: "The custom arose to use this particular vegetable because the Hebrew letters of the word *karpas* are an acronym describing the Jews' enslavement in Egypt: "ס" *samech* = 60; the other three letters spell out "*perach*" (פרח), which means "crushing labor". "Sixty" alludes to the sixty "*ribbo*" רבו (600,000) Jews who were oppressed by crushing labor in Egypt."

Which vegetables are acceptable?

Any vegetable whose blessing is "*borei p'ri ho'adama*" may be used for *karpas*. (*Magen Avraham*, O.C. 475:9)

There are contemporary *poskim* (decisors of Jewish Law) who maintain that a "green" vegetable is preferable, citing the *Talmud's* use of the word "yerek" (literally, "green") to identify the vegetable to be dipped. However, this opinion is found in none of the universally accepted codifications (*Chaye Odom, Mishnah Berurah,* and the *Aruch HaShulchan*). On the contrary, these authoritative works seem to indicate otherwise. The *Aruch HaShulchan*, for example (O.C.. 473:10),

בַּרְפַּס

says "For *karpas*, our custom is to take onions or radishes or a *yerek* whose blessing is '*borei p'ri ho'adama*', or potatoes."

Why do we dip the *Karpas* in salt water?

In line with the *Maharil's* interpretation of the word "*karpas*" as symbolic of the travail the Jews endured in Egypt, the dipping in salt water can now be understood. The salty water alludes to the sweat and tears shed by our subjugated forebears under the merciless oppression of their taskmasters.

Should one recline when eating *Karpas*?

The widespread contemporary practice is **not** to recline. This follows directly from the *Maharil's* thesis that *karpas* represents servitude. Only those Seder rituals which portray redemption and salvation require reclining; for those which depict our enslavement, one should not.

A question remains: if, as the *Talmud* says, *karpas* is eaten "in order to motivate the children to ask", why don't we do a juggling act, or some other outlandish stunt, to capture their attention?

The following answer gives us a new insight into all the sections of the Seder, and *karpas* in particular. The Rabbis never sought to capture the childrens' attention through the perpetration of some irrelevant, odd display. Rather, our progeny's inquisitiveness must be provoked through a purposeful recreation of the Exodus drama. Each section of the *Haggadah* is meant to be part of the retelling of the Exodus saga. *Kiddush* serves as the night's opening statement, thanking God for having taken us out of Egypt, and making us His chosen. *U'rechatz* references the Pascal lamb, requiring the highest level of ritual purity, *karpas* dipped in salt water denotes the "*Marror*" - bitterness - of our enslavement, as does the *Yachatz* soon to unfold.

When we eat *karpas*, the children wonder: Why are we eating a vegetable before the meal? The answer we intimate is: My dear child, tonight this **is** the meal. Just as a slave is happy to receive a simple, unprocessed vegetable which he scavenges from the ground after a day's crushing labor, so too we who are reliving the Egyptian enslavement eat this vegetable.

לגאולה

כרפס

משעבוד

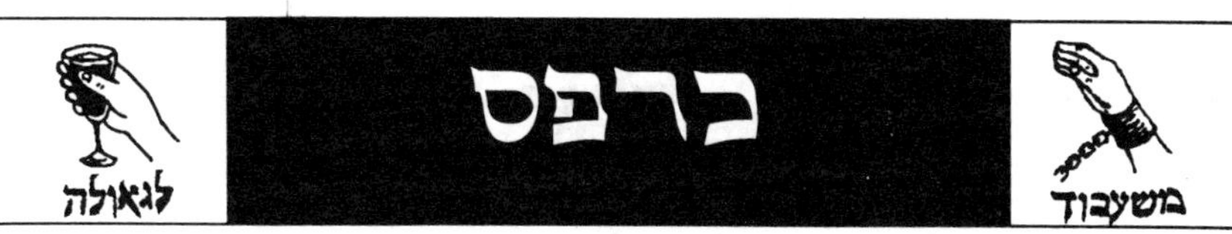

The karpas vegetable, (preferably not Marror) is dipped in the salt water. The blessing "borei p'ri ho'adama" is recited and less than an "olive size" of karpas vegetable is eaten. While reciting the "borei p'ri ho'adama" blessing have in mind the Marror vegetable, (to be eaten directly before the meal) as well. *(O.C. 473:6 with gloss of Mishnah Berurah)*

BLESSED ARE YOU ALMIGHTY, OUR GOD, KING OF THE UNIVERSE, WHO CREATES THE FRUIT OF THE EARTH.

בָּרוּךְ אַתָּה יהוה, אֱלֹהֵינוּ מֶלֶךְ הָעוֹלָם, בּוֹרֵא פְּרִי הָאֲדָמָה:

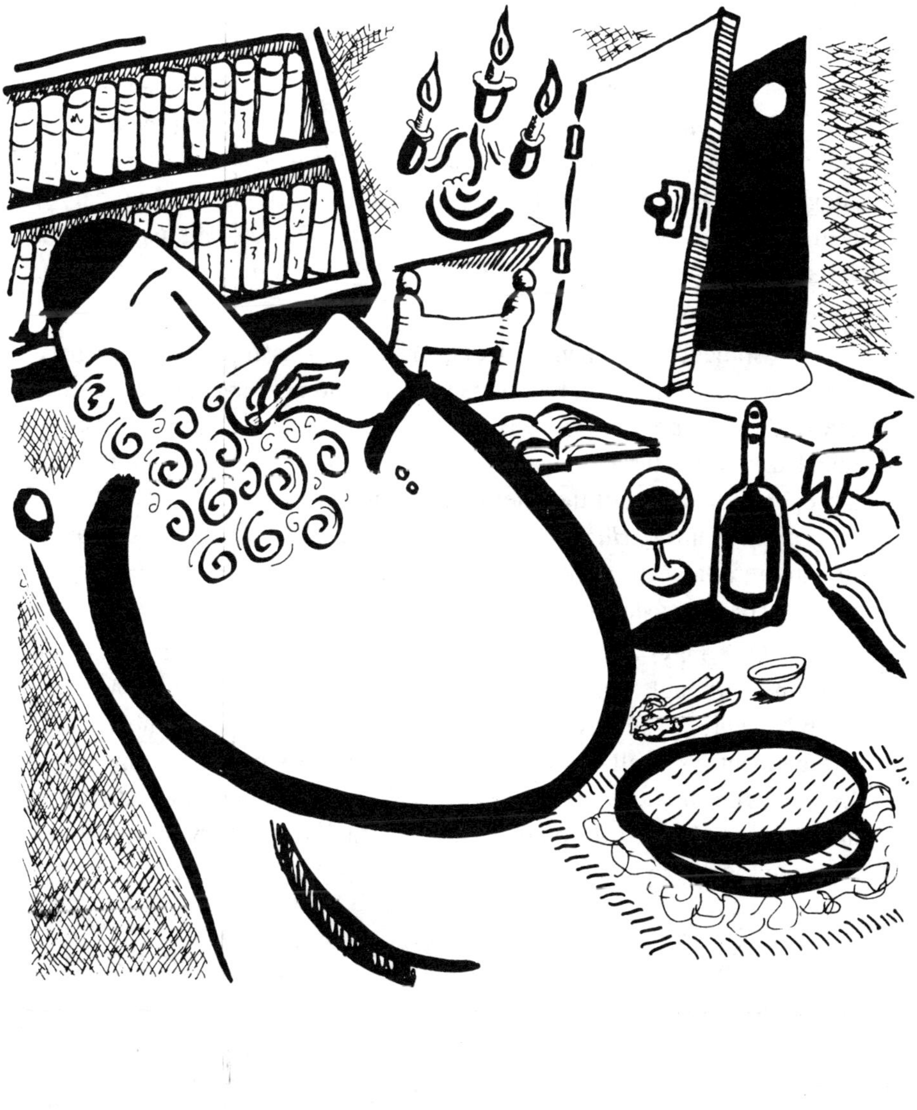

YACHATZ

The Breaking of the Middle Matzoh

Why do we break one of the *Matzohs*?

The *Torah* tells us "... seven days you shall eat *Matzohs*, '*lechem oni*', because you went forth from the land of Egypt in haste..." (*Deuteronomy XVI:3*) The *Torah* refers to *Matzoh* as "*lechem oni*". But what does *lechem oni* mean?

The simple interpretation is cited by *Rashi*: "Bread which reminds us of the afflictions with which we were afflicted in Egypt."

The *Talmud* gives two other interpretations. Noting the discrepancy between the spelling and the reading of the word "*oni*" (the spelling suggests the Hebrew word for "poor person", while the reading can be heard as the Hebrew word for "answer"), the *Talmud* tells us (Tractate *Pesachim* 36a): "Shmuel said: '*Lechem oni*', [is] bread over which we answer many things."

Shmuel's statement is to be understood as follows: our forefathers, oppressed in Egypt for so many years, did not have a whole loaf of bread; they ate broken *Matzohs*. We at the Seder table, Biblically commanded to relive the Passover saga, must utilize the *Matzoh* before us as a prop in our staging of the retelling. In final preparation for the *Maggid* section (next in the *Haggadah*), we break the *Matzoh* before us in order to conjure a tableau of poverty and oppression, and then begin to retell the story of our enslavement and eventual redemption.

One may wonder why a broken *Matzoh* is chosen to be the instrument through which we retell the Exodus narrative and not *Marror*, the bitter herb. The answer is: *Matzoh* conveys both the symbolism of enslavement as well as redemption, encompassing the entire saga. Broken *Matzoh* served as our diet when we were impoverished slaves, and later, whole *Matzohs* on our backs testified to the glory of God when we exited Egypt in great haste.

The leader takes the middle Matzoh and breaks it in two. The smaller half is replaced between the two whole Matzohs while the larger half is, by custom, hidden for later use as the afikomen. (O.C. 473:6 with gloss of Mishnah Berurah)

מַגִּיד

MAGGID

The Retelling of the Exodus Story

In his listing of Biblical commandments (positive command-ment 153), Maimonides (b. Spain 1135 - d. Egypt 1204) says: "[One is obligated] to retell [the story of] the Exodus from Egypt on the first night of Passover as it says [in the verse], 'You shall tell your son on that day, "Because of this did the Almighty do for me when I went out of Egypt." ' " (*Exodus XIII:8*) Clearly we are Biblically obligated to recount the story of the Exodus.

A comprehensive treatment of this obligation is presented in "The Premise", beginning on page 17. Nevertheless, a few additional points are in order.

Are women obligated in Maggid?

The *Sefer HaChinuch* (13th Century, Spain, *Mitzvah* 21) states explicitly that the obligation of *Maggid* rests on women as well as men. The great codifier *Chaye Odom* (130:12) so rules definitively. Therefore, if there are any men or women at the Seder who do not understand the Hebrew text, they should avail themselves of a transla-tion.

Many commentators ask: Why should women be obligated in *Maggid*, since it is time-bound, and therefore belonging to a category of *mitzvos* usually not incumbent upon women? The answer to this question follows directly from our commentary's premise, and can be found on page 28.

Is Maggid merely a verbal performance?

Even though on a Biblical level the accomplishment of *Maggid* need only be verbal, the Rabbis (and custom) added non-verbal embell-ishments to enhance the "retelling". This includes lifting of the *Matzoh*

מגיד

and *Marror* (during the recitation of "*Rabban Gamliel*"), removing drops of wine from the wine cup (at the mention of the plagues), the drinking of wine (the second of the four cups), the concealing and uncovering of the *Matzohs*, and raising our wine glass for the joyous singing of *Hallel*.

In fact, most of the non-verbal aspects of the Seder's other sections also serve to complement *Maggid*. For instance, drinking the four cups displays the newfound freedom of a slave redeemed. Eating the *Marror* relives the bitterness of our enslavement. Partaking of *karpas* and the broken *Matzoh* seats us among the slaves as they subsist on simple fare.

All of these depictions find their source in the *Torah's* directive for *Maggid* as quoted by the *Haggadah*: "In each generation, **a Jew is obligated to view himself as having gone out of Egypt** as it says in the verse: 'You shall tell your son on that day, "Because of this did the Almighty do for me when I went out of Egypt" '. [*Exodus XIII:8*] Not only were our forefathers redeemed from slavery by the Holy One, Blessed Be He, we too were redeemed with them." **Therefore we not only retell, but reenact.**

Are there guidelines for the retelling?

There certainly are. They include:

1. The need to **reenact,** not just retell, as mentioned above.

2. The requirement to **elaborate.** Whereas there is a Biblical obligation to "remember" the Exodus twice daily, on Passover night we must "retell".

3. The *Torah* demands that the retelling utilize the medium of **question and answer.** We thus begin the *Maggid* section with "*Ma Nishtana*", the four questions the child poses to the parent.

מגיד

The Matzoh is uncovered and raised for the recitation of the following paragraph. If the Matzohs are part of the Seder platter, the entire Seder platter may be raised. (O.C. 473:6)

If there are those who do not understand the Hebrew text of the Haggadah, the leader should explain what is being said. Obviously, the best way to follow the evening's proceedings is to read the English translation then the commentary and ask as many questions as time permits. (Ramah, O. C. 473:6)

הָא לַחְמָא עַנְיָא דִי אֲכָלוּ אַבְהָתָנָא בְּאַרְעָא דְמִצְרָיִם. כָּל דִּכְפִין יֵיתֵי וְיֵכֻל. כָּל דִּצְרִיךְ יֵיתֵי וְיִפְסַח. הַשַּׁתָּא הָכָא, לְשָׁנָה הַבָּאָה בְּאַרְעָא דְיִשְׂרָאֵל. הַשַּׁתָּא עַבְדֵי, לְשָׁנָה הַבָּאָה בְּנֵי חוֹרִין:

THIS IS THE POOR BREAD OUR FOREFATHERS ATE IN THE LAND OF EGYPT. ALL WHO ARE HUNGRY COME AND EAT. ALL WHO ARE IN NEED COME AND PARTAKE OF THE PASSOVER SEDER. NOW WE ARE HERE; NEXT YEAR IN THE LAND OF ISRAEL. NOW WE ARE SLAVES; NEXT YEAR FREEMEN.

COMMENTARY

This paragraph, although not part of *Maggid* per se, serves as its introduction. Its language and intent have mystified commentators. Some of the questions asked are:

1. Why is it written in Aramaic and not in Hebrew, as is all the rest of the *Haggadah*?

2. If indeed our intent is to call out and invite all in need of a Seder meal to our home, why don't we rise from the table, go out, and announce the invitation publicly? Of what use is it to call to the less fortunate from the walled, seated preserve of our dining room? They will surely not hear us!

Our thematic interpretation of *Maggid* as an annual declaration of our nation's ennobled chosen status discloses the true intent of this paragraph.

Maimonides points out that this introduction to the *Haggadah* was instituted only after the destruction of the first Temple, when the Jews were in Babylonia and their spoken tongue was Aramaic. Those at the holiday table about to celebrate their deliverance from the Egyptian bondage may ask: Why are we celebrating? Are we not today in exile, yet enduring oppression, and being chased from one country to another? Even if currently we enjoy some measure of security, we know this to be an aberration within the two-millennium history of the Diaspora. Would a freed prisoner celebrate the anniversary of his release if incarcerated again?

To this question the Haggadah answers:

The first deliverance was not just a freedom from bondage, but rather an active investiture - our election as God's nation. That being the case, we know for certain that He will have pity on us as a father pities his errant son, and deliver His chosen ones from this miserable exile as well. Therefore, even in the Diaspora we have great cause for celebration, because that first deliverance presages the final one.

(This understanding helps elucidate the phrase we say nightly in the evening prayer, "Who struck with His anger all the firstborn of Egypt and removed His nation from their midst **to eternal freedom**".)

With the above in mind, *we see our invitation to the poor as really dispatched to us*, i.e. those of us already in place at the Seder table. We strengthen our resolve with this consolation: "Let him [us] come and celebrate Passover! Now, we are here; next year may we be in the land of Israel! Now we are slaves; next year may we be freemen!"

*The Matzohs are removed from the table as if we had already eaten. This is
so the children's inquisitiveness should be aroused. (O.C. 473:6)
The second of the four cups of wine are now filled. (O.C. 473:7)
Having aroused the children's inquisitiveness, "Ma Nishtana" (the four questions) is now asked. If there are no children present, the adults ask each
other these questions. Even if only one person is making a Seder he still ver-
balizes the four questions aloud. (O.C. 473:7)*

WHY IS THIS NIGHT DIF-
FERENT FROM ALL OTHER
NIGHTS?

מַה נִּשְׁתַּנָּה הַלַּיְלָה הַזֶּה
מִכָּל הַלֵּילוֹת.

ON ALL OTHER NIGHTS WE
EAT CHOMETZ AND MATZOH.
ON THIS NIGHT -
ONLY **MATZOH**.

שֶׁבְּכָל הַלֵּילוֹת אָנוּ אוֹכְלִין
חָמֵץ וּמַצָּה. הַלַּיְלָה הַזֶּה
כֻּלּוֹ **מַצָּה**:

ON ALL OTHER NIGHTS WE
EAT ALL KINDS OF VEGETA-
BLES. ON THIS NIGHT -
MARROR.

שֶׁבְּכָל הַלֵּילוֹת אָנוּ אוֹכְלִין
שְׁאָר יְרָקוֹת. הַלַּיְלָה הַזֶּה
מָרוֹר:

ON ALL OTHER NIGHTS WE
DO NOT DIP EVEN ONCE. ON
THIS NIGHT -
WE **DIP** TWICE.

שֶׁבְּכָל הַלֵּילוֹת אֵין אָנוּ
מַטְבִּילִין אֲפִילוּ פַּעַם אֶחָת.
הַלַּיְלָה הַזֶּה שְׁתֵּי פְעָמִים:

ON ALL OTHER NIGHTS WE
EAT   EITHER   SITTING
UPRIGHT OR RECLINING. ON
THIS NIGHT -
WE ALL **RECLINE**.

שֶׁבְּכָל הַלֵּילוֹת אָנוּ אוֹכְלִין
בֵּין יוֹשְׁבִין וּבֵין מְסֻבִּין.
הַלַּיְלָה הַזֶּה כֻּלָּנוּ **מְסֻבִּין**.

--- COMMENTARY ---

Why does the *Haggadah* begin the *Maggid* section with children
asking questions? And why pose these specific four questions when in
fact the *Haggadah* will never answer them directly? Nowhere in the
Haggadah's exposition is there a mention of "*chometz*", "other herbs",
"dipping", or "reclining", all of which form the substance of the four
questions. Why prompt children to ask questions to which they never
receive answers?

מַה נִּשְׁתַּנָּה הַלַּיְלָה הַזֶּה

Applying our unifying theme of "chosenness", we begin to appreciate the *Haggadah's* approach. **The greatest gift Jewish parents can give their children is a sense of inheritance - an entitlement to a share in the chosen nation.** How indeed does a Jewish parent bestow that gift? The *Torah* tells us: we are commanded to teach our children the lesson of our "chosenness" on Passover eve. If this understanding is missing from the heart and mind of the child, how can he possibly appreciate his unique position in the world? What imperative is there for him to adhere to the *Torah* and all its laws if they are meaningless to him? Why should he strive to be different and unique?

The *Haggadah's* intent is to teach our children over and over again the great lesson that they are part of the chosen nation and have a special relationship with God. They must recognize that He chose *them* to serve Him as surely as their ancestors who left Egypt.

The sages prompted our children to ask, "Why is this night different?" *only as a means to an end.* This classic *Talmudic* methodology - "question and answer" - **involves** the children, by positioning them "center stage" in the historical epic of the Exodus. Thus they are alerted and sensitized to the great message we are about to transmit.

The exposition following the childrens' questions does not pretend to address the *questions* but rather the **children**. They can now feel fully a part of the Seder's message of "chosenness", having been recruited into the lead role of the *Maggid* drama.

The sages, masters of educational strategy, determinedly ignore the specific questions, refusing to answer them. By doing so, they focus the children on the foundational issue - *the election of the Jewish people, the historical fact that forms the very bedrock of Jewish faith.* Only when grounded in this indispensable certainty will all the details of observance follow. Without this foundation, the myriad laws and customs of Judaism have no permanent place in the heart and mind of a Jew, no matter how painstakingly explained.

The contemporary Hebrew after-school regimen, which surveys a spate of disconnected rituals culminating in a race through the *Haftorah* at *bar/bat mitzvah* time, is the antithesis of the *Torah's* holy approach. One would certainly not gather beautiful furnishings without having a sturdy house in which to install them. Any such attempt would expose the furnishings, as well as their owner, to the ravages of external destructive forces. So too, a Jewish child deserves the protection of a stalwart spiritual abode, which is an understanding of his "chosenness".

This message is especially compelling in contemporary society, which assails our children with all manner of pernicious influences. It falls to us - the parents - to furnish a protective environment by transmitting the message of the Exodus: we are the chosen of God, and must fulfill that mission by meticulously following the Almighty's *Torah*.

The Matzohs are brought back to the table and uncovered and we begin to recite the Maggid portion of the Haggadah. (O.C. 473:7) Reclining during the recitation of Maggid is not advised, rather it should be said with awe. (Mishnah Berurah 473:71)

We WERE SLAVES TO PHARAOH IN EGYPT. GOD TOOK US FROM THERE WITH A STRONG HAND AND AN OUTSTRETCHED ARM. IF THE HOLY ONE, BLESSED IS HE, HAD NOT TAKEN OUR FOREFATHERS FROM EGYPT, WE, OUR CHILDREN, AND OUR GRANDCHILDREN WOULD STILL BE ENSLAVED TO PHARAOH IN EGYPT. EVEN IF WE WERE ALL WISE, UNDERSTANDING, SAGE, AND KNOWLEDGEABLE IN THE TORAH; WE WOULD STILL BE COMMANDED TO TELL THE STORY OF THE EXODUS. AND ALL WHO EXPAND UPON THE STORY OF THE EXODUS, MERIT PRAISE.

עֲבָדִים הָיִינוּ לְפַרְעֹה בְּמִצְרַיִם, וַיּוֹצִיאֵנוּ יהוה אֱלֹהֵינוּ מִשָּׁם בְּיָד חֲזָקָה וּבִזְרוֹעַ נְטוּיָה. וְאִלּוּ לֹא הוֹצִיא הַקָּדוֹשׁ בָּרוּךְ הוּא אֶת אֲבוֹתֵינוּ מִמִּצְרַיִם, הֲרֵי אָנוּ וּבָנֵינוּ וּבְנֵי בָנֵינוּ מְשֻׁעְבָּדִים הָיִינוּ לְפַרְעֹה בְּמִצְרָיִם. וַאֲפִילוּ כֻּלָּנוּ חֲכָמִים, כֻּלָּנוּ נְבוֹנִים, כֻּלָּנוּ זְקֵנִים, כֻּלָּנוּ יוֹדְעִים אֶת הַתּוֹרָה, מִצְוָה עָלֵינוּ לְסַפֵּר בִּיצִיאַת מִצְרָיִם. וְכָל הַמַּרְבֶּה לְסַפֵּר בִּיצִיאַת מִצְרַיִם הֲרֵי זֶה מְשֻׁבָּח.

─────────── COMMENTARY ───────────

ואילו לנו הוציא

"If the Holy One, Blessed is He, had not taken our forefathers from Egypt, we, our children, and our grandchildren would still be enslaved to Pharaoh in Egypt."

All commentators struggle with the obvious question. How can the *Haggadah* be so sure that we would have remained slaves to Pharaoh if God had not redeemed us? Perhaps if the Jews had not been redeemed through the great miracles of the Exodus, their children or grandchildren

עֲבָדִים הָיִינוּ לְפַרְעֹה בְּמִצְרָיִם.

would have gained independence nevertheless. After all, an end to enslavement has come to numerous peoples within the last two centuries; why should the *Haggadah* assume a different prospective fate for the Jewish slaves in Egypt?

Following our unifying theme of "chosenness" the answer to this question comes almost intuitively. Having just asked the "four questions" the children are alert to and focused on our response. We use this moment of the childrens' greatest attentiveness *to introduce the "dramatis personae" of Maggid: the Jews, Pharaoh and God.*

The Jews and Pharaoh are presented respectively as slave and master, and God as the Divine Liberator. The Jews and Pharaoh are discussed at length throughout the rest of *Maggid*, while the paragraph before us, *"Avodim Hayinu"* - we were slaves in Egypt - expounds God's essence. The *Haggadah* describes God with that facet of His omnipotence which most relates to the Exodus: His absolute superintendency over human affairs, השגחה פרטית - *"Hasgacha P'ratis"*.

This Divine attribute is the one with which God introduces Himself in the first of the Ten Commandments: "I am the Lord your God who took you out of the land of Egypt." The Jewish understanding of "God" already presupposes that He is the Almighty Creator of heaven and earth; that need not be stated. We believe additionally, however, that God not only created the world but that His Divine rule constantly and continuously controls all happenings in it; **nothing** *"just happens"*. This belief is obligatory for every Jew, being the first of the Ten Commandments and a fundamental building block in the structure of our faith.

The *Haggadah's* phrase, "If the Holy One, Blessed is He, had not taken our forefathers from Egypt, we, our children, and our grandchildren would still be enslaved to Pharaoh in Egypt", is to be properly understood in this light. These words describe one of God's attributes - the attribute we learn from the Exodus itself. All we are really saying is that fate is in God's hands; **God is the Director of all the world's events.**

Heaven forbid we should even think for one second that our deliverance, or the release of any other enslaved people, was merely a natural process. *God's choosing us to be His, by miraculously delivering us from bondage, is the sole reason why we are a free and ennobled people today.*

This great lesson of God's ever-present hand in all that occurs in the world is the first one we teach our children when we begin our answer to them. Without this recognition, the Exodus is devoid of its Divine imprint and cannot serve as a proof of our "chosenness".

ואפילו כולנו חכמים

"Even if we were all wise, understanding, sage, and knowledgeable in the Torah: we would still be commanded to tell the story of the Exodus."

On the surface this statement of the *Haggadah* is very difficult, because it intimates that someone who is sage, understanding, old and wise in the knowledge of the *Torah*, should be exempt from adhering to the *mitzvos* found in it. How is this even thinkable? Would anyone suggest a sage be exempt from the prayer service, hearing the *Torah* readings or observing the myriad Shabbos rituals because his erudition has won him a waiver from these obligations?

The explanation is as follows: The *Torah* formulates the commandment to retell the story of the Exodus in terms of a father transmitting the Passover message of "chosenness" to his son.

Perhaps then, if one has already learned and passed on the message of our "chosenness" to the next generation, it can logically be argued that he should be exempt from participation in the *mitzvah*. This is why the *Haggadah* points out that, if there is no son to whom to transmit the message, or even if both father and son are very learned, and already apprised of the import and meaning of our Exodus, the *mitzvah* of *Maggid* must still be performed. As the *Sefer HaChinuch* states: "Even to oneself there is an obligation to verbalize this message, so that one should be impacted. Through speech the heart is awakened." (*Mitzvah* 21)

What the *Sefer HaChinuch* means to convey is as follows: If the message of "chosenness" was strictly intellectual, perhaps indeed, the wise and sage would be exempt from *Maggid*. After all, they already know that through the Exodus, God chose us as His nation. Why should they be compelled to repeat their knowledge year after year?

The answer is: That the Jews were chosen to be God's people is not just a **statement of fact**. It is much more - it is a **belief**. As true as a statement of fact can be, it does not necessarily create an imperative for a person's life's goals and actions. For example - one can say with absolute certainty that gravity is a "law of nature", yet it is totally external to the utterer. In no way will the person making the statement change his life because of that knowledge.

A **belief** on the other hand, becomes internalized - it directs the individual's very existence. A belief guides a person's life; the more profound the belief, the deeper the imprint on the individual.

The Exodus' message of "chosenness" is a belief. It must be ingested and digested, serving as the nutrients of a Jew's spiritual growth. Just as we repeat twice daily the foundational belief in God found in the "*Shema*" - Hear O Israel, the Lord is our God the Lord is One - so that it should become engraved on the tablets of our heart and shape our devotion, so too, the belief in our "chosenness" has to be before us constantly. This belief gives our lives special meaning and clear purpose. We were chosen to be God's ministers, devoting ourselves to His service through the *Torah*.

The *Haggadah* wants to teach us this lesson: *Maggid* is a statement of belief, not just a historical statement of fact. Therefore, even the wise and sage must reiterate the story of the Exodus, in order to strengthen their belief in our "chosenness".

וְכָל־הַמַּרְבֶּה לְסַפֵּר בִּיצִיאַת מִצְרַיִם הֲרֵי זֶה מְשֻׁבָּח

IT HAPPENED THAT RABBI ELIEZER, RABBI YEHOSHUAH, RABBI ELAZAR BEN AZARYA, RABBI AKIVA AND RABBI TARFON WERE CELEBRATING THE PASSOVER SEDER IN BNEI BRAK. THEY SPENT THE ENTIRE NIGHT RECOUNTING THE STORY OF THE EXODUS UNTIL THEIR STUDENTS CAME AND TOLD THEM, "MASTERS, THE TIME FOR RECITING THE MORNING SHEMA HAS ARRIVED."

מַעֲשֶׂה בְּרַבִּי אֱלִיעֶזֶר וְרַבִּי יְהוֹשֻׁעַ וְרַבִּי אֶלְעָזָר בֶּן עֲזַרְיָה וְרַבִּי עֲקִיבָא וְרַבִּי טַרְפוֹן שֶׁהָיוּ מְסֻבִּין בִּבְנֵי־בְרַק, וְהָיוּ מְסַפְּרִים בִּיצִיאַת מִצְרַיִם כָּל אוֹתוֹ הַלַּיְלָה, עַד שֶׁבָּאוּ תַלְמִידֵיהֶם וְאָמְרוּ לָהֶם, רַבּוֹתֵינוּ, הִגִּיעַ זְמַן קְרִיאַת שְׁמַע שֶׁל שַׁחֲרִית.

COMMENTARY

The *Haggadah* brings this anecdote to buttress the previous paragraph's point: even the very learned are obligated to review the lesson of our "chosenness".

The greatest sages of the *Talmud* participated fully in the *mitzvah* of *Maggid*, even when their children and students were not with them (the students in this instance only came to them in the morning). These sages were certainly intellectually appreciative of every nuance of Israel's specialness, yet, they discussed the import of the Exodus all night among themselves until the morning. These giants, more than anyone, wanted to spiritually elevate themselves and gain a closeness to God by imbibing the lesson of our nation's "chosenness".

There is a lesson to be learned: We must strengthen not only our children's understanding of our special position, but our own as well. We should leave the Seder with our belief and service invigorated. "The more one tells about the Exodus, the more one is praiseworthy."

RABBI ELAZAR BEN AZARYA SAID, "I AM LIKE A SEVENTY YEAR OLD MAN, EVEN SO, I WAS NEVER SUCCESSFUL IN FINDING THE SCRIPTURAL SOURCE FOR THE OBLIGATION TO MENTION THE EXODUS EVERY EVENING, UNTIL BEN ZOMA EXPOUNDED THE VERSE, 'SO THAT YOU WILL REMEMBER THE DAY OF YOUR DEPARTURE FROM EGYPT ALL THE DAYS OF YOUR LIFE'. *(Deuteronomy XVI:3)* THE PHRASE, 'DAYS OF YOUR LIFE', REFERS TO THE MENTION OF THE EXODUS IN THE DAY, THE SCRIPTURE'S ADDITION OF THE WORD 'ALL' INCLUDES THE NIGHTS AS WELL." THE SAGES DISAGREE [WITH BEN ZOMA] SAYING: "THE 'DAYS OF YOUR LIFE' REFERS TO THIS WORLD; '*ALL* THE DAYS OF YOUR LIFE' INCLUDES THE MESSIANIC ERA."

אָמַר רַבִּי אֶלְעָזָר בֶּן עֲזַרְיָה הֲרֵי אֲנִי כְּבֶן שִׁבְעִים שָׁנָה, וְלֹא זָכִיתִי שֶׁתֵּאָמֵר יְצִיאַת מִצְרַיִם בַּלֵּילוֹת, עַד שֶׁדְּרָשָׁהּ בֶּן זוֹמָא. שֶׁנֶּאֱמַר, לְמַעַן תִּזְכֹּר אֶת יוֹם צֵאתְךָ מֵאֶרֶץ מִצְרַיִם כֹּל יְמֵי חַיֶּיךָ. יְמֵי חַיֶּיךָ הַיָּמִים. כֹּל יְמֵי חַיֶּיךָ הַלֵּילוֹת. וַחֲכָמִים אוֹמְרִים, יְמֵי חַיֶּיךָ הָעוֹלָם הַזֶּה. כֹּל יְמֵי חַיֶּיךָ, לְהָבִיא לִימוֹת הַמָּשִׁיחַ.

―――――――― COMMENTARY ――――――――

If the retelling of the story of the Exodus is so critical to our identity as Jews, having determined our "chosenness", how can we possibly mention it but once a year?

This paragraph answers us: Indeed, we need make mention of the Exodus **every** day and night of the year, besides the more elaborate *mitzvah* to retell the story of our redemption in its entirety at the Seder.

"Hear O Israel...", the prayer that is recited twice daily, is a Jew's primary declaration of the acceptance of God as the Almighty. We mention the Egyptian Exodus in the final verse of this service: "I am the Lord your God, Who brought you out from the land of Egypt to be your God; I am the Lord your God." (*Numbers XV:41*) By placing the Exodus together with "Hear O Israel", we show its importance: **we equate the Exodus with the acceptance of God Himself.**

BLESSED IS THE ALL-PRE-
SENT GOD, BLESSED IS HE.
BLESSED IS THE ONE WHO
GAVE THE TORAH TO HIS
NATION, ISRAEL. BLESSED IS
HE. THE TORAH SPEAKS OF
FOUR TYPES OF CHILDREN:
ONE WISE, ONE WICKED,
ONE SIMPLE AND ONE WHO
DOES NOT KNOW HOW TO
ASK.

בָּרוּךְ הַמָּקוֹם, בָּרוּךְ הוּא,
בָּרוּךְ שֶׁנָּתַן תּוֹרָה לְעַמּוֹ
יִשְׂרָאֵל. בָּרוּךְ הוּא. כְּנֶגֶד
אַרְבָּעָה בָנִים דִּבְּרָה
תוֹרָה. אֶחָד חָכָם. וְאֶחָד
רָשָׁע. וְאֶחָד תָּם. וְאֶחָד
שֶׁאֵינוֹ יוֹדֵעַ לִשְׁאוֹל.

COMMENTARY

This introduction to the "four sons" has confounded all commentators. Why at this point in the *Haggadah* do we bless God for having
given us the *Torah*?

Our central theme of "chosenness" provides the answer. If we
indeed were chosen by God to be His nation, then in a Divine sense, we
are His ministers. How can we insure that our children who will succeed
us in His service will be prepared for their ministerial office?

The answer is: *The **Torah** is the chosen ministers' definitive manu-
al, containing not only all a Jew needs to know in order to serve the
Almighty King but also how best to instruct our children in His service.*

Looking to the *Torah* for guidance, we find that the word of God
recognizes children's different psyches and addresses four personality
types among them. Thus the Hagaddah says, "Blessed is the One who
gave the *Torah* to His nation Israel; Blessed is He. The *Torah* speaks Of
four types of children..."

Each one of the sons is instructed according to his ability and
frame of mind, but all are taught this most important lesson: they are part
of the chosen nation.

THE WISE SON, WHAT DOES HE SAY? "WHAT ARE THE RITUALS, RULES AND LAWS WHICH GOD OUR LORD HAS COMMANDED YOU?" *(Deuteronomy VI:20)* YOUR RESPONSE TO HIM SHOULD UTILIZE THE LAWS OF THE PASCAL LAMB: ONE MAY NOT EAT ANYTHING AFTER HAVING EATEN THE PASCAL LAMB.

THE WICKED SON, WHAT DOES HE SAY? "WHAT IS THIS SERVICE TO *YOU?*" *(Exodus XII:26)* [HIS CHOICE OF THE TERM "**YOU**" INDICATES] YOU AND NOT HIM! BY EXCLUDING HIMSELF FROM THE [JEWISH] COMMUNITY HE HAS DENIED THE BASIC PRINCIPLE [OF JUDAISM]. YOUR RESPONSE TO HIM SHOULD BLUNT HIS TEETH BY TELLING HIM, "BECAUSE OF THIS DID GOD DO FOR *ME* WHEN I WENT OUT OF EGYPT". *(Exodus XIII:8)* FOR *ME* BUT NOT FOR *HIM*. HAD HE BEEN THERE HE WOULD NOT HAVE BEEN LIBERATED.

THE SIMPLE SON, WHAT DOES HE SAY? "WHAT IS THIS?" TELL HIM: "WITH A

חָכָם מָה הוּא אוֹמֵר, מָה הָעֵדֹת וְהַחֻקִּים וְהַמִּשְׁפָּטִים אֲשֶׁר צִוָּה יהוה אֱלֹהֵינוּ אֶתְכֶם. וְאַף אַתָּה אֱמָר לוֹ כְּהִלְכוֹת הַפֶּסַח, אֵין מַפְטִירִין אַחַר הַפֶּסַח אֲפִיקוֹמָן.

רָשָׁע מָה הוּא אוֹמֵר, מָה הָעֲבוֹדָה הַזֹּאת לָכֶם. לָכֶם וְלֹא לוֹ, וּלְפִי שֶׁהוֹצִיא אֶת עַצְמוֹ מִן הַכְּלָל, כָּפַר בְּעִיקָר. וְאַף אַתָּה הַקְהֵה אֶת שִׁנָּיו וֶאֱמָר לוֹ, בַּעֲבוּר זֶה עָשָׂה יהוה לִי בְּצֵאתִי מִמִּצְרָיִם. לִי וְלֹא לוֹ, אִלּוּ הָיָה שָׁם לֹא הָיָה נִגְאָל.

תָּם מָה הוּא אוֹמֵר, מַה זֹּאת. וְאָמַרְתָּ אֵלָיו, בְּחוֹזֶק

כְּנֶגֶד אַרְבָּעָה בָנִים דִּבְּרָה תוֹרָה

STRONG HAND GOD TOOK US OUT OF EGYPT FROM THE HOUSE OF SLAVERY".

(Exodus XIII:14)

יָד הוֹצִיאָנוּ יהוה מִמִּצְרַיִם, מִבֵּית עֲבָדִים.

AND THE SON WHO DOES NOT KNOW HOW TO ASK YOU SHOULD INITIATE HIS INSTRUCTION, AS IT SAYS, "YOU WILL TELL YOUR SON ON THAT DAY SAYING: 'BECAUSE OF THIS DID GOD DO FOR ME WHEN I WENT OUT OF EGYPT' ".

(Exodus XIII:8)

וְשֶׁאֵינוֹ יוֹדֵעַ לִשְׁאוֹל אַתְּ פְּתַח לוֹ, שֶׁנֶּאֱמַר וְהִגַּדְתָּ לְבִנְךָ בַּיּוֹם הַהוּא לֵאמֹר, בַּעֲבוּר זֶה עָשָׂה יהוה לִי בְּצֵאתִי מִמִּצְרָיִם.

COMMENTARY

Part I

An Overview: **The *Torah* speaks of four sons...**

In four distinct passages (three in the Book of Exodus and one in Deuteronomy), the *Torah* instructs us how to answer our inquisitive children about the *mitzvos* of Passover. The Bible's depiction of the "four sons" contrasts notably with the *Haggadah's* portrayal. The reader will benefit from seeing the two in juxtaposition:

THE WISE SON

Biblical Passage	**Haggadah's Text**
Deuteronomy VI:10-25	**Question**: What are the rituals, rules and laws which God our Lord has commanded you?
When God, your Lord, brings you to the land that He swore to your fathers, Abraham, Isaac, and Jacob, that He will give to you, [you will find] great, flourishing cities... In the future, *your child may ask you,* **"what are the rituals, rules and laws which God our Lord has commanded you?"**	**Answer**: One may not eat anything after having eaten the Pascal lamb.

You will tell your son, **"We were slaves to Pharaoh in Egypt and God took us out of Egypt with a mighty hand.** God directed great and terrible miracles against Pharaoh and all his household before our very eyes.

We are the ones He brought out of there, to bring us to, and give us the land He promised to our forefathers.

God commanded us to keep all these rules so that we would remain in awe of God for all time, so that we would survive even as we are today. It is our privilege to safeguard and keep this entire mandate before God our Lord, as He commanded us."

THE WICKED SON

Biblical Passage

Exodus XII:25-27

When you come to the land that God will give you, as He promised, you must [also] keep this service. *Your children may [then] ask you,* **"What is this service to you?"** **You must answer, "It is the Passover service to God. He passed over the houses of the Israelites in Egypt when He struck the Egyptians, sparing our homes..."**

Haggadah's Text

Question: What is this service to you?

Answer: Because of this did God do for me when I went out of Egypt.

THE SIMPLE SON

Biblical Passage

Exodus XIII:11-14

When God will bring you to the land of Canaan, as He swore to you and your forefathers, and He will give it to you... *Your child may later ask you,* **"What is this?"** **You will tell him, "With a strong hand God took us out of Egypt from the house of slavery..."**

Haggadah's Text

Question: What is this?

Answer: With a strong hand God took us out of Egypt from the house of slavery.

THE SON WHO DOES NOT KNOW HOW TO ASK

Biblical Passage	**Haggadah's Text**
Exodus XIII:5-8	**Question:** None.

When God will bring you to the land of the Canaanites... As He swore to your forefathers, to give you a land flowing with milk and honey,

Answer: Because of this did God do for me when I went out of Egypt.

you should do this service in this month [*Nissan*]. Seven days you will eat *Matzohs... You will tell your son on that day saying,* **"Because of this did God do for me when I went out of Egypt."**

(*It is noteworthy and intriguing that each of the above passages alludes to the possession of the land, the bequeathment of which capped the process begun in Egypt on that first Passover night. For a full discussion of how the land of Israel figures in the "chosenness" of the Jewish people,* see our exposition *of Vayeired Mitzraima and Dayeinu.*)

A reader of these Biblical passages is puzzled. Why are four distinct father-son dialogues recorded in the *Torah*, when one would suffice?

The answer to this perplexing question was transmitted to the Rabbis through an oral tradition dating back to Sinai: these four excerpts reference four character types, each with a unique personality. The written *Torah* does not identify these character types; the oral tradition (the *Haggadah*), by teaching us which child speaks in each passages, does.

But there still remain some more basic questions, requiring our attention.

As explained in our commentary to the previous section, the *Torah* not only gives us the "what" to tell our children but the "how" to communicate it as well. The "what" is alike for all children; we have only one universal text of the *Haggadah*, not four! Moreover, nowhere in rabbinic literature do we find an obligation to categorize our children as wise, wicked, simple and not able to ask, so that we should be able to address the *Torah's* designated reply to them.

On the contrary, we find just the opposite. The answers given in the Torah to the wise and wicked sons are mentioned elsewhere in the *Haggadah* for all present at the Seder table to hear: "We were slaves to Pharaoh in Egypt and God took us out of Egypt with a mighty hand, (the *Torah's* answer to the Wise son) appears as the immediate reply to the "Four Questions" and "It is the Passover service to God. He passed over the houses of the Israelites in Egypt when He struck the Egyptians, sparing our homes", (the *Torah's* answer to the Wicked son) is part of *Rabban Gamliel's* exposition later in the *Haggadah* which is said by all. Were we indeed obligated to give four distinct answers, we would certainly have to direct each reply to its intended son. Obviously, we must tell **all** our children **alike** the same story of the Exodus. Why then do we find four distinct replies in the *Torah* when one long answer including the remarks to all the sons should suffice?

Also, and just as troubling, nowhere do we find an obligation for the sons to ask the specific questions which match their personality type. Shouldn't the children at the Seder table have to ask the questions the *Torah* says they will ask? Why did the Rabbis formulate four new questions to initiate the *Maggid* section ("Why is this night different from all other nights") when they could have easily posed those mentioned in the *Torah* itself?

We must deduce: there is in fact no obligation for our children to ask the questions posed by the *Torah* nor for us to identify them as wise, wicked, simple and unable to ask, so as to furnish the respective Biblical reply.

The *Torah* says something else altogether: every child has an inquisitiveness which is a basic part of their psyche. This inquisitiveness constantly produces questions which the *Torah* commands us to answer; not just those verbalized - those questions will surely be answered - but those unspoken questions, which if not addressed, will greatly retard and perhaps even pervert the child's spiritual (and emotional) growth.

A child's inquisitiveness prompts an unconscious pondering of every one of the questions posed by the sons in the *Torah*. *The Torah is not discussing four different children but **one** child with several different and quite normal facets to him.*

There is in each one of us all the characteristic traits represented by the four sons. God created us with multiple facets to our personality and it is our lifelong obligation to harness each of them to His service.

The truly important questions emanating from children, are rarely those which they ask in so many words. But these are precisely the ones a Jewish parent is Biblically obliged to address. These questions are fashioned by the various aspects of their psyche and must be answered properly so as to channel each component characteristic to the worship of the Almighty.

This is precisely why it is from the reply to the "son who does not know how to ask" that we draw the Biblical source for *Maggid*. The *Torah* teaches: your children may not verbalize any questions but you should surely realize they have questions and you must answer them.

This unverbalized, even subconscious, questioning, is an attempt to discover one's identity. For us Jews this is especially important; we wonder, "why are we different and what makes us special?" A Jewish child yearns to understand his "chosenness" and we are instructed by the *Torah* to satisfy this spiritual craving.

Having framed the "four sons" in their Biblical context, we are now ready to analyze the *Haggadah's* text in detail.

Part II

The Haggadah's Text Analyzed

Of the literally scores of textually based questions asked with regard to the four sons, we will focus on several which are perhaps the most glaringly difficult:

1. Why do the *Haggadah's* answers to the Wise and Wicked Sons differ from the *Torah's* replies to them?

2. The *Haggadah's* answers do not suffice to fulfill one's Biblical obligation of *Maggid*.

Any *Talmudic* student knows that the entire source for the commandment to retell the story of the Exodus stems from the four quoted passages above. If one does not follow the Biblical prescription for that retelling, how can one hope to fulfill the *mitzvah* of *Maggid*? Yet here, neither the learning of the laws of Passover with the Wise Son nor the admonition we give the Wicked Son adhere to the Biblical prescription. The *Haggadah's* replies have nothing to do with retelling the story of the Exodus. How then can the *Haggadah* offer its replies as a substitute for the *Torah's*?

3. What differentiates the Wise Son from the Wicked Son? (If it is because the Wicked Son says, "What is this service to *you*?", doesn't the Wise Son also say, "What are the rituals, rules and laws that God our Lord has commanded *you*?")

4. Why juxtapose "**Wicked**" with "**Wise**" and not with the more obvious characterological type "**Good**"? (Good : Wicked, Wise : Foolish)

Our commentary's theme of "chosenness" answers these questions with a new insight into the Wise and Wicked Sons' comments and our response to them.

The *Haggadah's* answers are not different than those found in the Bible but rather explain the *Torah's* pedagogical tactic.

Each of the four answers gives us historical facts about the Exodus and all of them should be told to every child present at the Seder - as indeed the *Haggadah* does! But our goal in retelling the story of the Exodus is not only to teach historical facts but to transmit an understanding - the understanding that we are the chosen nation. How indeed do we accomplish this critical transmission? How do we best reach each child with all their multiple personality traits? The *Haggadah* expounds: this is exactly the query the *Torah* comes to answer.

By splitting the historical retelling of the Exodus into four distinct replies and not lumping them all together, the *Torah* teaches us a great *lesson in pedagogy*. Imbedded into each of the four replies is not only the history of the Exodus but the *Torah's* educational strategy for teaching the great lesson of Israel's chosenness to four personality types.

As explained in Part I of this section, the *Torah* does not speak of four **different** sons but rather four different traits found in every one of our children. These traits are; (1) the intellectual, (2) the rebellious, (3) the pure and (4) the apathetic. The *Haggadah* teaches us: each one of these traits must be addressed individually **as if** we were talking to four different sons (children).

The *Haggadah* proceeds to set forth the *Torah's* education strategies to transmit the great lesson of the Exodus: our nation's "chosenness".

The wise son [the intellectual trait] seems to question only the details of his ministerial duties ("What are the rituals, rules, and laws...?"), not his appointment to "chosenness", but we must not be deluded by his apparent precociousness and intellectual understanding. He is not yet the "Good" son, only "Wise". Even though he knows we were given special "rituals, rules and laws" only applicable to the chosen ministers of the Almighty, the *Haggadah* teaches us that the knowledge of our "chosenness" alone is not enough; the **"taste"** of that "chosenness" must remain on our palate throughout life.

Looking back to the Bible, we see this interpretation clearly in the *Torah's* response to the "Wise son". He asks about rituals, rules and laws and the *Torah* instructs us to answer him, "We were slaves to Pharaoh in Egypt and God took us out of Egypt with a mighty hand." How does the answer address the question? The *Haggadah* explains the *Torah's* dialogue. This passage references the "Wise son" who seeks a purely intellectual understanding of "chosenness". The *Torah* answers him: an intellectual understanding of "chosenness" will not suffice, it must be experiential. We must experience our slavery in Egypt and our redemption by Divine intervention. Only such an understanding can imprint itself on our very soul and thus constantly be with us.

With this interpretation we also understand the perplexing literal meaning of the *Haggadah's* response to the Wise Son, "Tell him כ-הלכות *similar* to the laws of the Pascal lamb." Indeed our obligation on Passover night is not to teach the laws of the Pascal lamb but to borrow and utilize the lesson of its laws in fulfilling *Maggid*. The reason for not eating any food after partaking of the Pascal lamb is so the taste of the Pascal lamb should remain with us. So too, a purely intellectual awareness of our chosenness is insufficient. We must instill this lesson so deeply that its "taste" remains with us always.

The wicked son [the rebellious trait] sees the Exodus as a historical event only; even assuming our forefathers were chosen, it was only they who were so elected, but not all Jews for all time. This son refuses to see the current Jewish generation as part of an eternally chosen nation.

The *Haggadah* points out the profoundly serious implications of the wicked son's comments. Whether he realizes it or not, his denial of the Jewish nation's perpetual "chosenness" really repudiates the Divine aegis of the *Torah* itself, for the *Torah* explicitly cites God's consecration of Israel as His own forever.

Moreover, the *Haggadah* here asserts that denial of the Divinity of the *Torah* will eventually lead to a denial of God Himself; hence the

Haggadah states, "By excluding himself [the Wicked son] from the [Jewish] community, he has denied the basic principle [of Judaism]." The "basic principle" is belief in the Almighty Himself.

All this is alluded to in the *Torah* by the omission of God in the Wicked sons' question. Whereas the Almighty is prominent in the Wise son's query, the Wicked son does not acknowledge Him.

How accurate our Sages were! Those Jews who rejected Israel's eternal "chosenness" and special destiny invariably ended up rejecting the *Torah* and ultimately the Almighty Himself. Daily, our own eyes bear witness to this tragic progression.

The *Haggadah* explains the *Torah's* strategy for reaching the "Wicked son". He must be made to feel how strongly his own father believes in Israel's "chosenness." To him we retort, "We certainly were and **are** chosen by God. Not only the generation of the Exodus was chosen but 'God did this for **me** when **I** left Egypt'. I too was chosen, as were all Jews for eternity. Even you, who deny this, are chosen. Only those Jews, who at the time of the Exodus continued to cling to Egypt's culture and mores, and by so doing showed they did not want to be chosen, were granted their wicked wish and perished with the Egyptians."

This is precisely what the *Torah* means when replying to the "Wicked son", "It is the Passover service to God. He passed over the houses of the Israelites in Egypt when He struck the Egyptians, sparing our homes." The entire point of God's passing over our homes while killing the Egyptians was to choose the Jews by so doing. You who deny our "chosenness", would have certainly perished with the Egyptians.

The *Haggadah* continues: we must explain to him that his denial will avail him nought. The word "*hak'hei*" used in reply to the "Wicked son" is defined: to make blunt or to break the power of. We must show every Jew the futility of trying to shed his "chosenness" and its inherent mission; God-given, it is irrevocable.

Many Jews believe the Seder is an ecumenical event proclaiming universal freedom and thereby make the same mistake as the Wicked son. They invite gentiles to their home to share in what they take to be the evening's generic message.

Their good intentions are misplaced. Passover's message is not one of universal freedom. God did not free all the world's slaves on that night! Only the Jewish nation was liberated from their oppressors. The miraculous manner in which our nation achieved liberty was God's medium for declaring His choice of the Jews as the "Chosen People". Passover night is the time for Jews to celebrate proudly this "chosenness", without any self-denial.

Our presentation clarifies another perplexity. After blunting his argument we tell him, "Because of this did God do for me when I went out of Egypt". (*Exodus XIII:8*) Isn't this what we tell the son who does not know how to ask? Why then does the Hagaddah use this verse in the reply to the wicked son?

The *Haggadah* is giving us another profound lesson in pedagogy. How is it possible that the wicked son came to make such a grave mistake? The sages answer: his education must have been lacking. The only way to get through to him is to begin his Jewish education anew, from the very beginning, patiently and lovingly filling in all the gaps.

The *Haggadah's* simple son and son who does not know how to ask mirror exactly the text found in the *Torah* (see opening comments to this section).

The **simple son** [the pure trait] intuitively senses his election to "chosenness" without any confusion. He asks, "What is **this**?", only desiring a concretized articulation of his chosen status. The *Torah's* strategy is to tell him, "With a strong hand God took us out of Egypt from the house of slavery" - a clear and unadulterated statement.

Many Jews feel the need to apologize for our "chosenness", leading them to a pedagogic style which takes the sublime and makes it ridiculous. A Jewish child (or adult) does not accept obfuscation; he seeks the truth and will accept only that.

The son who does not know how to ask [the apathetic trait] is complacent about his current situation and does not want the bother that examination of his "chosenness" would demand. The *Torah* teaches us that we must challenge and thereby awaken him from this passive religious disposition.

Many parents feel they cannot impose a lifestyle on their children, maintaining that, "When they are older they will make their own decision about religion". The *Torah* both written and oral, instructs us differently. Basic beliefs and lessons of Judaism have to be part of a parent-initiated dialogue with a child from an early age. The earlier great truths are learned the better they are integrated. How can the grown child be expected to make an "educated" decision about religion without the benefit of a Jewish education? How telling, that we learn the entire *mitzvah* of *Maggid* from this son.

From the first three sons (wise, wicked and simple) we learn that we must instruct our children about their Jewish identity not only on Passover but throughout the entire year. This is clearly stated in the verses themselves, "when your son will ask you" i.e. whenever he will ask you. Additionally, from the *Torah's* wise son we learn even a greater lesson. Whereas the verses of the wicked and simple son clearly indicate they are asking about Passover, the wise son is certainly not; he is asking about the *Torah* in general. We must instruct our children about their chosen status in connection with the entirety of their religious devotion.

Instruction in Judaism cannot and should not be restricted to a few hours at the Passover Seder but must be an ongoing and comprehensive pursuit.

The specific instruction of our children, associated with the retelling of the Exodus, is derived from the son who does not know how to ask. Having just mentioned this source verse, the *Haggadah* proceeds in the next section to analyze its wording in order to determine when precisely the retelling must occur.

IF ONE ASKS: PERHAPS THE OBLIGATION TO RETELL THE STORY OF THE EXODUS BEGINS FROM THE FIRST DAY OF THE MONTH OF NISSAN? WE COUNTER BY QUOTING THE BIBLE, "YOU SHALL TELL YOUR SON ON THAT DAY,". *(Exodus XIII:8)* IF ONE STILL ARGUES, PER-HAPS "ON THAT DAY" REFERS TO THE DAYTIME [AND NOT THE NIGHTTIME], WE AGAIN QUOTE THE BIBLE, "BECAUSE OF **THIS**" [THE DIRECT CONTINUATION OF THE ABOVE QUOTED VERSE, "YOU SHALL TELL YOUR SON..."]. "THIS" REFERS TO THE MATZOH AND THE MARROR, PLACED BEFORE YOU AT NIGHT [AT THE SEDER].

יָכוֹל מֵרֹאשׁ חֹדֶשׁ. תַּלְמוּד לוֹמַר בַּיּוֹם הַהוּא. אִי בַּיּוֹם הַהוּא יָכוֹל מִבְּעוֹד יוֹם. תַּלְמוּד לוֹמַר בַּעֲבוּר זֶה. בַּעֲבוּר זֶה, לֹא אָמַרְתִּי אֶלָּא בְּשָׁעָה שֶׁיֵּשׁ מַצָּה וּמָרוֹר מוּנָחִים לְפָנֶיךָ.

—————————— *COMMENTARY* ——————————

The *Haggadah* suggests three possible dates for retelling the saga of our Exodus: the first day in the month of *Nissan (Rosh Chodesh)*, the 14th of *Nissan* (the day before Passover night) or the 15th of *Nissan* at night (Passover night itself).

The Jews were liberated from Egypt Passover night. Logically, the retelling of the Exodus saga should be on its anniversary, the night of the 15th of *Nissan*. Why does the *Haggadah* propose any other time besides Passover night for the *mitzvah* of *Maggid*? Even more perplexing is the *Haggadah's* conclusion. It chooses the 15th of *Nissan* (Passover night) not because it is the anniversary of the Exodus but because it is then that we are Biblically commanded to eat of the *Matzoh, Marror* and Pascal lamb.

Why doesn't the Haggadah deduce that it is indeed on the 15th at night we retell the story of the Exodus because on that date the Exodus occurred?

Using our thematic premise, that the commandment to retell the Exodus saga is really a fundamental statement of belief in our "chosenness", we understand the *Haggadah's* approach.

Yes, God initiated the Exodus on Passover night, but that is not what we commemorate. We celebrate our being chosen as His nation. Therefore, we must determine the exact date this "chosenness" occurred.

Perhaps, the *Haggadah* suggests, our "chosenness" was conferred on *Rosh Chodesh* (the first day of *Nissan*). On that date the Jewish nation received its first commandment. Commandments are our ministerial duties to the Almighty King, suggesting a chosen status. Or perhaps, it was not until the Jews actually performed a commandment that "chosenness" devolved upon them, in which case the 14th of *Nissan*, when the Jews sacrificed the Pascal lamb, should be the date when *Maggid* is to be fulfilled. The *Haggadah* concludes that neither one of these suggestions is correct. Rather, "chosenness" took place on the 15th of *Nissan* at night - Seder night.

The commandments of the first and fourteenth of *Nissan* were not sufficient to establish our "chosenness" because these commandments do not require the participation of every individual Jew. These two commandments are performed by an agent: (1) the Jewish calendar is set through the *Sanhedrin HaGadol*, the High Court composed of seventy-one great sages acting on behalf of the Jewish nation and (2) the Pascal lamb for an entire family or group is slaughtered by a delegated member. It was not until the fifteenth at night, Passover night, that each individual Jew was required to actively participate in a *mitzvah*; there could be no proxy. Each Jew had to eat *Matzoh* and *Marror* as well as the Pascal lamb.

It is for this reason we transmit to our children the message of our "chosenness" specifically on Passover night. A Jewish child must know his "chosenness" is neither optional nor assignable; it is mandatory and he is personally responsible. This is what the *Haggadah* suggests when it says, "Because of **this**, "this" refers to the *Matzoh* and the *Marror*, placed before you at night" The *mitzvos* of *Matzoh* and *Marror* are set before **each** Jew to perform, indicative of his individual chosen status.

The lesson learned is: not only was the Jewish people chosen as

a "national body", but "chosenness" devolved upon each and every Jew as an individual. No Jew can exempt himself from his ministerial responsibilities by assigning them to another Jew or the national body. They are his alone to perform.

Jews who are complacent about their spiritual state because they wax nostalgic over a pious forebear do themselves a great injustice. Reliance on an observant grandparent or uncle (or cousin) does not address **their own** "chosenness".

ORIGINALLY OUR FOREFATHERS WORSHIPED IDOLS, BUT NOW THE ALMIGHTY HAS BROUGHT US NEAR TO HIS SERVICE, AS THE VERSE SAYS: "JOSHUA SAID TO THE ENTIRE NATION, 'SO SAID THE ALMIGHTY, GOD OF ISRAEL, IN DAYS OF OLD, YOUR ANCESTORS LIVED BEYOND THE [EUPHRATES] RIVER. [THOSE ANCESTORS WERE] TERACH, THE FATHER OF ABRAHAM AND NACHOR, AND THEY WORSHIPED IDOLS. AND I TOOK YOUR FOREFATHER, ABRAHAM, FROM BEYOND THE [EUPHRATES] RIVER AND LED HIM THROUGHOUT THE ENTIRE LAND OF CANAAN. I MULTIPLIED HIS OFFSPRING AND GAVE HIM [A SON] ISAAC. TO ISAAC I GAVE JACOB AND ESAU. TO ESAU, I GAVE MOUNT SEIR AS AN INHERITANCE BUT JACOB AND HIS SONS WENT DOWN TO EGYPT.'"

מִתְּחִלָּה עוֹבְדֵי עֲבוֹדָה זָרָה הָיוּ אֲבוֹתֵינוּ, וְעַכְשָׁיו קֵרְבָנוּ הַמָּקוֹם לַעֲבוֹדָתוֹ. שֶׁנֶּאֱמַר, וַיֹּאמֶר יְהוֹשֻׁעַ אֶל כָּל הָעָם, כֹּה אָמַר יהוה אֱלֹהֵי יִשְׂרָאֵל, בְּעֵבֶר הַנָּהָר יָשְׁבוּ אֲבוֹתֵיכֶם מֵעוֹלָם, תֶּרַח אֲבִי אַבְרָהָם וַאֲבִי נָחוֹר, וַיַּעַבְדוּ אֱלֹהִים אֲחֵרִים: וָאֶקַּח אֶת אֲבִיכֶם אֶת אַבְרָהָם מֵעֵבֶר הַנָּהָר וָאוֹלֵךְ אוֹתוֹ בְּכָל אֶרֶץ כְּנָעַן, וָאַרְבֶּה אֶת זַרְעוֹ, וָאֶתֶּן לוֹ אֶת יִצְחָק: וָאֶתֶּן לְיִצְחָק אֶת יַעֲקֹב וְאֶת עֵשָׂו, וָאֶתֶּן לְעֵשָׂו אֶת הַר שֵׂעִיר לָרֶשֶׁת אוֹתוֹ, וְיַעֲקֹב וּבָנָיו יָרְדוּ מִצְרָיִם.

(Joshua XXIV: 2-4)

--------------------------------- COMMENTARY ---------------------------------

When discussing key elements of the obligation to retell the story of the Exodus, the *Mishnah* in Tractate *Pesachim* 116a states, "One commences with shame and concludes with praise".

The *Talmud* goes on to explain that this principle precipitates our stating in the *Haggadah*: "Originally our forefathers worshipped idols, but now the Almighty has brought us near to His service, as the verse says: 'Joshua said to the entire nation, "So said the Almighty, God of Israel, in days of old, your ancestors lived beyond the [Euphrates] river. [Those ancestors were] Terach, the father of Abraham and Nachor, and they worshipped idols..." ' "

This component of the commandment to retell the story of the Exodus has always been a mystery. What does Abraham's ancestor's worship of idols have to do with the Exodus?

Our definition of *Maggid*, as a declaration of belief that God chose us to be His nation through the Exodus, gives us the full answer. **The Haggadah seeks to explain why the Jews were chosen from among all the peoples of the earth**. Why not some other nation? *In this paragraph the Haggadah tells us: It is because we had a great forefather, Abraham.*

Even as the entire world defamed itself through idol worship, with his own father, Terach, in the vanguard (the "shame" cited above in the *Mishnah*), Abraham rose above the rest of humanity, recognizing and devoting himself to the service of the one true God - the Creator of heaven and earth (the "praise"). It is in Abraham's merit that his children, the Jews, became the chosen nation. Abraham's ability to transcend his idolatrous environment resulted in his descendants' election as the chosen people.

Rabbi Moshe Chaim Luzzato ("The Way Of God", Part II, Chapter IV, subsection 3) points this out clearly:

According to the Highest Judgment, none of humanity deserved to rise above the base level to which Adam and his children had fallen as a result of their sin.

There was, however, one exception: Abraham. He had succeeded in elevating himself, and as a result of his deeds was chosen by God. Abraham, was therefore, permanently made into a superior excellent "Tree", conforming to man's highest level. It was further provided that he would be able to produce "branches" (**father a nation**) possessing his characteristics.

The world was then divided into seventy nations, each with its own particular place in the general scheme. All of them, howev-

וְיַעֲקֹב וּבָנָיו יָרְדוּ מִצְרָיִם

er, remained on the level of man in his fallen state while only Israel rose to an elevated state.

ואתן לעשו את הר שעיר ויעקב ובניו ירדו מצרים

"To Esau I gave Mount Seir to inherit but Jacob and his children went down to Egypt."

What is the purpose of the verse juxtaposing Esau's inheritance of Mount Seir to Jacob's sojourn in Egypt? What possible connection is there between these two disparate historical incidents?

The answer is: In our introduction to the *Haggadah* (The Premise), we explained the conversation that took place between God and Abraham at the time of the Covenant Between the Halves. Abraham requested assurance that **all** his children would be chosen, not only the saintly among them. God answered that this could only be accomplished by the Jews first attaining nationhood, for which the Egyptian experience would be a prerequisite.

The verse quoted now in the *Haggadah* tells us this point exactly. Esau's family became a nation immediately, indicated by their inheriting a national homeland. Israel, however, needed the Egyptian experience to attain nationhood.

BLESSED IS HE WHO KEEPS HIS PROMISE TO ISRAEL, BLESSED IS HE! FOR THE HOLY ONE PRECISELY CALCULATED THE "END" IN ORDER TO FULFILL THE PROMISE MADE TO ABRAHAM IN THE COVENANT BETWEEN THE HALVES, AS THE VERSE SAYS: "AND [GOD] SAID TO ABRAHAM, 'KNOW FOR SURE THAT YOUR DESCENDANTS WILL BE FOREIGNERS IN A LAND THAT IS NOT THEIRS FOR FOUR HUNDRED YEARS. THEY WILL BE ENSLAVED AND OPPRESSED. BUT I WILL FINALLY BRING JUDGEMENT AGAINST THE NATION THAT ENSLAVES THEM AND THEY WILL THEN LEAVE WITH GREAT WEALTH.' "

(Genesis XV:13-14)

בָּרוּךְ שׁוֹמֵר הַבְטָחָתוֹ לְיִשְׂרָאֵל, בָּרוּךְ הוּא, שֶׁהַקָּדוֹשׁ בָּרוּךְ הוּא חִשַּׁב אֶת הַקֵּץ, לַעֲשׂוֹת כְּמָה שֶׁאָמַר לְאַבְרָהָם אָבִינוּ בִּבְרִית בֵּין הַבְּתָרִים, שֶׁנֶּאֱמַר, וַיֹּאמֶר לְאַבְרָם יָדֹעַ תֵּדַע כִּי גֵר יִהְיֶה זַרְעֲךָ בְּאֶרֶץ לֹא לָהֶם וַעֲבָדוּם וְעִנּוּ אֹתָם, אַרְבַּע מֵאוֹת שָׁנָה: וְגַם אֶת הַגּוֹי אֲשֶׁר יַעֲבֹדוּ דָן אָנֹכִי, וְאַחֲרֵי כֵן יֵצְאוּ בִּרְכֻשׁ גָּדוֹל:

─────────── **COMMENTARY** ───────────

Why do we say, "Blessed is He who keeps His promise to **Israel**"? The "promise" of which the *Haggadah* speaks was made to Abraham, so we should really say, "Blessed is He Who Keeps His promise to **Abraham**".

Our interpretation of *Maggid*, as a statement of belief that God chose us, again provides the answer. We thank God Who kept His promise to Abraham **concerning** the creation and choosing of the "nation Israel." (Maimonides' text of the *Haggadah* strongly supports this interpretation. His text reads: "Who keeps His promise to Israel *His* *nation."*)

When the time came and the Egyptian experience had molded us into a nation, God did as He had promised Abraham, and that is stated clearly in the *Haggadah*:

> "Blessed is He, Who keeps His promise to Israel; blessed is He! For the Holy One, precisely calculated the "end" in order to fulfill the promise made to Abraham in the Covenant Between the Halves..."

Our interpretation also illuminates the phrase, "for the Holy One, precisely calculated the *end*." What is the "end", and why did it require precise calculation? The answer is that God promised Abraham that He would forge a nation from Abraham's descendants and then choose that nation as His own. The entire Egyptian experience was necessary only because it served to create that nation. Once nationhood was realized the Egyptian experience had served its purpose. The "end" refers to "that moment" when Israel attained nationhood.

God calculated the moment of nationhood so the Exodus would coincide precisely with it. This was so Israel should not have to be in Egypt even one moment longer than necessary. This is the kindness for which we thank God.

We cover the Matzohs and raise our wine cups for the recitation of this paragraph. Afterwards, we put down our wine cups and uncover the Matzohs.
(*Mishnah Berurah 473:73 citing Sh'La HaKadosh*)

AND IT IS THIS WHICH HAS STOOD BY OUR FOREFATHERS AND US. MANY HAVE RISEN UP AGAINST US TO DESTROY US IN EACH AND EVERY GENERATION BUT THE HOLY ONE, BLESSED IS HE, SAVES US FROM THEIR HAND.

וְהִיא שֶׁעָמְדָה לַאֲבוֹתֵינוּ וְלָנוּ. שֶׁלֹּא אֶחָד בִּלְבָד עָמַד עָלֵינוּ לְכַלּוֹתֵינוּ. אֶלָּא שֶׁבְּכָל דּוֹר וָדוֹר עוֹמְדִים עָלֵינוּ לְכַלּוֹתֵינוּ. וְהַקָּדוֹשׁ בָּרוּךְ הוּא מַצִּילֵנוּ מִיָּדָם.

———————— COMMENTARY ————————

All classical commentators ask: what is the *Haggadah* referring to in the phrase, "and it is **this** which has stood by our forefathers and us"? What precisely is "*this*"?

Drawing upon the interpretation we gave to the *Haggadah's* previous paragraph, which recounts the promise to Abraham at the Covenant Between the Halves and God's fulfillment of that promise by choosing the Jews as His nation, the reference becomes clear. "This" refers to our elevated status as chosen nation.

Being His chosen children has saved us generation after generation. As each new enemy sought to annihilate us we were saved by the Almighty. Just as an errant son whose father, even while punishing him, makes certain not to inflict permanent harm, so too, God Almighty, even while expiating Israel's sins, makes certain that no mortal blow is inflicted through the chastisement.

"This" is precisely what Abraham wanted from God. He realized his progeny would sin. Had "chosenness" only devolved upon the righteous of Abraham's descendants, the Jewish people would have never survived. *Abraham requested an **unqualified** chosenness.*

God, fulfilling His promise, conferred "chosenness" upon the "nation" Israel. As a nation, we are eternal, membership being automatic and irrevocable. Even though we are held accountable for our errant deeds, our chosen status can never be negated.

The *Talmud* in Tractate *Sanhedrin* 44a makes this point clearly:"**Israel has sinned**" (Joshua VII:11), [commenting upon this verse] **Rabbi Aba the son of Savda, said, "Even though they sin they are Israelites."**

שֶׁבְּכָל דּוֹר וָדוֹר, עוֹמְדִים עָלֵינוּ לְכַלּוֹתֵנוּ

See Commentary page 96

GO AND LEARN WHAT LABAN, THE ARAMEAN, ATTEMPTED TO DO TO OUR FOREFATHER, JACOB. FOR PHARAOH DECREED ONLY AGAINST THE NEWBORN MALES, WHEREAS LABAN ATTEMPTED TO UPROOT EVERYTHING, AS IT SAYS IN THE VERSE:

צֵא וּלְמַד, מַה בִּקֵשׁ לָבָן הָאֲרַמִי לַעֲשׂוֹת לְיַעֲקֹב אָבִינוּ, שֶׁפַּרְעֹה לֹא גָזַר אֶלָּא עַל הַזְּכָרִים וְלָבָן בִּקֵשׁ לַעֲקוֹר אֶת הַכֹּל, שֶׁנֶּאֱמַר:

VERSE I

"AN ARAMEAN ATTEMPTED TO DESTROY MY FATHER. THEN HE DESCENDED TO EGYPT AND SOJOURNED THERE, WITH FEW PEOPLE; AND THERE HE BECAME A NATION - GREAT, MIGHTY, AND NUMEROUS."

(Deuteronomy XXVI:5)

אֲרַמִי אֹבֵד אָבִי, וַיֵּרֶד מִצְרַיְמָה וַיָּגָר שָׁם בִּמְתֵי מְעָט, וַיְהִי שָׁם לְגוֹי גָּדוֹל, עָצוּם וָרָב.

See Commentary page 97

"HE DESCENDED TO EGYPT" - COMPELLED TO DO SO BY DIVINE COMMAND.

וַיֵּרֶד מִצְרַיְמָה, אָנוּס עַל פִּי הַדִּבּוּר.

"AND SOJOURNED THERE" - THIS TEACHES THAT OUR FOREFATHER, JACOB, DID NOT DESCEND TO EGYPT TO SETTLE PERMANENTLY, BUT ONLY TO SOJOURN TEMPORARILY. AS IT SAYS IN THE VERSE: "THEY [JACOB'S SONS] SAID TO PHARAOH: 'WE HAVE COME TO LIVE IN THE LAND TEM-

וַיָּגָר שָׁם, מְלַמֵּד שֶׁלֹּא יָרַד יַעֲקֹב אָבִינוּ לְהִשְׁתַּקֵעַ בְּמִצְרַיִם, אֶלָּא לָגוּר שָׁם. שֶׁנֶּאֱמַר, וַיֹּאמְרוּ אֶל פַּרְעֹה, לָגוּר בָּאָרֶץ בָּאנוּ, כִּי אֵין מִרְעֶה לַצֹּאן אֲשֶׁר לַעֲבָדֶיךָ, כִּי כָבֵד הָרָעָב

PORARILY SINCE THERE IS NO PASTURE FOR YOUR SERVANT'S FLOCKS; BECAUSE THE FAMINE IS SEVERE IN CANAAN. AND NOW PLEASE LET YOUR SERVANTS RESIDE IN THE LAND OF GOSHEN.'"
(Genesis XLVII:4)

בְּאֶרֶץ כְּנָעַן, וְעַתָּה יֵשְׁבוּ נָא עֲבָדֶיךָ בְּאֶרֶץ גֹּשֶׁן.

"WITH FEW PEOPLE" - AS IT SAYS IN THE VERSE: "WITH SEVENTY PEOPLE YOUR FOREFATHERS DESCENDED TO EGYPT, AND NOW THE ALMIGHTY, YOUR GOD, HAS MADE YOU AS NUMEROUS AS THE HEAVENLY STARS."
(Deuteronomy X:22)

בִּמְתֵי מְעָט, כְּמָה שֶׁנֶּאֱמַר, בְּשִׁבְעִים נֶפֶשׁ יָרְדוּ אֲבֹתֶיךָ מִצְרָיְמָה, וְעַתָּה שָׂמְךָ יהוה אֱלֹהֶיךָ כְּכוֹכְבֵי הַשָּׁמַיִם לָרֹב.

"THERE HE BECAME A NATION" - WHICH TEACHES US THAT THE JEWS WERE A DISTINCTIVE PEOPLE THERE.

וַיְהִי שָׁם לְגוֹי מְלַמֵּד שֶׁהָיוּ יִשְׂרָאֵל מְצֻיָּנִים שָׁם.

"GREAT, MIGHTY" - AS IT SAYS IN THE VERSE: "AND THE CHILDREN OF ISRAEL WERE FRUITFUL AND INCREASED ABUNDANTLY AND MULTIPLIED AND BECAME VERY, VERY MIGHTY; AND THE LAND WAS FILLED WITH THEM."
(Exodus I:7)

גָּדוֹל עָצוּם, כְּמָה שֶׁנֶּאֱמַר, וּבְנֵי יִשְׂרָאֵל פָּרוּ וַיִּשְׁרְצוּ וַיִּרְבּוּ וַיַּעַצְמוּ בִּמְאֹד מְאֹד, וַתִּמָּלֵא הָאָרֶץ אֹתָם.

"NUMEROUS" - AS IT SAYS IN THE VERSE: "I MADE YOU AS NUMEROUS AS

וָרָב, כְּמָה שֶׁנֶּאֱמַר, רְבָבָה כְּצֶמַח הַשָּׂדֶה נְתַתִּיךְ,

PLANTS OF THE FIELD, AND YOU MULTIPLIED AND GREW AND YOU BECAME CHARMING; YOUR BREASTS WERE FIRM AND YOUR HAIR GREW LONG; YET YOU WERE NAKED AND BARE." *(Ezekiel XVI:7)* "AND I PASSED OVER YOU AND I SAW YOU WALLOWING IN YOUR BLOOD, AND I SAID TO YOU, 'THROUGH YOUR BLOOD YOU SHALL LIVE! AND I SAID TO YOU, THROUGH YOUR BLOOD YOU SHALL LIVE.'"

(Ezekiel XVI:6)

וַתִּרְבִּי וַתִּגְדְּלִי וַתָּבוֹאִי בַּעֲדִי עֲדָיִים, שָׁדַיִם נָכוֹנוּ וּשְׂעָרֵךְ צִמֵּחַ, וְאַתְּ עֵרֹם וְעֶרְיָה. וָאֶעֱבוֹר עָלַיִךְ וָאֶרְאֵךְ מִתְבּוֹסֶסֶת בְּדָמָיִךְ, וָאֹמַר לָךְ בְּדָמַיִךְ חֲיִי וָאֹמַר לָךְ בְּדָמַיִךְ חֲיִי.

VERSE II "THE EGYPTIANS DID EVIL TO US AND THEY AFFLICTED US, AND IMPOSED UPON US HARD LABOR."
(Deuteronomy XXVI:6)

וַיָּרֵעוּ אֹתָנוּ הַמִּצְרִים וַיְעַנּוּנוּ, וַיִּתְּנוּ עָלֵינוּ עֲבֹדָה קָשָׁה.

"THE EGYPTIANS DID EVIL TO US" - AS IT SAYS IN THE VERSE: "COME LET US OUTWIT THEM, LEST THEY INCREASE, AND IN THE EVENT OF WAR THEY WILL JOIN WITH OUR ENEMIES AND FIGHT AGAINST US, CAUSING US TO FLEE FROM OUR LAND." *(Exodus I:10)*

וַיָּרֵעוּ אֹתָנוּ הַמִּצְרִים, כְּמָה שֶׁנֶּאֱמַר הָבָה נִתְחַכְּמָה לוֹ, פֶּן יִרְבֶּה וְהָיָה כִּי תִקְרֶאנָה מִלְחָמָה וְנוֹסַף גַּם הוּא עַל שֹׂנְאֵינוּ וְנִלְחַם בָּנוּ וְעָלָה מִן הָאָרֶץ.

"THEY AFFLICTED US" - AS IT SAYS IN THE VERSE: "[THE EGYPTIANS] PLACED

וַיְעַנּוּנוּ כְּמָה שֶׁנֶּאֱמַר, וַיָּשִׂימוּ עָלָיו שָׂרֵי מִסִּים

וַיָּרֵעוּ אֹתָנוּ הַמִּצְרִים

TASKMASTERS OVER THEM TO AFFLICT THEM WITH HEAVY LABOR; [THE JEWS] BUILT TREASURE CITIES FOR PHARAOH: PITHOM AND RAAMSES."

(Exodus I:11)

לְמַעַן עַנֹּתוֹ בְּסִבְלֹתָם, וַיִּבֶן עָרֵי מִסְכְּנוֹת לְפַרְעֹה אֶת פִּתֹם וְאֶת רַעַמְסֵס:

"IMPOSED UPON US HARD LABOR" - AS IT SAYS IN THE VERSE: "THE EGYPTIANS WORKED THE ISRAELITES WITH CRUSHING LABOR."

(Exodus I:13)

וַיִּתְּנוּ עָלֵינוּ עֲבֹדָה קָשָׁה, כְּמָה שֶׁנֶּאֱמַר, וַיַּעֲבִדוּ מִצְרַיִם אֶת בְּנֵי יִשְׂרָאֵל בְּפָרֶךְ:

VERSE III   **"WE CRIED OUT TO THE ALMIGHTY GOD OF OUR FATHERS; AND GOD HEARD OUR VOICE, SAW OUR AFFLICTION, OUR BURDEN, AND OUR OPPRESSION."**

(Deuteronomy XXVI:7)

וַנִּצְעַק אֶל יהוה אֱלֹהֵי אֲבֹתֵינוּ, וַיִּשְׁמַע יהוה אֶת קֹלֵנוּ, וַיַּרְא אֶת עָנְיֵנוּ וְאֶת עֲמָלֵנוּ וְאֶת לַחֲצֵנוּ:

"WE CRIED OUT TO THE ALMIGHTY GOD OF OUR FATHERS" - AS IT SAYS IN THE VERSE: "AND IT CAME TO PASS IN THE COURSE OF THOSE MANY DAYS, THE KING OF EGYPT DIED, AND THE ISRAELITES MOANED BECAUSE OF THEIR SERVITUDE; THEY CRIED OUT AND THEIR CRY ROSE TO THE ALMIGHTY FROM THE WORK."

(Exodus II:23)

וַנִּצְעַק אֶל יהוה אֱלֹהֵי אֲבֹתֵינוּ כְּמָה שֶׁנֶּאֱמַר, וַיְהִי בַיָּמִים הָרַבִּים הָהֵם וַיָּמָת מֶלֶךְ מִצְרַיִם וַיֵּאָנְחוּ בְנֵי יִשְׂרָאֵל מִן הָעֲבֹדָה וַיִּזְעָקוּ, וַתַּעַל שַׁוְעָתָם אֶל הָאֱלֹהִים מִן הָעֲבֹדָה:

"GOD HEARD OUR

וַיִּשְׁמַע יהוה אֶת קֹלֵנוּ,

וַנִּצְעַק אֶל־יְיָ אֱלֹהֵי אֲבֹתֵינוּ.

VOICE" - AS IT SAYS IN THE VERSE: "THE ALMIGHTY HEARD THEIR GROANING AND REMEMBERED HIS COVENANT WITH ABRAHAM, ISAAC AND JACOB."

(Exodus II:24)

כְּמָה שֶׁנֶּאֱמַר, וַיִּשְׁמַע אֱלֹהִים אֶת נַאֲקָתָם, וַיִּזְכֹּר אֱלֹהִים אֶת בְּרִיתוֹ אֶת אַבְרָהָם אֶת יִצְחָק וְאֶת יַעֲקֹב:

"SAW OUR AFFLICTION" - THIS REFERS TO A FORCED SEPARATION BETWEEN HUSBAND AND WIFE, AS IT SAYS IN THE VERSE: "THE ALMIGHTY SAW THE ISRAELITES AND THE ALMIGHTY KNEW".

(Exodus II:25)

וַיַּרְא אֶת עָנְיֵנוּ, זוֹ פְּרִישׁוּת דֶּרֶךְ אֶרֶץ, כְּמָה שֶׁנֶּאֱמַר, וַיַּרְא אֱלֹהִים אֶת בְּנֵי יִשְׂרָאֵל, וַיֵּדַע אֱלֹהִים:

"OUR BURDEN" - THIS REFERS TO [THE DROWNING OF] THE CHILDREN, AS IT SAYS IN THE VERSE: "EVERY SON THAT IS BORN YOU WILL CAST INTO THE RIVER, AND EVERY DAUGHTER YOU WILL LET LIVE."

(Exodus I:22)

וְאֶת עֲמָלֵנוּ, אֵלוּ הַבָּנִים, כְּמָה שֶׁנֶּאֱמַר, כָּל הַבֵּן הַיִּלּוֹד הַיְאֹרָה תַּשְׁלִיכֻהוּ, וְכָל הַבַּת תְּחַיּוּן.

"OUR OPPRESSION" - THIS REFERS TO THE PERSECUTION, AS IT SAYS IN THE VERSE: "I HAVE SEEN HOW THE EGYPTIANS ARE PERSECUTING THEM."

(Exodus III:9)

וְאֶת לַחֲצֵנוּ, זוֹ הַדְּחַק כְּמָה שֶׁנֶּאֱמַר, וְגַם רָאִיתִי אֶת הַלַּחַץ אֲשֶׁר מִצְרַיִם לֹחֲצִים אֹתָם:

VERSE IV   **"GOD BROUGHT US OUT OF EGYPT WITH A MIGHTY HAND AND AN**

וַיּוֹצִאֵנוּ יהוה מִמִּצְרַיִם בְּיָד חֲזָקָה וּבִזְרֹעַ נְטוּיָה וּבְמֹרָא

See
Commentary
page 99

גָּדֹל, וּבְאֹתוֹת וּבְמֹפְתִים:

OUTSTRETCHED ARM, WITH GREAT AWE, SIGNS AND WONDERS."
(Deuteronomy XXVI:8)

וַיּוֹצִאֵנוּ יהוה מִמִּצְרַיִם, לֹא עַל יְדֵי מַלְאָךְ, וְלֹא עַל יְדֵי שָׂרָף, וְלֹא עַל יְדֵי שָׁלִיחַ, אֶלָּא הַקָּדוֹשׁ בָּרוּךְ הוּא בִּכְבוֹדוֹ וּבְעַצְמוֹ, שֶׁנֶּאֱמַר, וְעָבַרְתִּי בְאֶרֶץ מִצְרַיִם בַּלַּיְלָה הַזֶּה, וְהִכֵּיתִי כָל בְּכוֹר בְּאֶרֶץ מִצְרַיִם מֵאָדָם וְעַד בְּהֵמָה, וּבְכָל אֱלֹהֵי מִצְרַיִם אֶעֱשֶׂה שְׁפָטִים אֲנִי יהוה.

"GOD BROUGHT US OUT OF EGYPT" - WE WERE NOT BROUGHT OUT OF EGYPT BY AN ANGEL, SERAPH, OR MESSENGER, BUT BY THE HOLY ONE, BLESSED IS HE, HIMSELF, IN HIS GLORY AS IT SAYS IN THE VERSE: "I WILL PASS THROUGH THE LAND OF EGYPT ON THIS NIGHT; I WILL STRIKE DOWN ALL THE FIRSTBORN IN THE LAND OF EGYPT, MAN AND BEAST ALIKE; UPON ALL THE GODS OF EGYPT I WILL EXECUTE JUDGEMENTS, I AM THE ALMIGHTY." *(Exodus XII:12)*

וְעָבַרְתִּי בְאֶרֶץ מִצְרַיִם בַּלַּיְלָה הַזֶּה - אֲנִי וְלֹא מַלְאָךְ; וְהִכֵּיתִי כָל בְּכוֹר בְּאֶרֶץ מִצְרַיִם - אֲנִי וְלֹא שָׂרָף; וּבְכָל אֱלֹהֵי מִצְרַיִם אֶעֱשֶׂה שְׁפָטִים - אֲנִי וְלֹא הַשָּׁלִיחַ; אֲנִי יהוה - אֲנִי הוּא וְלֹא אַחֵר.

"I WILL PASS THROUGH THE LAND OF EGYPT ON THIS NIGHT" - I, NOT AN ANGEL. "I WILL STRIKE DOWN ALL THE FIRSTBORN IN THE LAND OF EGYPT" - I, NOT A SERAPH. "UPON ALL THE GODS OF EGYPT I WILL EXECUTE JUDGEMENTS" - I, NOT A MESSENGER. "I AM THE ALMIGHTY" - I AM HE, NONE OTHER.

בְּיָד חֲזָקָה, זוֹ הַדֶּבֶר,

"WITH A MIGHTY

HAND" - THIS REFERS TO PESTILENCE [AMONG THE EGYPTIANS' CATTLE], AS IT SAYS IN THE VERSE: "BEHOLD, THE HAND OF THE ALMIGHTY WILL STRIKE YOUR CATTLE IN THE FIELD: HORSES, DONKEYS, CAMELS, THE HERDS AND THE FLOCKS - A VERY HEAVY PESTILENCE".

(Exodus IX:3)

"**AN OUTSTRETCHED ARM**" - THIS REFERS TO THE SWORD, AS IT SAYS IN THE VERSE: "HIS DRAWN SWORD IN HIS HAND, OUTSTRETCHED OVER JERUSALEM."

(I Chronicles XXI:16)

"**WITH GREAT AWE**" - THIS REFERS TO THE REVELATION OF THE DIVINE PRESENCE, AS IT SAYS IN THE VERSE: "HAS THE ALMIGHTY EVER SOUGHT TO TAKE FOR HIMSELF A NATION FROM THE MIDST OF ANOTHER NATION WITH TRIALS, SIGNS AND WONDERS, BY BATTLE, AND WITH A MIGHTY HAND AND OUTSTRETCHED ARM AND WITH GREAT AWE, JUST AS THE ALMIGHTY YOUR GOD DID FOR YOU IN EGYPT, BEFORE YOUR EYES?"

(Deuteronomy IV:34)

כְּמָה שֶׁנֶּאֱמַר, הִנֵּה יַד יהוה הוֹיָה בְּמִקְנְךָ אֲשֶׁר בַּשָּׂדֶה, בַּסּוּסִים בַּחֲמֹרִים בַּגְּמַלִים בַּבָּקָר וּבַצֹּאן, דֶּבֶר כָּבֵד מְאֹד:

וּבִזְרֹעַ נְטוּיָה, זוֹ הַחֶרֶב, כְּמָה שֶׁנֶּאֱמַר, וְחַרְבּוֹ שְׁלוּפָה בְּיָדוֹ נְטוּיָה עַל יְרוּשָׁלָיִם:

וּבְמֹרָא גָּדֹל, זוֹ גִּלּוּי שְׁכִינָה, כְּמָה שֶׁנֶּאֱמַר, אוֹ הֲנִסָּה אֱלֹהִים לָבוֹא לָקַחַת לוֹ גוֹי מִקֶּרֶב גּוֹי, בְּמַסֹּת בְּאֹתֹת וּבְמוֹפְתִים וּבְמִלְחָמָה וּבְיָד חֲזָקָה וּבִזְרוֹעַ נְטוּיָה וּבְמוֹרָאִים גְּדֹלִים, כְּכֹל אֲשֶׁר עָשָׂה לָכֶם יהוה אֱלֹהֵיכֶם בְּמִצְרַיִם לְעֵינֶיךָ:

"SIGNS" - THIS REFERS TO THE STAFF [OF MOSES], AS IT SAYS IN THE VERSE: "THIS STAFF TAKE IN YOUR HAND, WITH IT YOU SHALL PERFORM THE SIGNS."

(Exodus IV:17)

וּבְאֹתוֹת, זֶה הַמַּטֶּה, כְּמָה שֶׁנֶּאֱמַר, וְאֶת הַמַּטֶּה הַזֶּה תִּקַּח בְּיָדֶךָ, אֲשֶׁר תַּעֲשֶׂה בּוֹ אֶת הָאֹתֹת.

"WONDERS" - THIS REFERS TO THE [PLAGUE OF] BLOOD, AS IT SAYS IN THE VERSE: "I WILL PLACE WONDERS IN THE HEAVENS AND ON THE EARTH, * *BLOOD, FIRE* AND *PILLARS OF SMOKE.*"

(Joel III:3)

וּבְמֹפְתִים זֶה הַדָּם, כְּמָה שֶׁנֶּאֱמַר, וְנָתַתִּי מוֹפְתִים בַּשָּׁמַיִם וּבָאָרֶץ, * דָּם וָאֵשׁ וְתִימְרוֹת עָשָׁן:

See Commentary page 100

** A little wine is removed from our cups with the index finger and sprinkled onto our plates 16 times: at the mention of each one of the words - blood, fire and pillars of smoke (3), each plague (10), and each acronym for the plagues (3). (Ramah, O.C. 473:7)*

─────────── COMMENTARY ───────────

צא ולמד מה בקש לבן הארמי לעשות ליעקב אבינו

"Go and learn what Laban, the Aramean, attempted to do to our forefather Jacob."

What interest does the *Haggadah* have in Laban, the wicked father-in-law of the patriarch Jacob? What impact did Laban have on the Exodus from Egypt?

The *Talmud* in Tractate *Berachos* 16b states, "the Rabbis learned you cannot refer to anyone as a patriarch except for Abraham, Isaac and Jacob, and you cannot refer to anyone as a matriarch except for Sarah, Rebecca, Rachel and Leah."

The *Talmud* is telling us: all the spiritual traits necessary to make up the Jewish personality are inherited from the three patriarchs and four matriarchs. Each one of these giants of humanity worked their entire lives to perfect those traits which they passed on. Abraham and Sarah perfected kindness and outreach to their fellow man. Isaac and Rebecca spent a lifetime perfecting awe and fear of God. Jacob, together with Rachel and Leah, achieved the strength to survive as a Jew against all adversity.

We are taught that the Jews who left Egypt didn't assimilate into the Egyptian culture. The Israelites retained their Hebrew language, names, and distinctive ethnic dress, even while brutally oppressed by their Egyptian taskmasters. How did the Israelites, enslaved in Egypt, have the inner strength to survive as a unique people, keeping their identity as Jews?

The answer is: They inherited their strength from Jacob. Jacob himself perfected this trait, having to overcome Laban's trickery and intimidation while living with him for twenty years. Laban, the *Haggadah* points out, was far more wicked than Pharaoh and yet, not only did Jacob survive, but he managed to fortify his spiritual strength. This inner strength was passed down to his progeny, making it possible for them to endure Egypt's immoral culture and physical enslavement.

With the above in mind, we understand why assimilation and intermarriage bring upon the Jewish nation the greatest wrath of God. Such acts directly spurn that very special relationship God has granted us with Him. He chose us from all the nations, making us separate and unique. Heaven forbid that we should wish to divest ourselves of our ennobled status by trying to blend back into the rest of humanity from which we were chosen. Having spent five hundred years (from the birth of Abraham to the Exodus) perfecting our spiritual characteristics, how can we, and why should we, abandon our elevated station?

וירד מצרימה

"... as it says in the verse: An Aramean attempted to destroy my father. Then he descended to Egypt and sojourned there, with few people; and there he became a nation - great, mighty, and numerous."

At this point, the Haggadah begins to cite and explain in classic *"midrashic"* style, four verses in Deuteronomy XXVI:5-8, expounding the import of each word. This exposition encompasses approximately one third of the entire *Maggid* portion of the Haggadah.

Verse 1:   [You shall speak and say before your Almighty God] an Aramean attempted to destroy my father. Then he descended to Egypt and sojourned there, with few people; and there he became a nation - great, mighty, and numerous.

Verse 2:   The Egyptians did evil to us and they afflicted us, and imposed upon us hard labor.

Verse 3:   We cried out to the Almighty God of our fathers; and God heard our voice, saw our affliction, our burden, and our oppression.

Verse 4:   God brought us out of Egypt with a mighty hand and an outstretched arm, with great awe, signs and wonders.

These verses are the declaration made by a Jewish farmer who comes to Jerusalem and offers the first fruits of his field in the Holy Temple.

The *Talmud* specifically instructs us to cite these verses Passover night, to fulfill our obligation to retell the story of the Exodus.

Why is this paragraph about the first fruits so integral to the story of the Exodus? Why doesn't the Haggadah instead cite the detailed historical narration of our enslavement and redemption found in the first thirteen chapters of the Book of Exodus? And why does the Jewish farmer, bringing his first fruits, mention the Exodus altogether? *Why is the Exodus critical to the thanks he gives for the bounty God has bestowed upon him?* What possible connection could there be between the "first fruits" and the Exodus from Egypt?

We return again to our thesis for the answer. On Passover night we don't merely "retell" the story of the Exodus. Were we to do so, the Hagaddah would certainly confine its focus to the historical account in the Book of Exodus. Rather, the *mitzvah* of *Maggid* is to declare that, by taking us out of Egypt on Passover night, God chose the Jewish nation from among all others to be His.

But the Exodus only **initiated** the choosing of Israel, a process that continued until the Jews entered the "Promised Land". Being chosen means we merit a special closeness to God. **Only in the land of Israel do the Jews achieve this closeness. When we find ourselves in the land of Israel with Jerusalem and the Holy Temple resonating to God's earthly presence, our chosenness is indeed consummated.**

The Jewish farmer declares how fortunate we are to have been chosen by God in Egypt and to have merited His sacred proximity. The ultimate **proof** of our "chosenness" is the fact that we live, work and derive sustenance from the same land where God's presence is most apparent.

(With this concept we can also understand Israel's being punished with exile. Why was exile from the Land of Israel decreed as a punishment for our sins, and not some other expiation? The answer is: when we sin we forfeit the special closeness to God that residence in His holy land confers, and must surrender for a time our right to it. Although our chosen status remains irrevocable even when we sin, we no longer merit all its spiritual benefits.)

The Jewish farmer thanks God for having chosen the Jewish nation and granting us the great privilege of closeness to Him. Our closeness to God is a direct function of our "chosenness" with which we were invested Passover night in Egypt. This was the primary goal of the Exodus. For precisely this reason, the farmer, after mentioning our sojourn in Egypt, our affliction, our crying out to the Almighty God, and that God brought us out of Egypt with a mighty hand, concludes, "He brought us to this place [the Land of Israel] and gave us this land, a land flowing with milk and honey." (*Deuteronomy* XXIV:9)

The Haggadah, looking to express our "chosenness" through the Exodus, naturally focuses on the *Torah*-prescribed words of the Jewish farmer, for therein lies the greatest declaration of that "chosenness".

ויוציאנו ה' ממצרים

"God brought us out of Egypt with a mighty hand and an outstretched arm, with great awe, signs and wonders."

Why did the Exodus have to be effected by the use of miracles? Could not a more "natural" chain of events have brought about the same redemption?

Answer: God created the world ex nihilo. Not only was all matter and space created but the very "laws of nature" were brought into being. Thus, the natural laws can be said to be the Almighty's agents. A miracle occurs when the Creator affects this world **without** resort to the agency of the "laws of nature".

All of the events constituting the Exodus were miraculous. God wished to demonstrate His choice of Israel with absolute clarity. He manifested Himself to choose His beloved, even as a human king exhibits affection for his queen by personally attending her without calling upon his royal servants. Redemption achieved through the "laws of nature" (although themselves a divine instrument) would have shown a lack of affection.

The miracles of the Exodus were the heralding trumpets of Royalty, declaring to humanity God's choice of the Jews as His. Were the miracles meant just to facilitate the Jewish nation's release from bondage, they would have been unnecessary. The Exodus could have been accomplished through the agency of natural events. Thus, the Haggadah tells us: "**With great awe**" - this refers to the revelation of the Divine Presence, as it says in the verse: "Has the Almighty ever sought to take for Himself a nation from the midst of another nation with trials, signs and wonders, by battle, and with a mighty hand and outstretched arm and with great awe, just as the Almighty your God did for you in Egypt, before your eyes?" (*Deuteronomy IV:34*)

דם ואש ותמרות עשן

*"I will place wonders in the heavens and on the earth, **blood**, **fire** and **pillars of smoke**."*

The *Torah* gives the plagues main billing in the drama of the Exodus, describing each one in detail. The Haggadah, on the other hand, reduces them to a mere mention. Why?

A proper answer to this question requires a brief introduction to the role of the plagues in the Exodus saga. Classical commentators have separated the plagues into two groups: The first nine, ending with the plague of darkness, and the tenth, the killing of the Egyptian firstborn.

The first nine plagues were meant to punish the Egyptians for the viciousness with which they enslaved the Israelites, but not to effect the Jews' release from bondage. Many verses in the Bible specifically point out that God would repeatedly harden Pharaoh's heart and thus his resolve not to release the Jews, preventing him from succumbing to the pressure of the plagues. Obviously, God did not intend for these nine plagues to accomplish the Jews' redemption.

In addition, it must be pointed out that the first nine plagues were meant to cleanse the Jewish slaves of the awe in which they held their Egyptian masters and civilization. The sons and daughters of Abraham had to be readied to declare only God their Master and none other. In fact, tradition tells us that only a small minority of the Jews were able to psychologically break with the Egyptians and their culture. The vast majority remained dazzled by the civilization of their oppressors and perished during the plague of darkness.

We can now appreciate why the plagues play only a subdued role in the Haggadah.

As we have pointed out time after time, *Maggid* is a declaration of our "chosenness", to which we were elected at the time of the Exodus. The first nine plagues play only an ancillary role in God's choice of Israel. Therefore, the Haggadah mentions them only in passing.

The above distinction between the first nine plagues and the tenth is evidenced in the *Dayeinu* section that follows in the Haggadah. The first nine plagues are included there wholesale by the general term "wrought judgements against them", while the tenth plague, the slaying of the firstborn, is absolutely critical to the choosing of Israel and is therefore mentioned specifically and separately from the others: "and not slain their firstborn".

AN ALTERNATE INTERPRE-TATION [OF THE ABOVE MEN-TIONED VERSE, *(Deuteronomy XXVI:8)*, IS THAT EACH PHRASE REPRESENTS TWO PLAGUES INFLICTED UPON THE EGYPTIANS, THUS]: THE PHRASE, "WITH A MIGHTY HAND" - SIGNIFIES TWO PLAGUES; THE PHRASE "AN OUTSTRETCHED ARM" - SIGNIFIES TWO PLAGUES; THE PHRASE "WITH GREAT AWE" - SIGNIFIES TWO PLAGUES; THE PHRASE "SIGNS" - SIGNIFIES TWO PLAGUES; AND THE PHRASE, "WONDERS" SIGNIFIES TWO PLAGUES.

CUMULATIVELY, THESE ARE THE TEN PLAGUES WHICH THE HOLY ONE, BLESSED IS HE, BROUGHT UPON THE EGYPTIANS IN EGYPT, SPECIFICALLY THEY ARE:

BLOOD. FROGS. VERMIN. WILD BEASTS. PESTILENCE. BOILS. HAIL. LOCUSTS. DARKNESS.

SLAYING OF THE FIRSTBORN

דָּבָר אַחֵר, בְּיָד חֲזָקָה שְׁתַּיִם. וּבִזְרֹעַ נְטוּיָה שְׁתַּיִם. וּבְמֹרָא גָּדֹל שְׁתַּיִם, וּבְאֹתוֹת שְׁתַּיִם. וּבְמֹפְתִים שְׁתַּיִם:

אֵלוּ עֶשֶׂר מַכּוֹת שֶׁהֵבִיא הַקָּדוֹשׁ בָּרוּךְ הוּא עַל הַמִּצְרִים בְּמִצְרַיִם וְאֵלוּ הֵן:

דָּם. צְפַרְדֵּעַ. כִּנִּים. עָרוֹב. דֶּבֶר. שְׁחִין. בָּרָד. אַרְבֶּה. חֹשֶׁךְ.

מַכַּת בְּכוֹרוֹת.

RABBI YEHUDAH ABBREVI-
ATED THE PLAGUES BY THE
ACRONYM [OF THEIR HEBREW
INITIALS]:

רַבִּי יְהוּדָה הָיָה נוֹתֵן בָּהֶם
סִמָּנִים:

D"TZACH. ADASH. B'ACHAB.

דְּצַ"ךְ. עֲדַ"שׁ.
בְּאַחַ"ב.

———————— COMMENTARY ————————

All the commentators are mystified. What is Rabbi Yehudah's intention in reducing the plagues to an acronym?

The answer is: On Passover night, in order to fulfill the *mitzvah* of *Maggid*, we elaborate on the saga of the Exodus, but our elaboration extends only to those events which played a role in our being chosen as God's special nation.

Since the plagues are of only secondary importance in the process of choosing Israel (as explained in depth in our commentary above), Rabbi Yehudah emphasizes this subdued role by reducing them to their initials.

More important is: whatever the number of plagues brought upon the Egyptians in Egypt, there were five times as many brought upon them when the Red Sea was split. What happened at the Red Sea is more critical because there the act of choosing Israel was at a dramatic high. This explains why Rabbi Yose the Galilean, Rabbi Eliezer and Rabbi Akiva expend effort trying to account for the precise number of plagues at the Red Sea.

One may wonder, if Rabbi Yehudah's intent is as our commentary suggests, why does he include in his acronym the tenth plague - the killing of the firstborn, since that plague was indeed critical to "chosenness" (as explained above)?

The answer is: the tenth plague was a plague like the other nine in that it (a) punished the Egyptians and (b) showed the Jews how power-less their masters were before the Almighty. Therefore, the killing of the firstborn could and should be included in a listing of plagues. It had, however, a second dimension - God Himself came to inflict the tenth plague upon the Egyptians, thereby choosing Israel as his nation. This second dimension, the fact that God Himself meted out the plague, is unique and is not addressed by Rabbi Yehudah, who focuses here only on the plagues' first dimension.

דצ״ך

צְפַרְדֵעַ

דָם

כִּנִּים

עֶדִי"ש

דֶּבֶר

עָרוֹב

שְׁחִין

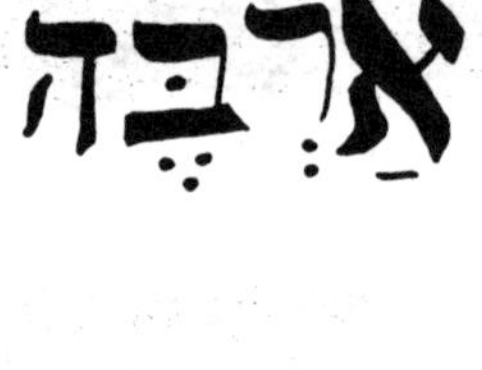
אַרְבֶּה

בָּרָד

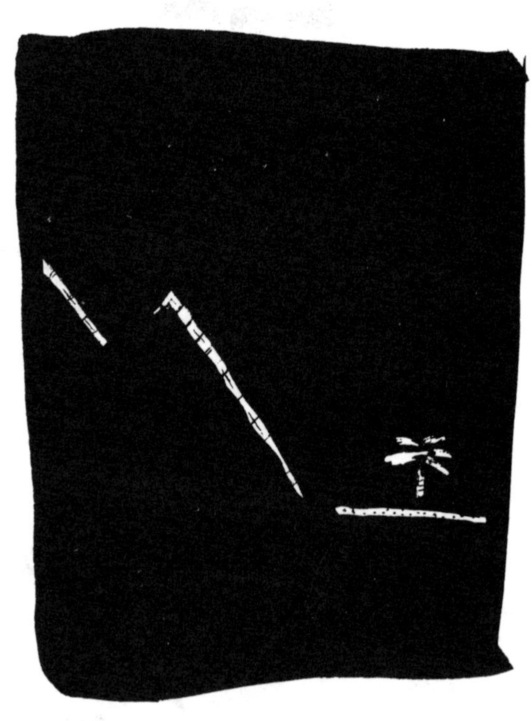

מַכַּת בְּכוֹרוֹת

חֹשֶׁךְ

RABBI YOSE THE GALILEAN SAYS: ONE CAN PROVE THAT THE EGYPTIANS WERE SMITTEN WITH TEN PLAGUES IN EGYPT AND FIFTY PLAGUES AT THE RED SEA. CONCERNING THE PLAGUES IN EGYPT THE TORAH STATES, "THE MAGICIANS SAID TO PHARAOH, 'IT IS THE FINGER OF GOD' ". *(Exodus VIII:15)* WHEREAS AT THE RED SEA THE TEXT READS, "ISRAEL SAW THE GREAT HAND WHICH THE ALMIGHTY WIELDED AGAINST THE EGYPTIANS, AND THE ISRAELITES FEARED THE ALMIGHTY, AND THEY BELIEVED IN HIM AND HIS SERVANT MOSES". *(Exodus XIV:31)* ONE CAN DEDUCE: IF TEN PLAGUES IS REPRESENTED BY THE TERM "FINGER", THEN FIFTY PLAGUES IS REPRESENTED BY THE TERM "HAND" (A HAND HAVING FIVE FINGERS).

RABBI ELIEZER SAYS: ONE CAN PROVE THAT EACH OF THE PLAGUES THE HOLY ONE, BLESSED IS HE, INFLICTED UPON THE EGYPTIANS IN EGYPT WAS IN

רַבִּי יוֹסֵי הַגְּלִילִי אוֹמֵר, מִנַּיִן אַתָּה אוֹמֵר שֶׁלָּקוּ הַמִּצְרִים בְּמִצְרַיִם עֶשֶׂר מַכּוֹת, וְעַל הַיָּם לָקוּ חֲמִשִּׁים מַכּוֹת. בְּמִצְרַיִם מָה הוּא אוֹמֵר, וַיֹּאמְרוּ הַחַרְטֻמִּם אֶל פַּרְעֹה אֶצְבַּע אֱלֹהִים הִוא. וְעַל הַיָּם מָה הוּא אוֹמֵר, וַיַּרְא יִשְׂרָאֵל אֶת הַיָּד הַגְּדֹלָה אֲשֶׁר עָשָׂה יהוה בְּמִצְרַיִם, וַיִּירְאוּ הָעָם אֶת יהוה, וַיַּאֲמִינוּ בַּיהוה וּבְמֹשֶׁה עַבְדּוֹ. כַּמָּה לָקוּ בָאֶצְבַּע, עֶשֶׂר מַכּוֹת, אֱמוֹר מֵעַתָּה, בְּמִצְרַיִם לָקוּ עֶשֶׂר מַכּוֹת, וְעַל הַיָּם לָקוּ חֲמִשִּׁים מַכּוֹת:

רַבִּי אֱלִיעֶזֶר אוֹמֵר, מִנַּיִן שֶׁכָּל מַכָּה וּמַכָּה, שֶׁהֵבִיא הַקָּדוֹשׁ בָּרוּךְ הוּא עַל הַמִּצְרִים בְּמִצְרַיִם, הָיְתָה

FACT FOUR PLAGUES. THE VERSE SAYS: "HE SENT AGAINST [THE EGYPTIANS] HIS BURNING ANGER [CONSISTING OF]: WRATH, INDIGNATION, TROUBLE AND MESSENGERS OF EVIL". *(Psalms LXXVIII:49)* [SINCE EACH PLAGUE IS REFERRED TO AS "HIS BURNING ANGER" AND COMPOSED OF]:

[1]   "WRATH",

[2]   "INDIGNATION",

[3]   "TROUBLE" AND

[4]   "MESSENGERS OF EVIL".

WE MAY CONCLUDE [USING THE "FINGER" AND "HAND" FORMULA PRESENTED ABOVE BY RABBI YOSE THE GALILEAN]: THE ALMIGHTY INFLICTED FORTY PLAGUES IN EGYPT AND TWO HUNDRED BY THE RED SEA.

RABBI AKIVA SAYS: ONE CAN PROVE THAT EACH OF THE PLAGUES THE HOLY ONE, BLESSED IS HE, INFLICTED UPON THE EGYPTIANS IN EGYPT WAS IN FACT FIVE PLAGUES. THE VERSE [QUOTED ABOVE BY RABBI ELIEZER] SHOULD BE EXPLAINED THUS: "HE SENT AGAINST [THE EGYPTIANS]:

[1]   "HIS BURNING ANGER"

שֶׁל אַרְבַּע מַכּוֹת. שֶׁנֶּאֱמַר, יְשַׁלַּח בָּם חֲרוֹן אַפּוֹ עֶבְרָה וָזַעַם וְצָרָה מִשְׁלַחַת מַלְאֲכֵי רָעִים.

עֶבְרָה אַחַת.
וָזַעַם שְׁתַּיִם.
וְצָרָה שָׁלֹשׁ.
מִשְׁלַחַת מַלְאֲכֵי רָעִים אַרְבַּע. אֱמוֹר מֵעַתָּה, בְּמִצְרַיִם לָקוּ אַרְבָּעִים מַכּוֹת. וְעַל הַיָּם לָקוּ מָאתַיִם מַכּוֹת:

רַבִּי עֲקִיבָא אוֹמֵר, מִנַּיִן שֶׁכָּל מַכָּה וּמַכָּה, שֶׁהֵבִיא הַקָּדוֹשׁ בָּרוּךְ הוּא עַל הַמִּצְרִים בְּמִצְרַיִם, הָיְתָה שֶׁל חָמֵשׁ מַכּוֹת. שֶׁנֶּאֱמַר, יְשַׁלַּח בָּם חֲרוֹן אַפּוֹ, עֶבְרָה וָזַעַם וְצָרָה, מִשְׁלַחַת מַלְאֲכֵי רָעִים.

חֲרוֹן אַפּוֹ אַחַת.

[2] "WRATH",

[3] "INDIGNATION",

[4] "TROUBLE" AND

[5] "MESSENGERS OF EVIL".

WE MAY CONCLUDE [USING THE "FINGER" AND "HAND" FORMULA PRESENTED ABOVE BY RABBI YOSE THE GALILEAN]: THE ALMIGHTY INFLICTED FIFTY PLAGUES IN EGYPT AND TWO HUNDRED AND FIFTY BY THE RED SEA.

HOW NUMEROUS ARE THE EXALTED FAVORS THE OMNIPRESENT HAS BESTOWED UPON US!

HAD [THE ALMIGHTY] BROUGHT US OUT OF EGYPT AND NOT WROUGHT JUDGEMENTS AGAINST THEM [THE EGYPTIANS],

IT WOULD HAVE SUFFICED.

HAD HE WROUGHT JUDGEMENTS AGAINST THEM AND NOT DESTROYED THEIR GODS,

IT WOULD HAVE SUFFICED.

HAD HE DESTROYED THEIR GODS AND NOT SLAIN THEIR FIRSTBORN,

IT WOULD HAVE SUFFICED.

HAD HE SLAIN THEIR FIRSTBORN AND NOT GIVEN US

עֶבְרָה שְׁתַּיִם. וָזַעַם שָׁלֹשׁ. וְצָרָה אַרְבַּע. מִשְׁלַחַת מַלְאֲכֵי רָעִים חָמֵשׁ.

אֱמוֹר מֵעַתָּה, בְּמִצְרַיִם לָקוּ חֲמִשִּׁים מַכּוֹת. וְעַל הַיָּם לָקוּ חֲמִשִּׁים וּמָאתַיִם מַכּוֹת:

כַּמָּה מַעֲלוֹת טוֹבוֹת לַמָּקוֹם עָלֵינוּ.

אִלּוּ הוֹצִיאָנוּ מִמִּצְרַיִם, וְלֹא עָשָׂה בָהֶם שְׁפָטִים **דַּיֵּנוּ:**

אִלּוּ עָשָׂה בָהֶם שְׁפָטִים, וְלֹא עָשָׂה בֵאלֹהֵיהֶם **דַּיֵּנוּ:**

אִלּוּ עָשָׂה בֵאלֹהֵיהֶם, וְלֹא הָרַג אֶת בְּכוֹרֵיהֶם **דַּיֵּנוּ:**

אִלּוּ הָרַג אֶת בְּכוֹרֵיהֶם, וְלֹא נָתַן לָנוּ אֶת מָמוֹנָם

קָרַע לָנוּ אֶת־הַיָּם דַּיֵּנוּ

THEIR WEALTH,

IT WOULD HAVE SUFFICED.

HAD HE GIVEN US THEIR WEALTH AND NOT SPLIT THE RED SEA FOR US,

IT WOULD HAVE SUFFICED.

HAD HE SPLIT THE RED SEA FOR US AND NOT LED US THROUGH IT DRY-SHOD,

IT WOULD HAVE SUFFICED.

HAD HE LED US THROUGH IT DRY-SHOD AND NOT DROWNED OUR OPPRESSORS IN IT,

IT WOULD HAVE SUFFICED.

HAD HE DROWNED OUR OPPRESSORS IN IT AND NOT SUSTAINED US IN THE DESERT FORTY YEARS,

IT WOULD HAVE SUFFICED.

HAD HE SUSTAINED US IN THE DESERT FORTY YEARS AND NOT FED US MANNA,

IT WOULD HAVE SUFFICED.

HAD HE FED US MANNA AND NOT GIVEN US THE SABBATH,

IT WOULD HAVE SUFFICED.

HAD HE GIVEN US THE SABBATH AND NOT BROUGHT US TO MOUNT SINAI,

IT WOULD HAVE SUFFICED.

דַּיֵּנוּ:

אִלּוּ נָתַן לָנוּ אֶת מָמוֹנָם, וְלֹא קָרַע לָנוּ אֶת הַיָּם דַּיֵּנוּ:

אִלּוּ קָרַע לָנוּ אֶת הַיָּם, וְלֹא הֶעֱבִירָנוּ בְּתוֹכוֹ בֶּחָרָבָה דַּיֵּנוּ:

אִלּוּ הֶעֱבִירָנוּ בְּתוֹכוֹ בֶּחָרָבָה, וְלֹא שִׁקַּע צָרֵינוּ בְּתוֹכוֹ דַּיֵּנוּ:

אִלּוּ שִׁקַּע צָרֵינוּ בְּתוֹכוֹ, וְלֹא סִפֵּק צָרְכֵּנוּ בַּמִּדְבָּר אַרְבָּעִים שָׁנָה דַּיֵּנוּ:

אִלּוּ סִפֵּק צָרְכֵּנוּ בַּמִּדְבָּר אַרְבָּעִים שָׁנָה, וְלֹא הֶאֱכִילָנוּ אֶת הַמָּן דַּיֵּנוּ:

אִלּוּ הֶאֱכִילָנוּ אֶת הַמָּן, וְלֹא נָתַן לָנוּ אֶת הַשַּׁבָּת דַּיֵּנוּ:

אִלּוּ נָתַן לָנוּ אֶת הַשַּׁבָּת, וְלֹא קֵרְבָנוּ לִפְנֵי הַר סִינַי דַּיֵּנוּ:

HAD HE BROUGHT US TO MOUNT SINAI AND NOT GIVEN US THE TORAH,

IT WOULD HAVE SUFFICED.

HAD HE GIVEN US THE TORAH AND NOT BROUGHT US INTO THE LAND OF ISRAEL,

IT WOULD HAVE SUFFICED.

HAD HE BROUGHT US INTO THE LAND OF ISRAEL AND NOT BUILT THE HOLY TEMPLE FOR US,

IT WOULD HAVE SUFFICED.

[**O**UR OBLIGATION TO BE GRATEFUL IS] CERTAINLY INCREASED BY THE DOUBLE AND REDOUBLED BLESSINGS WHICH THE OMNIPRESENT HAS BESTOWED UPON US:

HE BROUGHT US OUT OF EGYPT

WROUGHT JUDGEMENTS AGAINST THEM

DESTROYED THEIR GODS

SLEW THEIR FIRSTBORN

GAVE US THEIR WEALTH

SPLIT THE RED SEA FOR US

LED US THROUGH DRY-SHOD

DROWNED OUR OPPRESSORS

אִלוּ קֵרְבָנוּ לִפְנֵי הַר סִינַי, וְלֹא נָתַן לָנוּ אֶת הַתּוֹרָה **דַּיֵּנוּ:**

אִלוּ נָתַן לָנוּ אֶת הַתּוֹרָה, וְלֹא הִכְנִיסָנוּ לְאֶרֶץ יִשְׂרָאֵל **דַּיֵּנוּ:**

אִלוּ הִכְנִיסָנוּ לְאֶרֶץ יִשְׂרָאֵל, וְלֹא בָנָה לָנוּ אֶת בֵּית הַבְּחִירָה **דַּיֵּנוּ:**

עַל אַחַת כַּמָּה וְכַמָּה, טוֹבָה כְפוּלָה וּמְכֻפֶּלֶת לַמָּקוֹם עָלֵינוּ. שֶׁהוֹצִיאָנוּ מִמִּצְרַיִם, וְעָשָׂה בָהֶם שְׁפָטִים. וְעָשָׂה בֵאלֹהֵיהֶם. וְהָרַג אֶת בְּכוֹרֵיהֶם. וְנָתַן לָנוּ אֶת מָמוֹנָם, וְקָרַע לָנוּ אֶת הַיָּם. וְהֶעֱבִירָנוּ בְּתוֹכוֹ בֶּחָרָבָה. וְשִׁקַע צָרֵינוּ בְּתוֹכוֹ. וְסִפֵּק צָרְכֵנוּ בַּמִּדְבָּר אַרְבָּעִים שָׁנָה. וְהֶאֱכִילָנוּ אֶת הַמָּן. וְנָתַן לָנוּ אֶת הַשַּׁבָּת. וְקֵרְבָנוּ לִפְנֵי הַר סִינַי. וְנָתַן לָנוּ אֶת הַתּוֹרָה. וְהִכְנִיסָנוּ לְאֶרֶץ

SUSTAINED US IN THE
DESERT FORTY YEARS
FED US MANNA
GAVE US THE SABBATH
BROUGHT US TO MOUNT
SINAI
GAVE US THE TORAH
BROUGHT US INTO THE
LAND OF ISRAEL
BUILT THE HOLY TEMPLE
FOR US;
TO ATONE FOR ALL OUR
SINS.

יִשְׂרָאֵל. וּבָנָה לָנוּ אֶת בֵּית
הַבְּחִירָה לְכַפֵּר עַל כָּל
עֲוֹנוֹתֵינוּ:

--- ***COMMENTARY*** ---

All commentators are perplexed with the statements in *Dayeinu*. For example, the Haggadah says, "had He split the Red Sea for us and not led us through it dry-shod - it would have sufficed". Had that happened, the Jews would have drowned!

Also, how can we state, "had He brought us to Mount Sinai and not given us the *Torah* - it would have sufficed"? What good would coming near Him at Mount Sinai have been had God not given us the *Torah*?

Following our thematic, that the miraculous events of the Exodus were meant to establish and proclaim to the entire world Israel's status as the chosen nation, the answer is as follows:

A king chooses his queen, not by a singular act but by many. First, he selects one woman from many possible candidates. After selecting her, he showers her with presents fit for royalty. Then he makes a party in her honor. These acts of affection are done not only to please and honor but have a wider aim as well - to establish this woman as the one chosen to be the queen.

At the party in her honor the king may place a crown on the future queen's head. The king both shows how much he favors his future queen and at the same time demonstrates that she alone will be the queen and no other.

All the king's acts of courtship fall into two categories: (1) an intimate show of affection which is of concern only to the sovereign and his queen-to-be (2) a public show of regalia necessary to usher in his beloved before the entire kingdom in order to have her accepted as the future queen.

Eventually the marriage takes place and the chosen bride comes to live in the palace with the king, sharing his royal chambers, thereby not only consummating the marriage but also her queenly election.

So too the "nation Israel" and God. Our sages tell us that the relationship between the King of the universe and Israel is to be compared to a groom and his chosen bride. The Exodus from Egypt is when the courtship first began, the *Torah* given at Mount Sinai corresponds to the wedding and settling the land of Israel is reflective of residing together in the palace.

In *Dayeinu* we enumerate each step in the process through which God chose the Jewish nation to be His; i. e. the King of Kings' courtship of His beloved people. God first began his selection of the Jews by taking them from servitude with great miracles. As a token present to His beloved, He shifted the wealth of the Egyptian civilization to them. With great affection He changed His own established rules of nature in their honor by splitting the Red Sea to save them from the Egyptian cavalry. He supported us and gave us manna from heaven. The King then gave from His treasure house a gift He was saving for His future queen from the time of creation - the Sabbath. He placed His crown upon us and gave us the keys to His royal chambers at the time of our wedding celebration when we stood together at Mount Sinai.

We were then brought to the royal palace to live side by side with the King. We came to the land of Israel where God had ordained that His Divine Presence should rest in the Holy Temple. (Appropriately, the rabbis instituted that we read "The Song of Songs" on Passover because it speaks of the relationship between the King and his beloved.)

In no way are we to misconstrue the statement in *Dayeinu*, "it would have sufficed", to mean that God did not have to do these miracles; without each and every one of them, we would have been either physically or spiritually lost!

God however, at the time of the Exodus, not only saved us through miracles time and time again, but used those very same miracles to proclaim our "chosenness". Certainly some of the miracles mentioned in *Dayeinu* could have been performed without public fanfare, as were many Divine kindnesses shown Israel. But God employed every one of them not only to save His beloved and thereby show His affection in a private manner, but also as a herald, publicly proclaiming to all humanity - "Israel is the Almighty's chosen".

In *Dayeinu*, we express our gratitude for the "public" aspect of each miraculous event; every one of the miracles proclaims the King's choice of his queen.

Had He taken us out of Egypt and through that event alone proclaimed our "chosenness" to the world, that would have sufficed. How much more jubilant should we be that God repeatedly publicized our ennobled status through each and every one of the miracles mentioned in *Dayeinu*.

Dayeinu, in fact, is possibly the strongest proof of our thesis that *Maggid* is more than just a command to retell the story of the Exodus. If retelling is all we do, why do we mention in *Dayeinu* all the miracles which transpired in the desert for forty years; the manna, the revelation at Mount Sinai, the giving of the *Torah*, being led into the land of Israel and the building of the Holy Temple? Clearly, these events have nothing to do with the Exodus. The building of the Temple took place a full four hundred and eighty years after the Jews' departure from Egypt!

But given our fundamental premise in the Haggadah that we are obligated to retell how God chose us through the events of the Exodus, every one of the miracles mentioned in *Dayeinu* is clearly in place. Each of them was part of the process of choosing Israel, evidencing the special relationship between God and the Jewish nation.

Our wine cups should be refilled to replace the wine removed when we recalled the plagues. The spilled wine should not be used. (The source for this is not in Shulchan Aruch but rather is an accepted custom and tradition.)

For the recitation of "Rabban Gamliel" everyone should be present and attentive. As stated in the Haggadah, "Whoever has not explained these three things on Passover [seder night] has not fulfilled his obligation [of remembering the Exodus]". (Mishnah Berurah, O.C. 473:64)

RABBI GAMLIEL WAS OFT TO SAY, "WHOEVER HAS NOT EXPLAINED THESE THREE THINGS ON PASSOVER [SEDER NIGHT] HAS NOT FULFILLED HIS OBLIGATION. THESE THREE THINGS ARE:

רַבָּן גַּמְלִיאֵל הָיָה אוֹמֵר. כָּל שֶׁלֹּא אָמַר שְׁלֹשָׁה דְבָרִים אֵלּוּ בַּפֶּסַח, לֹא יָצָא יְדֵי חוֹבָתוֹ, וְאֵלּוּ הֵן.

PESACH - *(the Pascal lamb)*

פֶּסַח.

MATZOH - *(the unleavened bread)*

מַצָּה.

MARROR - *(the bitter herbs)*

וּמָרוֹר:

We only look at the shankbone on the Seder plate which represents the Pascal lamb while reciting the following passage but we don't lift it. (Mishnah Berurah, 474:72)

THE PASCAL LAMB OFFERING THAT OUR FATHERS ATE WHEN THE HOLY TEMPLE STOOD - WHY DID THEY DO SO? BECAUSE THE HOLY ONE, BLESSED IS HE, PASSED OVER THE HOUSES OF OUR FOREFATHERS IN EGYPT, AS IT SAYS IN THE VERSE: "YOU SHALL SAY: 'IT IS A PASCAL SACRIFICE TO THE ALMIGHTY WHO PASSED OVER THE ISRAELITES'

פֶּסַח שֶׁהָיוּ אֲבוֹתֵינוּ אוֹכְלִים בִּזְמַן שֶׁבֵּית הַמִּקְדָּשׁ הָיָה קַיָּם, עַל שׁוּם מָה, עַל שׁוּם שֶׁפָּסַח הַקָּדוֹשׁ בָּרוּךְ הוּא עַל בָּתֵּי אֲבוֹתֵינוּ בְּמִצְרַיִם. שֶׁנֶּאֱמַר, וַאֲמַרְתֶּם זֶבַח פֶּסַח הוּא לַיהוה, אֲשֶׁר פָּסַח עַל בָּתֵּי בְנֵי יִשְׂרָאֵל בְּמִצְרַיִם, בְּנָגְפּוֹ אֶת

HOUSES IN EGYPT WHEN HE SMOTE THE EGYPTIANS AND SPARED OUR HOMES.' THE NATION BOWED AND PROSTRATED THEMSELVES."

(Exodus XII: 27)

מִצְרַיִם וְאֶת בָּתֵּינוּ הִצִּיל, וַיִּקֹּד הָעָם וַיִּשְׁתַּחֲווּ:

The middle Matzoh is raised for everyone to see while reciting this passage.
(O.C. 473:7 and Ramah)

WHY DO WE EAT THIS MATZOH (UNLEAVENED BREAD)? BECAUSE THE SUPREME KING OF KINGS, THE HOLY ONE, BLESSED IS HE, REVEALED HIMSELF TO OUR ANCESTORS AND REDEEMED THEM EVEN BEFORE THEIR DOUGH HAD TIME TO LEAVEN, AS IT SAYS IN THE VERSE: "THEY BAKED THE DOUGH WHICH THEY TOOK OUT OF EGYPT INTO MATZOH CAKES AS IT DID NOT RISE, FOR THEY WERE DRIVEN FROM EGYPT AND COULD NOT LINGER; NOR HAD THEY PREPARED ANY PROVISIONS FOR THEMSELVES."

(Exodus XII:39)

מַצָּה זוֹ שֶׁאָנוּ אוֹכְלִים, עַל שׁוּם מָה. עַל שׁוּם שֶׁלֹּא הִסְפִּיק בְּצֵקָם שֶׁל אֲבוֹתֵינוּ לְהַחֲמִיץ. עַד שֶׁנִּגְלָה עֲלֵיהֶם מֶלֶךְ מַלְכֵי הַמְּלָכִים הַקָּדוֹשׁ בָּרוּךְ הוּא וּגְאָלָם. שֶׁנֶּאֱמַר, וַיֹּאפוּ אֶת הַבָּצֵק אֲשֶׁר הוֹצִיאוּ מִמִּצְרַיִם עֻגֹת מַצּוֹת כִּי לֹא חָמֵץ, כִּי גֹרְשׁוּ מִמִּצְרַיִם וְלֹא יָכְלוּ לְהִתְמַהְמֵהַּ וְגַם צֵדָה לֹא עָשׂוּ לָהֶם:

The Marror (bitter herb) is raised for everyone to see while reciting this passage. *(O.C. 473:7)*

WHY DO WE EAT THIS BITTER HERB? BECAUSE THE EGYPTIANS EMBITTERED THE LIVES OF OUR FOREFA-

מָרוֹר זֶה שֶׁאָנוּ אוֹכְלִים, עַל שׁוּם מָה. עַל שׁוּם שֶׁמֵּרְרוּ הַמִּצְרִים אֶת חַיֵּי

THERS IN EGYPT, AS IT SAYS IN THE VERSE: "THEY EMBITTERED THEIR LIVES WITH HARD LABOR, WITH MORTAR AND BRICKS, AND ALL MANNER OF WORK IN THE FIELD; THEY IMPOSED UPON THEM CRUSHING LABOR.

(Exodus I:14)

אֲבוֹתֵינוּ בְּמִצְרַיִם, שֶׁנֶּאֱמַר, וַיְמָרְרוּ אֶת חַיֵּיהֶם בַּעֲבֹדָה קָשָׁה, בְּחֹמֶר וּבִלְבֵנִים וּבְכָל עֲבֹדָה בַּשָּׂדֶה, אֵת כָּל עֲבֹדָתָם אֲשֶׁר עָבְדוּ בָהֶם בְּפָרֶךְ:

——————— COMMENTARY ———————

The following questions demand our attention:

1.   If the thrust of *Maggid* is only to retell the events of the Exodus, why does *Rabban Gamliel* omit from his list of "musts": Moses, Pharaoh and the plagues?

2.   Since *Rabban Gamliel* postulates the minimum fulfillment of *Maggid*, why doesn't the *Haggadah* advance his ruling to the section's introduction, instead of consigning it to the conclusion?

3.   (i) Why the insistence on mentioning *Matzoh*? While the Pascal lamb and *Marror* were key elements in the Jews' Egyptian experience and redemption, *Matzoh* seems on the surface so very incidental to the Exodus. True, it symbolizes the Jews' hastened exit from slavery but why use the relatively minor incident of the dough not rising, to evidence the point? Why not simply state: God took us out of Egypt in great haste?

(ii) More fundamentally, why is leaving in great haste so significant? On first analysis, it seems to detract from the miracle of the Exodus. A slave who is escaping runs away; freemen take leave at their leisure. Surely a much greater miracle would have been effected if the Israelites had more time to prepare provisions for their Exodus, leaving without haste as freemen.

4.   In his exposition of the role of *Matzoh*, *Rabban Gamliel* attributes the haste with which the Jews left Egypt to God: "... because the supreme King of Kings, the Holy One, Blessed is He, revealed Himself

to our ancestors and redeemed them even before their dough had time to leaven, as it says in the verse: '... for they were driven from Egypt and could not linger...'". (*Exodus XII:39*)

A quick overview of the surrounding verses in the Bible makes it explicitly clear that it was in fact the **Egyptians** who drove the Israelites out of Egypt:

> **"And the Egyptians were urgent upon the people, to hasten to send them out of the land; for they said; 'We are all dead men.'"** (*Exodus XII:33*)

What compels *Rabban Gamliel* to deviate from the simple explanation of the Biblical text?

The answer to all the above questions follows directly from our commentary's central theme: *Maggid* is a great deal more than a chronology of the Exodus; it is primarily a declaration of belief that God took us out of Egypt **to be His chosen nation.**

This premise in place, our first question is immediately settled; Moses, Pharaoh and the plagues play no role in Israel's "chosenness".

The second of our questions is most trenchantly answered by the recent *Talmudic* genius, Rav Chaim Soloveichik (b. 1853 Russia - d. 1918, Poland). Reb Chaim (as he is affectionately known) in his elucidation of a variant text found in Maimonides (*Chometz U'Matzoh* 7:6), states that a key element of *Maggid* is the obligation of every Jew to "act out" the Exodus, not merely speak about it.

The chief manner in which we "act out" the Exodus is by eating the Pascal lamb, *Matzoh* and *Marror*. These three foods are our props for physically portraying the enslavement, Divine intervention and redemption. But how is one to know that our eating is indeed also part of *Maggid*? Perhaps, partaking of the *Matzoh* and *Marror* is done solely to fulfill the obligation to eat these foods, a commandment unto itself and not tied to *Maggid*.

That problem is precisely the one *Rabban Gamliel* comes to answer, says Reb Chaim. The way to incorporate the eating of the Pascal lamb, *Matzoh*, and *Marror* into the retelling of the Exodus is to point to them at the end of our narrative, directly before eating them, and explain: "This Pascal lamb that I am about to eat, what will I be portraying by its consumption? I will be reenacting God's passing over our forefathers' homes in Egypt..." Similarly we point to the *Matzoh* and *Marror* and explain what eating them will portray in the story of the Exodus.

Reb Chaim's elucidation explains why *Rabban Gamliel's* statement must come at the conclusion of *Maggid*. *Rabban Gamliel's* statement serves as the nexus **joining** the retelling of the Exodus saga to the eating of the Pascal lamb, *Matzoh* and *Marror*, therefore, it must be at the conclusion of the one, and directly before the other. This answers our second question.

As explained in our commentary to the Haggadah's next section, "In each generation, a Jew is obligated to view himself as having gone out of Egypt...", a Jew must feel the Haggadah's retelling as an autobiographical account. Because even Jews yet unborn were chosen at the Exodus, the "chosenness" that devolved upon the Jewish nation when we left Egypt, actually did occur to us. To exhibit belief in our chosenness we "act out" those events as if we were reliving then.

It follows, self-evidently, that the reenactment of the Exodus which takes place through the eating of the Pascal lamb, *Matzoh* and *Marror*, comprises the major motifs in the Exodus saga. *Rabban Gamliel* foretells which motif will be performed respectively through the eating of the Pascal lamb, *Matzoh*, and *Marror*. These are:

Pesach

*The Pascal lamb: **God literally chose us by singling out the Jewish nation as His**.* He passed over our homes where the Pascal lamb was being eaten, leaving us in peace and security, while killing the Egyptian firstborn wherever they were found.

Matzoh

*The Unleavened Bread: **During the Exodus the laws of nature themselves attested that God took the Jewish people to be His**.*

Laws of nature dictate that fermentation occurs when dough is left unattended, causing it to rise. That being the case, why is it (as the verse informs us) the dough brought out of Egypt was baked into *Matzoh* cakes **before it could rise?** (*Exodus XII:39*) The dough which was baked, was the same dough previously wrapped in the Jews' robes and placed on their shoulders as they were leaving Egypt. The Israelites then took time to request of the Egyptians silver, gold and clothing, and traveled from Rameses toward Sukkoth. (*Exodus XII:34-37*) Surely the time elapsed to do all this should have allowed for the zymologic process to take place and caused the dough to rise. So why didn't it rise? We are forced to conclude: at the time of the Exodus "natural law" was suspended.

"Natural law" serves as the **agent** of God's will. Therefore, when God directly intercedes, natural law is suspended; the servant serves no purpose when the master performs the task. Symbolic and demonstrative of God's direct intercession to choose Israel was the dough taken out of Egypt by the Israelites which did not rise in contravention of the natural fermentation process. This decisively answers question 3(i).

Kabbalistically, we know *Matzoh* represents a higher spiritual level, while leavened dough symbolizes a baser plane. Once chosen to be God's people, the Jews were spiritually elevated and no longer belonged among the base Egyptians. This explains the great significance attached by the Haggadah to the Almighty bringing out the nation Israel in haste and answers question 3(ii).

Following through with the above reasoning we also are able to answer question 4. On careful analysis of the verses in Exodus XII:30-42 one clearly sees it was the Egyptians who urged the Jews to leave quickly. The Jews, however, did not respond at all to their pleas. How could they? With the Almighty's superseding presence clearly visible to all, the Jews were far beyond accepting any directives from their former masters, so they took their time. It is God who then caused the nation Israel to leave in haste, wishing to separate His chosen children from the base, idolatrous and immoral Egyptians.

The reason for the Jews' flight from Egypt clearly presents us with an important contemporary lesson: assimilating into the prevailing culture is certainly not God's desire for His chosen.

Marror

Bitter Herbs: **The Jews merited the ennobled status of chosen nation because on a national level, they maintained their distinctive spiritual excellence inherited from their forefathers.**

How did the misery of enslavement figure into the Jews' selection as the Chosen Nation?

The answer is: The Egyptian experience was the crucible in which the Jewish people was forged into a nation.

While suffering the crushing blows of their taskmasters, the Jews managed to retain their own language (Hebrew), ethnic dress and personal names. **They didn't let themselves assimilate into their masters' culture but proudly kept their own.** They spoke the holy language of the patriarchs, their conduct in dress was fashioned by modesty, the names they chose reflected a desire to define their very being as in the service of God (*Mechiltah, Bo, Parsha* 5). As a result of this national spiritual resolve and inner strength, they truly merited becoming a nation; one whole and indivisible entity worthy of being chosen by God.

There is a contemporary lesson to be learned from our ancestor's resolute example: a Jew must comport himself as a Jew. If one has never worn a *yarmulke* (skullcap), or donned a *talis* (four-cornered fringed garment), or fails to dress with modesty, or gives his child a distinctly non-Jewish name, or speaks crudely, or is wholly illiterate in our national language (Hebrew), he is in danger of renouncing his heritage.

Indeed, the surest way to guarantee Jewish continuity is to dress as Jews, give ourselves and our children Jewish names, and to be versed in our holy tongue.

Why do modern Jews feel so queasy about bestowing a Hebrew name upon their children but so guiltless about choosing one that sounds as if it has been culled from the roster of soap opera characters? Why do we suffer the bizarre blandishments of a clothes industry that dupes us into wearing torn garments and pink hair and countless other sartorial practical jokes? And why are we so quick to take on the argot of other groups in the name of being "cool", while remaining oblivious to our own language?

By falling prey to assimilation we forfeit the very characteristic that caused God to choose us. We callously spurn the great love shown us by the Almighty. We should seek to learn from our forefathers, not our gentile contemporaries.

IN EACH GENERATION, A JEW IS OBLIGATED TO VIEW HIMSELF AS HAVING GONE OUT OF EGYPT, AS IT SAYS IN THE VERSE: "YOU SHALL TELL YOUR SON ON THAT DAY, 'BECAUSE OF THIS DID THE ALMIGHTY DO FOR ME WHEN I WENT OUT OF EGYPT' ". *(Exodus XIII:8)* NOT ONLY WERE OUR FOREFATHERS REDEEMED FROM SLAVERY BY THE HOLY ONE, BLESSED IS HE, WE TOO WERE REDEEMED WITH THEM. AS IT SAYS IN THE VERSE: "HE BROUGHT US FROM THERE THAT HE MIGHT BRING US [TO] AND GIVE US THE LAND HE HAD PROMISED TO OUR ANCESTORS."

(Deuteronomy VI:23)

בְּכָל דּוֹר וָדוֹר חַיָּב אָדָם לִרְאוֹת אֶת עַצְמוֹ כְּאִלּוּ הוּא יָצָא מִמִּצְרַיִם, שֶׁנֶּאֱמַר, וְהִגַּדְתָּ לְבִנְךָ בַּיּוֹם הַהוּא לֵאמֹר, בַּעֲבוּר זֶה עָשָׂה יהוה לִי בְּצֵאתִי מִמִּצְרָיִם: לֹא אֶת אֲבוֹתֵינוּ בִּלְבָד גָּאַל הַקָּדוֹשׁ בָּרוּךְ הוּא, אֶלָּא אַף אוֹתָנוּ גָּאַל עִמָּהֶם. שֶׁנֶּאֱמַר, וְאוֹתָנוּ הוֹצִיא מִשָּׁם, לְמַעַן הָבִיא אֹתָנוּ לָתֶת לָנוּ אֶת הָאָרֶץ אֲשֶׁר נִשְׁבַּע לַאֲבֹתֵינוּ:

COMMENTARY

The Haggadah instructs us: "In each generation, a Jew is obligated to view himself as having gone out of Egypt, as it says in the verse: 'You should tell your son on that day, "because of this did the Almighty do for *me* when *I* went out of Egypt." ' "

The Hagaddah, quoting the source verse of the commandment to retell the story of the Exodus, speaks of a parent, his child, and the message the one imparts to the other. But as the Haggadah points out, the verse discussing the substance of the message never says anything about the historical epic of the Exodus itself, only that it happened to "me", i.e., the parent. The Haggadah deduces that this is in fact the critical message to be transmitted: **it happened to me**.

וְהִגַּדְתָּ לְבִנְךָ

The Haggadah derives from the above *Torah* verse, that a fulfillment of the Biblical injunction to retell the story of the Exodus to the next generation, is accomplished only by an autobiographical account; if the substance of the transmission is "it happened to me" it can only be imparted through a personalized recounting. Indeed, it must be so for the message to have any meaning for the child. The events of the Exodus are historical trivia and meaningless to the child, without a Jew internalizing and reliving that very event. Only when a parent says, "My child, it happened to me", does it assume a life-directing character.

But how is it possible for someone at the Seder, who is living hundreds or thousands of years after the Exodus, to say, "when **I** left Egypt," much less believe it?

The answer comes with an understanding of the message of the Exodus. True, the miracles the message recounts are historical, having occurred in the year 2448. However, in each generation, our obligation at the Seder is much more than mere remembrance. Every Jew must recognize that when God took us out of Egypt with great miracles, He chose us as his special nation. This "chosenness" was bestowed upon the Jewish nation as a whole and devolved upon each individual Jew for all time. In that sense, Jews in every generation can truly say, "I was 'chosen' at the Exodus."

The importance of the Exodus and the reason why we are instructed to recount its events for ourselves and to our children, lies not in its history but in its modern and eternal relevance to the Jewish people; we were chosen to be God's nation through the Exodus and we, therefore, continue to be His chosen today and for all eternity.

This personal interaction with the Exodus is critical to *Maggid*. Without this feeling on the part of the parent, a Jewish child will never accept the message of his "chosenness". Logically, a Jewish child reasons, if his parents were not chosen at the time of the Exodus, why should he be so endowed?

The Matzoh, which has been uncovered throughout the recitation of Maggid, is now covered. We raise our wine cups until after the recitation of "Hallel" and the conclusion of the "Asher G'alanu" blessing. (O.C. 473:7 and Ramah)

THEREFORE IT IS OUR DUTY TO THANK, PRAISE, LAUD, GLORIFY, EXALT, HONOR, BLESS, EXTOL AND ADORE, HE WHO PERFORMED ALL THESE MIRACLES FOR OUR FOREFATHERS AND FOR US. HE BROUGHT US FROM SLAVERY TO FREEDOM, FROM SORROW TO JOY, FROM MOURNING TO FESTIVITY, FROM DARKNESS TO GREAT LIGHT AND FROM BONDAGE TO REDEMPTION. LET US RECITE A NEW SONG BEFORE HIM, HALLELUYAH!

לְפִיכָךְ אֲנַחְנוּ חַיָּבִים לְהוֹדוֹת, לְהַלֵּל, לְשַׁבֵּחַ, לְפָאֵר, לְרוֹמֵם, לְהַדֵּר, לְבָרֵךְ, לְעַלֵּה, וּלְקַלֵּס. לְמִי שֶׁעָשָׂה לַאֲבוֹתֵינוּ וְלָנוּ אֶת כָּל הַנִּסִּים הָאֵלוּ. הוֹצִיאָנוּ מֵעַבְדוּת לְחֵרוּת. מִיָּגוֹן לְשִׂמְחָה. וּמֵאֵבֶל לְיוֹם טוֹב. וּמֵאֲפֵלָה לְאוֹר גָּדוֹל. וּמִשִׁעְבּוּד לִגְאֻלָּה. וְנֹאמַר לְפָנָיו שִׁירָה חֲדָשָׁה הַלְלוּיָה:

--- **COMMENTARY** ---

What does the Haggadah mean by the phrase "from darkness to great light"?

When God redeemed us from Egypt, He not only brought us out physically, but also bestowed a spiritual elevation upon us. The *Talmud* compares this Divinely-granted uplifting to a king selecting his queen. Just as a king bedecks his chosen with precious stones and royal apparel befitting her new status, so too, God adorned his "queen" - the Jewish nation.

This concept is developed in "The Way of God", Part IV, Chapter 4, Subsection 9:

And after this [a Jew] remembers the Exodus from Egypt. [The reason for this remembrance is] because the Exodus was the great event through which Israel was rectified.

After Adam's sin, mankind was left degraded and imperfect... Even though our patriarch Abraham was chosen so that he and his progeny would be set apart from all nations to be God's people, still, they had no ability... to gain possession of their appropriate crown. This was because of the prevalent spiritual darkness and the initial pollution of which they had not yet rid themselves. Therefore, they needed to be exiled to Egypt.

When the proper time came, God increased His influence and illumination over the Jews, denying evil access to them. [God] lifted them from degradation and brought them up to Him... They were established as a nation, attached to God and crowned by Him.

With this in mind we understand the Haggadah's phrase, "from darkness to great light." "Darkness" is the spiritual night which envelops mankind, and "light" is the spiritual splendor with which God crowned Israel, elevating His chosen nation. God lavished this gift upon the Jews so that we would be appropriately attired to be His queen.

Taking stock of God's gift to us imparts a contemporary lesson. How can we spurn the Divine conferral of spiritual illumination by descending to the dark abyss of assimilation and intermarriage? Our aim should be much higher, targeting levels of religious commitment long established by our history and destiny.

לְפִיכָךְ אֲנַחְנוּ חַיָּבִים לְהוֹדוֹת

PRAISE THE ALMIGHTY! O SERVANT OF THE ALMIGHTY, PRAISE THE NAME OF THE LORD. BLESSED BE THE NAME OF THE ALMIGHTY NOW AND EVERMORE. FROM THE RISING SUN UNTIL ITS SETTING, PRAISED BE THE NAME OF THE ALMIGHTY. HIGH ABOVE ALL NATIONS IS THE LORD, ABOVE THE HEAVENS, HIS GLORY. WHO IS LIKE UNTO THE ALMIGHTY, OUR LORD WHO DWELLS ON HIGH YET LOOKS DOWN UPON THE HEAVENS AND EARTH. HE RAISES THE IMPOVERISHED MAN FROM DUST, THE POOR MAN FROM THE DUNGHILL, TO SEAT HIM WITH PRINCES, WITH THE PRINCES OF HIS PEOPLE. HE TRANSFORMS THE BARREN WOMAN INTO A JOYFUL MOTHER OF CHIL- DREN. HALLELUYAH!

(Psalm 113)

WHEN ISRAEL WENT FORTH FROM EGYPT, THE HOUSE OF JACOB FROM A NATION OF STRANGE TONGUE, YEHU- DAH BECAME HIS HOLY ONE, ISRAEL HIS GOVERNORS. THE SEA LOOKED AND FLED, THE JORDAN WAS DRIVEN

הַלְלוּיָהּ, הַלְלוּ עַבְדֵי יהוה, הַלְלוּ אֶת שֵׁם יהוה: יְהִי שֵׁם יהוה מְבֹרָךְ, מֵעַתָּה וְעַד עוֹלָם: מִמִּזְרַח שֶׁמֶשׁ עַד מְבוֹאוֹ, מְהֻלָּל שֵׁם יהוה: רָם עַל כָּל גּוֹיִם, יהוה, עַל הַשָּׁמַיִם כְּבוֹדוֹ: מִי כַּיהוה אֱלֹהֵינוּ, הַמַּגְבִּיהִי לָשָׁבֶת: הַמַּשְׁפִּילִי לִרְאוֹת, בַּשָּׁמַיִם וּבָאָרֶץ: מְקִימִי מֵעָפָר דָּל, מֵאַשְׁפֹּת יָרִים אֶבְיוֹן: לְהוֹשִׁיבִי עִם נְדִיבִים, עִם נְדִיבֵי עַמּוֹ: מוֹשִׁיבִי עֲקֶרֶת הַבַּיִת, אֵם הַבָּנִים שְׂמֵחָה, הַלְלוּיָהּ:

בְּצֵאת יִשְׂרָאֵל מִמִּצְרָיִם, בֵּית יַעֲקֹב מֵעַם לֹעֵז: הָיְתָה יְהוּדָה לְקָדְשׁוֹ, יִשְׂרָאֵל מַמְשְׁלוֹתָיו: הַיָּם רָאָה וַיָּנֹס, הַיַּרְדֵּן יִסֹּב לְאָחוֹר: הֶהָרִים רָקְדוּ

BACKWARD. THE MOUNTAINS SKIPPED LIKE RAMS, THE HILLS LIKE YOUNG SHEEP. WHAT AILS YOU, O SEA, THAT YOU DID FLEE, JORDAN THAT YOU WERE DRIVEN BACK? YE MOUNTAINS THAT SKIPPED LIKE RAMS, YE HILLS LIKE YOUNG SHEEP? TREMBLE, O EARTH, BEFORE THE MASTER, BEFORE THE GOD OF JACOB, WHO TURNED THE ROCK INTO A POOL OF WATER, THE FLINTY ROCK INTO A FLOWING FOUNTAIN.

(Psalm 114)

כְּאֵילִים, גְּבָעוֹת כִּבְנֵי צֹאן: מַה לְּךָ הַיָּם כִּי תָנוּס, הַיַּרְדֵּן תִּסֹּב לְאָחוֹר: הֶהָרִים תִּרְקְדוּ כְאֵילִים, גְּבָעוֹת כִּבְנֵי צֹאן: מִלִּפְנֵי אָדוֹן חוּלִי אָרֶץ, מִלִּפְנֵי אֱלוֹהַ יַעֲקֹב: הַהֹפְכִי הַצּוּר אֲגַם מָיִם, חַלָּמִישׁ לְמַעְיְנוֹ מָיִם:

COMMENTARY

All commentators wonder why the *Hallel* service, always recited as a unit, is split into halves by the Haggadah. The first half is incorporated in the *Maggid* section before the holiday meal, while the concluding half follows our repast.

The great medieval sage, Don Yitzchak Abarbanel (Lisbon b. 1437 - d. 1508, Padua), answers this question. The *Talmud* (Tractate *Pesachim* 118a) asks: "Once we have the Great *Hallel* (Psalms 136), why do we recite this other *Hallel*? (Psalms 113 - 118). [The *Talmud* proceeds to answer] Because it mentions five events critical to Jewish belief: (1) the Exodus from Egypt, (2) the splitting of the Red Sea, (3) the giving of the *Torah*, (4) the resurrection of the dead, and (5) the pains of the coming of the Messiah."

Only the first three events cited by the *Talmud* have to do with the Exodus. (See our explanation of *Dayeinu* to understand why the splitting of the Red Sea, which occurred a week after the Jews left Egypt, and the giving of the *Torah*, which took place forty-three days after that, are still considered part of the Exodus.) All of them appear in Psalm 114, the second of the two paragraphs comprising the first half of *Hallel*.

Therefore, before the meal, when we are engaged in *Maggid*, retelling the saga of the Exodus as it relates to our being chosen as God's nation, we only recite the first two paragraphs of *Hallel*; only they relate to the story of the Exodus.

The coming of the Messiah and the resurrection of the dead, on the other hand, are **future** events, which we speak about and pray for only after the *mitzvos* of the evening, which commemorate the Exodus, are performed. We therefore recite the second half of *Hallel* containing these beliefs, after having accomplished *Maggid* and eaten the *Matzoh* and *Marror*, as a means of separating the Exodus saga from future events.

A question remains: Isn't the evening devoted to the obligation to retell the story of our Egyptian experience? Where do the Messiah and the resurrection of the dead figure in that experience? Why bother to mention these future events at all? They seem extraneous to the Seder's agenda.

But these future glories are likewise dependent on the story of the Exodus! The Exodus event - the creation of the chosen nation Israel - set in motion the destiny of the world until the end of days. Only for the benefit of His chosen ones will God bring the Messiah and the resurrection of the dead. This explains why the second half of *Hallel* is included in the Haggadah. Although set in the future, these majestic events nevertheless emanate from the great love God proclaimed when He chose Israel at the Exodus.

With great happiness and feeling for having been chosen as the Almighty's nation through the events of the Exodus, we proudly recite the following blessing with which we conclude the Maggid portion of the Haggadah.

BLESSED ARE YOU GOD, ALMIGHTY KING OF THE UNIVERSE, WHO HAS REDEEMED US, AND REDEEMED OUR ANCESTORS FROM EGYPT, AND HAS BROUGHT US TO THIS NIGHT TO EAT MATZOH AND MARROR. SO TOO, THE ALMIGHTY, OUR GOD AND GOD OF OUR FATHERS, BRING US ALSO TO OTHER FESTIVALS AND HOLIDAYS IN PEACE; HAPPY IN THE REBUILDING OF YOUR CITY, AND HAPPY IN YOUR SERVICE. MAY WE THERE PARTAKE OF SACRIFICES AND THE PASCAL LAMB, WHOSE BLOOD WILL REACH THE WALL OF YOUR ALTAR IN ACCEPTANCE. WE WILL THANK YOU WITH A NEW SONG FOR OUR REDEMPTION AND FOR THE EMANCIPATION OF OUR SOULS. BLESSED ARE YOU GOD, WHO REDEEMED ISRAEL.

בָּרוּךְ אַתָּה יהוה, אֱלֹהֵינוּ מֶלֶךְ הָעוֹלָם, אֲשֶׁר גְּאָלָנוּ וְגָאַל אֶת אֲבוֹתֵינוּ מִמִּצְרַיִם, וְהִגִּיעָנוּ הַלַּיְלָה הַזֶּה לֶאֱכָל בּוֹ מַצָּה וּמָרוֹר. כֵּן יהוה אֱלֹהֵינוּ וֵאלֹהֵי אֲבוֹתֵינוּ יַגִּיעֵנוּ לְמוֹעֲדִים וְלִרְגָלִים אֲחֵרִים הַבָּאִים לִקְרָאתֵנוּ לְשָׁלוֹם. שְׂמֵחִים בְּבִנְיַן עִירֶךְ וְשָׂשִׂים בַּעֲבוֹדָתֶךָ. וְנֹאכַל שָׁם מִן הַזְּבָחִים וּמִן הַפְּסָחִים (במוצ״ש אומרים: מִן הַפְּסָחִים וּמִן הַזְּבָחִים) אֲשֶׁר יַגִּיעַ דָּמָם עַל קִיר מִזְבַּחֲךָ לְרָצוֹן. וְנוֹדֶה לְךָ שִׁיר חָדָשׁ עַל גְּאֻלָּתֵנוּ וְעַל פְּדוּת נַפְשֵׁנוּ: בָּרוּךְ אַתָּה יהוה, גָּאַל יִשְׂרָאֵל:

We now recite the blessing over the second cup of wine. *(Ramah, O. C. 474:1)*

BLESSED ARE YOU ALMIGHTY, OUR GOD, KING OF THE UNIVERSE, WHO CREATES THE FRUIT OF THE VINE.

בָּרוּךְ אַתָּה יהוה, אֱלֹהֵינוּ מֶלֶךְ הָעוֹלָם, בּוֹרֵא פְּרִי הַגָּפֶן.

One must drink the wine while leaning to the left. *(O.C. 473:2)* *The minimum halachic requirement is to drink a majority of the cup; it is preferable to drink the entire cup.* *(O.C. 472:9 with the gloss of Mishnah Berurah)*

— COMMENTARY —

It is a well-known *Talmudic* formula that, prior to performing a *mitzvah*, a blessing must be recited. Why then, don't we recite a blessing before beginning *Maggid*? If "*Asher G'alanu*" is to be understood as the blessing over *Maggid*, should it not precede it?

Following our thematic of "chosenness", one may answer that in fact, we recite not only one but two blessings for *Maggid*.

"*Kiddush*", the sanctification over wine that initiates Seder night, serves as the blessing prior to the *mitzvah* of *Maggid*. A review of its text makes it clear that *Kiddush* acts not only to sanctify the holiday but as the "*Birchas Ha'mitzvah*" (blessing over a *mitzvah*) of *Maggid* as well:

> "Blessed are You God, Almighty King of the universe, Who has **chosen us from all nations,** and raised us above all tongues and has made us holy by His commandments... A holy convocation **in memory of the Exodus from Egypt. For You have chosen us, and sanctified us above all nations...**"

"*Asher G'alanu*" serves as a second blessing at the conclusion of *Maggid*. It is a blessing of thanks, appropriately following a narration of God's choice and redemption of Israel through great miracles.

One may wonder why **two** blessings are necessary. The answer is: The first blessing (*Kiddush*) is a "*Birchas Hamitzvah*" (blessing over a *mitzvah*), while the second blessing (*Asher G'alanu*) is a *"Birchas Ho'daah"* (blessing of thanks). Whereas other *mitzvos* don't require the giving of thanks after their performance, *Maggid* certainly does. We have just retold the entire story of our being chosen as God's people and stated that, "a Jew is obligated to view himself as having gone out of Egypt". If one has just been miraculously redeemed from slavery, a giving of thanks is in order.

A major question that still remains regards the text of the *"Asher G'alanu"* blessing. If our theme of "chosenness" is correct, then, one would certainly expect to thank God **for choosing us**, not merely our physical redemption. Perusing the text of *"Asher G'alanu"* we find no mention of our being chosen; instead, the blessing focuses on our physical redemption. For our commentary's unifying premise, this poses a major question indeed.

The answer to follow provides us with a profound lesson in Jewish ethics and can be illustrated by the following story.

A king wished to reward a servant who had distinguished himself through his matchless loyalty to the crown. As a means of affirming his esteem, the king pledged to bestow his largesse upon the servant and his descendants, guaranteeing their support even after the servant's death.

The king was true to his word. When the servant died, his children, who had in the interim fallen upon desperate times, having been victimized by the local authorities, were placed under royal guardianship. The king housed, clothed, and fed them in a style befitting his own family. In addition, the king beheaded their tormentors, a just retribution, to which the children bore witness. The king saw to their education personally, making sure they acquired both nobility of character and outstanding erudition. When they became of age, the king brought them into his castle, and appointed them ministers to the court.

When the royal ceremony was held to invest them with their ministerial status, the loyal servant's children knelt before the king and said, "We, the children of our dear father, would like to thank the king, not only for this great honor, but for every single act of kindness your Majesty has continually bestowed upon us. We can never forget the countless benefactions the king has showered upon us all these years."

The king smiled pridefully and said, "I have chosen wisely. Truly you are fit for the office to which I have named all of you. By your sensitivity to **all** that others have done for you, you have demonstrated your worthiness for the task for which I have chosen you."

And so it is with us on Seder night. It is not enough for us to thank the Almighty for the new, profoundly distinctive status of "chosenness" with which He graced us in Egypt. We must thank Him for all the good He did: for saving us from our physical oppression, exacting retribution from our tormentors, and bringing us to freedom. To be truly sensitive to the Almighty's ceaseless benevolence, we must open our mouths to thank Him for the mundane and as well as the sublime, the daily miracles of subsistence paired with the spiritual glories.

The blessing of "*Asher G'alanu*" is such a thanks, a remembrance of those kindnesses we are likely to take for granted after having experienced the overwhelming exaltation of "chosenness".

Till now, everything we have said is "*p'shat*", the simple understanding of the text. I would like to end our commentary with a homiletical interpretation.

Why is this night alone referred to as "Seder" night? After all, many elements of Jewish service are done in a prescribed order, and yet we do not entitle them "**Seder**".

We know we were chosen by God to be His nation. We know He gave us the holy *Torah* and its wonderful *mitzvos*. We should also know that "the how" of transmitting our "chosenness" and the holy *Torah* that accompanies that elevated status to the next generation - our children - is also taught to us by the *Torah*. To follow any other format or procedure then that outlined by the *Torah* will not be effective.

This is why we refer to Passover eve as "Seder" night. To achieve a transmission of Judaism to the next generation we must follow the *Torah's* procedure as outlined and detailed by our sages.

In Conclusion

Ultimately every thinking person searches for meaning in life, something that will give value to existence. We Jews are indeed fortunate. Through living the holy directives of the *Torah*, which has been transmitted to us generation after generation from Moses, who himself received it from God on Mount Sinai, every nuance of both our physical and mental endeavors has cosmic import.

God demands of us, His chosen nation, to do His will by performing the *Torah's* commandments. Every aspect of our lives relates to some commandment and we are therefore constantly serving the Creator Himself. Can life have any greater meaning? Certainly not!

It was on Passover night 3,300 years ago that God chose us - the Jewish people - to be His for all eternity. It is this election which we celebrate tonight. But its celebration requires much of us, not just on Seder night but for our entire lives. Honesty dictates that we follow through on the Divine status to which we were elevated. We are ministers to the King of Kings and must serve Him with our very lives.

From the Seder we should go forth, with our resolve strengthened to perfect our ministerial duties to God by undertaking the meticulous observance of every one of the *Torah's* laws. Indeed, it was for this that we were chosen.

We know the goal of the Haggadah, and we know how to achieve it. Let us pray that we merit its accomplishment.

May we merit to be next year in Jerusalem, a chosen nation reunited with God in His chosen land.

 רחצה

RACHTZA

Washing of the Hands Before Eating the Matzohs

Why do we wash our hands?

We wash before eating *Matzoh* as we do before eating any bread throughout the year.

Although the halachic foundations of the ritual washing of the hands are quite complicated, involving a knowledge of "*Tumah* and *Tahara*" (ritual purity) with its myriad intricacies, some general comments are in order. *Terumah*, the tithe given the *Kohanim* (priests) from produce harvested in Israel, must not become ritually defiled. The Rabbis of the oral tradition worried that the *Kohanim* might inadvertently defile the *Terumah*. They therefore established restrictions to guard against this possibility. First, they decreed that all hands must be washed and ritually purified before being allowed to touch *Terumah*. Second, so that the *Kohanim* should remember to wash their hands for *Terumah*, the Rabbis demanded that **any** Jew who eats bread - even non-*Terumah* - must wash his hands before eating (see *Mishnah Zavim*, 5:12 and *Mishnah Chagiga*, 2:5).

With this background in place, we must now confront a simple but important question: why is *Rachtza* - washing the hands preparatory to eating the *Matzohs* - included in the Passover "*Seder*" listing? Don't we wash before eating any bread year-round? Why include in our list of Seder obligations an act which is, after all, incumbent upon us daily?

If one wants to propose a simple reply - namely, that the mnemonic (*Kadesh*, *U'rechatz*, *Karpas*, etc...) merely supplies an all-inclusive Passover checklist identifying **every** Seder element, whether or not it also appears throughout the year - we must counter: It was *Rashi*, the greatest *Torah* commentator, who authored the listing of Seder elements (See page 31). Any *Talmudist* knows that *Rashi's* authorship implies a precise halachic intent, not merely a simple mnemonic. So what indeed did *Rashi* have in mind by his inclusion of *Rachtza* in the "Seder"?

רחצה

The answer we are about to set forth at once lays our question to rest and inspires us with awe at the precision of *halacha* and the greatness of its masters.

There is a long-standing dispute among the authorities whether the kind of *Matzohs* we eat - thin, dry and crisp - are considered "bread" in the halachic sense. One view maintains that *Matzohs* are simply thin breads, necessitating all the rituals halachically applicable to bread (washing, "*Hamotzi*" and Grace After Meals). A second view holds that our *Matzohs* do not qualify as bread, but are rather considered a cracker. Those so maintaining do not wash their hands before eating *Matzohs*, nor do they make "*Hamotzi*" or say Grace After Meals (substituting instead the "*Al HaMichya*" blessing). *Ashkenazim*, on the whole, conform to the first opinion, while *Sephardim* subscribe to the latter (see responsa *Yechaveh Daas*, Vol. 3:12).

What is the great *Rashi's* opinion?

If we turn to Tractate *Berachos* 42a we see clearly that *Rashi*, though *Ashkenaz* by geography, sides here with *Sephardic* tradition. His opinion is that *Matzoh* falls within the class of foods called "*Pas Habo'ah b'Kissnin*" - pastries or crackers not considered bread. (See the *MeTargeim* on "*Lachmonious*"). *Tosafos*, however, strongly disputes *Rashi's* view, maintaining that *Matzoh* is indeed bread.

According to *Rashi*, *Matzoh* year-round is not bread, and accordingly does not require ritual washing. Only for Passover does *Rashi* demand that we wash for *Matzoh*, since the *Torah* refers to it as "bread of affliction" and commands its consumption, thus elevating it to the status of bread.

It is for **this** reason that *Rashi* includes *Rachtza* in his list of Seder-inspired obligations.

רחצה

All present ritually wash their hands and then make the following blessing.
(O.C. 475:1)

בָּרוּךְ אַתָּה יהוה אֱלֹהֵינוּ מֶלֶךְ הָעוֹלָם, אֲשֶׁר קִדְּשָׁנוּ בְּמִצְוֹתָיו, וְצִוָּנוּ עַל נְטִילַת יָדָיִם.

BLESSED ARE YOU ALMIGHTY, OUR GOD, KING OF THE UNIVERSE, WHO HAS SANCTIFIED US WITH HIS COMMANDMENTS, AND HAS COMMANDED US CONCERN-ING THE WASHING OF THE HANDS.

מוֹצִיא מַצָה

MOTZI MATZOH

Fulfilling the Biblical Obligation to Eat Matzoh

Our Biblical obligation

The *Torah* says "In the first [month] on the fourteenth day of the month at night you should eat *Matzohs...*" (*Exodus* XII:18). This verse obligates us to partake of *Matzoh* Seder night.

There is another verse, "And you shall eat the meat [of the Pascal lamb] roasted on this night, with *Matzohs* and *Marror* shall you eat it" (*Exodus* XII:8). This verse seems to imply that *Matzoh* is obligatory when we have the Pascal lamb, a sacrifice brought only when the Temple is standing. The *Talmud*, however, infers from the first verse (XII:18) that *Matzoh* must be eaten even in the absence of the Pascal lamb, as *Matzoh* alone is stipulated there. We will discuss the meaning of the second verse (XII:8) in the introduction to the sections *Marror* and *Koreich*.

Why does this section have two names?

On Seder night we must fulfill two obligations with *Matzoh*: (1) the required eating of bread common to every Sabbath and *Yom Tov* meal and (2) the specific *Matzoh* obligation unique to Passover night.

We thus entitle this section with the double name *"Motzi Matzoh"*, respectively noting both obligations about to be fulfilled.

Who is obligated in *Matzoh*?

Both men and women are equally obligated to eat *Matzoh*. Again, the question of time-bound *mitzvos* must be asked, since the requirement to eat *Matzoh* of course falls only on Passover, so why indeed is a woman obligated?

The *Talmud* in Tractate *Pesachim* (43b) cites an oral tradition

מוֹצִיא מַצָה

which teaches "Anyone who is included in the prohibition to eat leavened bread is admonished to eat *Matzoh*. 'Said Rabbi Elazar, therefore, women are Biblically obligated to eat *matzoh*.'"

Do we recline when we eat *Matzoh*?

The *Talmud* in Tractate *Pesachim* (108a) rules "one is required to recline when eating *Matzoh*", and so it is recorded in the *Shulchan Aruch* (O.C. 475:1).

 מוֹצִיא מַצָּה 

The leader takes all three Matzohs (the two whole and the broken half) with the broken Matzoh between the two whole and makes the following blessing. (O.C. 475:1) While reciting the "ha'motzi lechem" and the "achilas Matzoh" blessing have in mind the Koreich sandwich, which follows - because of this, one should not speak until the Koreich sandwich has been eaten. (O.C. 475:1)

BLESSED ARE YOU ALMIGHTY, OUR GOD, KING OF THE UNIVERSE, WHO BRINGS FORTH BREAD FROM THE EARTH.

בָּרוּךְ אַתָּה יהוה, אֱלֹהֵינוּ מֶלֶךְ הָעוֹלָם, הַמּוֹצִיא לֶחֶם מִן הָאָרֶץ.

The leader lets go of the bottom whole Matzoh, remaining with the top whole and middle broken Matzoh in his hands. He then makes the following blessing. (Mishnah Berurah 475:2).

BLESSED ARE YOU ALMIGHTY, OUR GOD, KING OF THE UNIVERSE, WHO SANCTIFIED US WITH HIS COMMANDMENTS AND COMMANDED US CONCERNING EATING MATZOH.

בָּרוּךְ אַתָּה יהוה, אֱלֹהֵינוּ מֶלֶךְ הָעוֹלָם, אֲשֶׁר קִדְּשָׁנוּ בְּמִצְוֹתָיו, וְצִוָּנוּ עַל אֲכִילַת מַצָּה.

All present at the seder should eat an olive-sized portion from each of the two Matzohs (the top and middle Matzoh). Since it is impossible for a single Matzoh to have enough "olived-sized" portions for everyone, other Matzos (besides the original three) should be used in addition. The leader should distribute at least a small piece from the top and middle Matzoh to everyone present. One should recline while eating the prescribed amount of Matzoh. (Mishnah Berurah 475:8-9)

מרור

MARROR

Fulfilling the obligation to eat bitter herbs

Is our obligation Biblical or Rabbinic?

The *Torah* says, "And you shall eat the meat [of the Pascal lamb] roasted on this night, with *Matzohs* and *Marror* shall you eat it" (*Exodus XII:8;* see also *Numbers IX:11*). The sage *Rava* deduces from the above verse (Tractate *Pesachim*, 120a): "[our present-day obligation to eat] *Marror* is only Rabbinic, because it says, '[one should eat the Pascal lamb] with *Matzoh* and *Marror.*' When there is a Pascal lamb, there is [an obligation to eat] *Marror*, but when there is no Pascal lamb, there is no [obligation to eat] *Marror.*"

From the above it is clear that our contemporary obligation to eat *Marror* is only Rabbinic.

What is *Marror*?

The *Mishnah* in Tractate *Pesachim* (2:6; also see 39a) says, "And these are the herbs with which one fulfills his obligation on *Pesach*, with lettuce, endives, horseradish, or charchavinah, and *Marror*. One fulfills his obligation with them whether moist or dry, but not preserved, nor stewed, nor boiled. [All of the above varieties may be combined] to aggregate to the size of an olive. The obligation may be fulfilled with their stalk..."

In the opinion of *Rashi* (*Exodus XII:8*), *Sefer HaChinuch* (*Mitzvah* 381) and others (*Rabbeinu David, Ritva,* and *Meiri* in *Pesachim* 39a), the *Mishnah's* listing is only a recommendation but not exhaustive. According to these authorities, any vegetation which is bitter constitutes *Marror*.

The *Magen Avraham*, however (O.C. 473:15) rules decisively that the *Mishnah's* list **is** exhaustive, and one should therefore fulfill his obligation by eating from among the above varieties only.

"Lettuce", the first of the five cited varieties, is commonly taken to mean romaine lettuce.

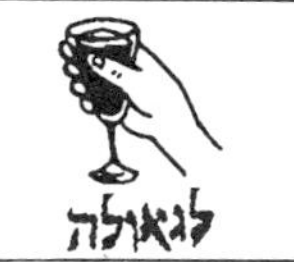

לגאולה

מרור

משעבוד

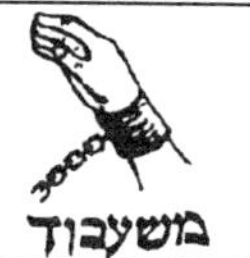

All present take an olived-sized portion of Marror dipping it in the charoses (being careful not to put on so much charoses that the taste of the bitter Marror is masked). The following blessing is recited. (O.C. 475:1)

BLESSED ARE YOU ALMIGHTY, OUR GOD, KING OF THE UNIVERSE, WHO SANCTIFIED US WITH HIS COMMANDMENTS AND COMMANDED US CONCERNING EATING MARROR.

בָּרוּךְ אַתָּה יהוה, אֱלֹהֵינוּ מֶלֶךְ הָעוֹלָם, אֲשֶׁר קִדְּשָׁנוּ בְּמִצְוֹתָיו, וְצִוָּנוּ עַל אֲכִילַת מָרוֹר.

One should eat the Marror without reclining. (O.C. 475:1)

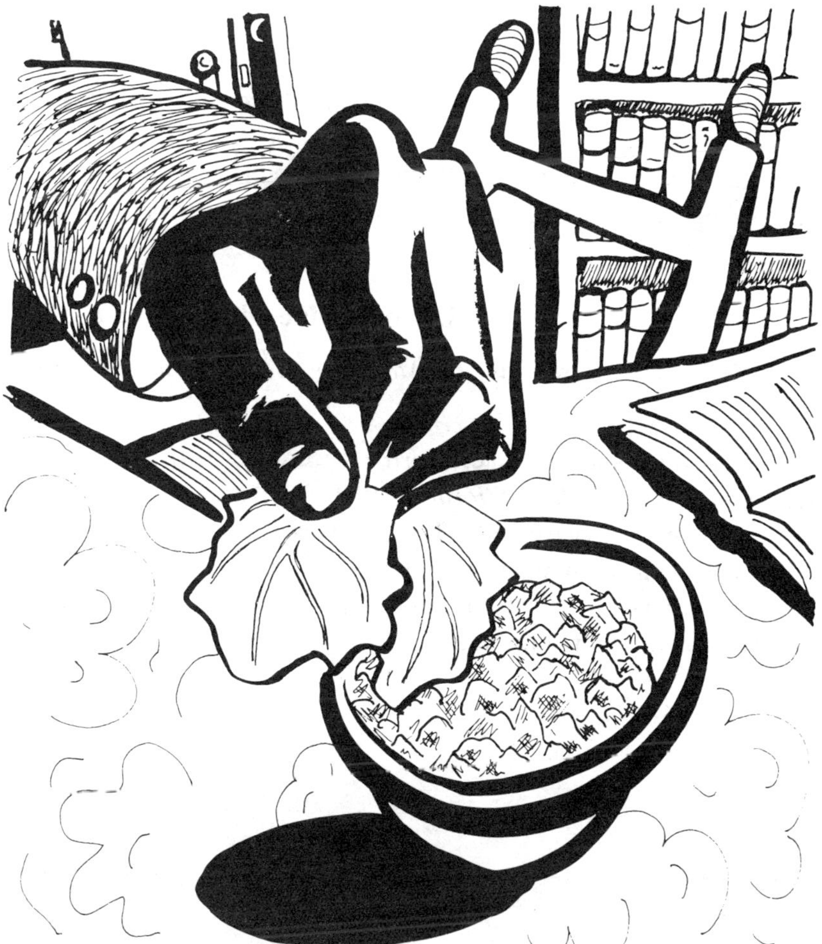

KOREICH

Eating Matzoh and Marror together as a sandwich

What is the source for *Koreich*?

The Bible says: "And you shall eat the meat [of the Pascal lamb] roasted on this night, with *Matzohs* and *Marror* shall you eat it" (*Exodus XII:8*). And again: "... and [you] shall eat it with *Matzohs* and *Marror*" (*Numbers IX:11*).

The *Talmud* in *Pesachim* 115a tells us of a dispute between *Hillel* and the Rabbis whether "with *Matzohs* and bitter herbs" denotes a Biblical **commandment** to eat the Pascal lamb, *Matzoh* and *Marror* together as a sandwich, or suggests only a Biblical **option**.

Since the dispute between *Hillel* and the Rabbis remains unresolved, the *Talmud* teaches us how to practically conduct ourselves at the Seder. First, we eat *Matzoh* and *Marror* each by itself in accordance with the majority opinion (the Rabbis). Thereafter we eat *Matzoh* and *Marror* together as a sandwich in accordance with *Hillel's* prescription.

Do we recline while eating *Koreich*?

Yes! Since we are eating the *Marror* with *Matzoh*, not by itself, we recline.

It is interesting to note: *Marror,* according to *Hillel,* should be tempered with *Matzoh;* the *Torah* doesn't want us to relive the unmitigated pain of the enslavement. This is precisely the reason why we use *Hillel's* opinion to commemorate the Holy Temple; albeit in exile and devoid of God's sanctuary, our pain is mitigated because the Almighty envelops us, lessening our bitter suffering.

The bottom Matzoh is now taken. From it, with the addition of other Matzohs if needed, each participant receives an olive-sized portion together with an olive-sized portion of Marror, (the Marror is dipped into charoses), making a sandwich of the Matzoh and Marror. The following paragraph is recited and the "sandwich" is eaten while reclining. (O.C. 475:1)

זֵכֶר לְמִקְדָּשׁ כְּהִלֵּל. כֵּן עָשָׂה הִלֵּל בִּזְמַן שֶׁבֵּית הַמִּקְדָּשׁ הָיָה קַיָּם. הָיָה כּוֹרֵךְ (פֶּסַח) מַצָּה וּמָרוֹר וְאוֹכֵל בְּיַחַד. לְקַיֵּם מַה שֶׁנֶּאֱמַר עַל מַצוֹת וּמְרֹרִים יֹאכְלֻהוּ:

IN COMMEMORATION OF THE BEIS HAMIKDASH ACCORDING TO HILLEL: THIS IS WHAT HILLEL WOULD DO WHEN THE BEIS HAMIKDASH WAS IN EXISTENCE - HE WOULD JOIN [THE MEAT OF THE] PASCAL LAMB, MATZOH, AND MARROR, AND EAT THEM TOGETHER TO FULFILL THE VERSE: "AND [YOU] SHALL EAT IT [THE PASCAL LAMB] WITH MATZOHS AND MARROR."

(Numbers IX:11)

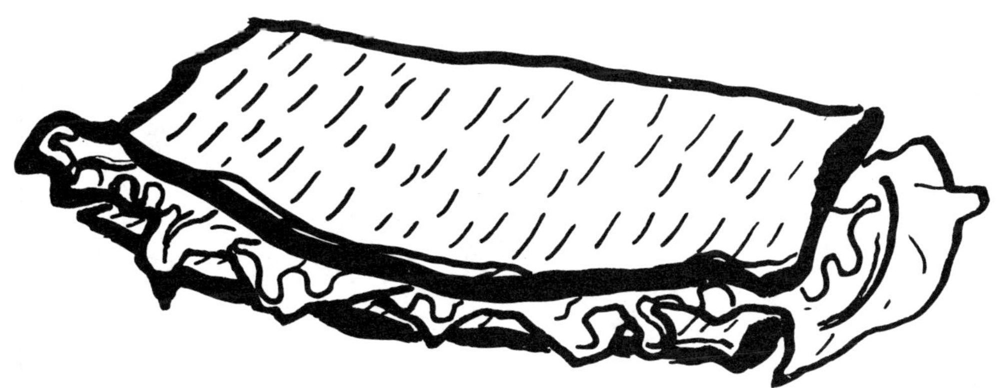

שֻׁלְחָן עוֹרֵךְ

SHULCHAN OREICH

Shulchan Oreich: The Prepared Evening Meal

This element of the Seder confronts us with an obvious question: What is uniquely "*Pesachdik*" about a dinner? After all, we eat an evening meal **every** night; why should a recurring element of our daily routine suddenly acquire a special ritual character?

The answer follows from an understanding of the novel context into which the Seder laws place the meal. Tonight, the *Shulchan Oreich* acts as a **preparation** for the eating of the Pascal lamb.

We are commanded by the *Torah* to eat the Pascal lamb only after we are sated; it is the *Shulchan Oreich* - the meal we are about to eat - that serves to sate us.

So understood, this evening's meal is indeed uniquely linked to Seder night.

By custom, dating back to Talmudic times, we do not eat meat or fowl roasted on a spit or in an oven, seder night. This custom came about to avoid even the appearance that we are eating the Pascal lamb (which is prohibited since we do not have the Temple in our day). (O.C. 476:1)

One should not overeat to the point of being gorged, thereby not being able to eat the Afikomen. (O.C. 476:1)

It is customary to eat hard boiled eggs (prior to the festive meal), symbolically mourning the destruction of the Temple and our inability to sacrifice the Pascal lamb. (Ramah 476:2)

צפון

TZAFON

The Eating of the Afikomen

To what does the word *Tzafon* refer?

It literally means "hidden," and alludes to the tradition of hiding the *Matzoh*, which the children try to find and (by custom) only return in exchange for a gift.

According to one view, the *Afikomen* symbolizes the Pascal lamb. Others, however, (*Rashi* and *Rashbam*, Tractate *Pesachim* 119b) say the *Afikomen* is not a remembrance of the Pascal lamb, but rather the medium through which we carry out our Biblical obligation to eat *Matzoh*. These medieval commentators here invoke the Biblical verse, "And [you] shall eat it [the Pascal lamb] with *Matzohs* and *Marror*" (*Numbers IX:11*). Thus, they maintain, when we reach the point in the Seder at which we eat the Pascal lamb, we must accompany the eating with *Matzoh* and *Marror*. The *Afikomen*, according to this opinion, serves as that *Matzoh*.

Do we recline when we eat the *Afikomen*?

We certainly do, irrespective of which opinion we endorse. Whether we designate the *Afikomen* as a proxy for the Pascal lamb, or as the instrument of the *mitzvah* to eat *Matzoh*, we recline, because in either case our leaning attests to our freedom from slavery.

After the meal, the afikomen is distributed to all (with the addition of other Matzohs if needed). Each participant must eat an olive-sized portion of the afikomen before midnight. Preferably, two olive-sized portions should be eaten: in memory of the Pascal lamb and the Matzoh that was eaten with it.
(O.C. 477:1 with gloss of Mishnah Berurah)

After the afikomen, one should not eat or drink (except for the two wine cups that are part of the Seder ritual), so its taste should remain on the palate.
(O.C. 478:1 with gloss of Mishnah Berurah)

בריך

BAREICH

Grace After Meals

A companion question to the one we asked in the introduction to *Shulchan Oreich* suggests itself here. The Biblical commandment to thank God at the completion of a meal, when it includes bread, is year round. Why then, does this daily *mitzvah* find a place in the enumeration of specific Seder obligations?

Again, as with *Shulchan Oreich*, we find that the Seder casts this daily commandment into a new role, one that requires the following brief preface.

The Seder is divided into two parts:

1) **An autobiographical recounting** of the Exodus, ("In each generation a Jew is obligated to view himself as having gone out of Egypt...").

2) **A retrospective view** of the Exodus, placing it in an historical perspective. This retrospective view has great ramifications for us today because what God did in Egypt 3300 years ago ensures our eternal chosenness. It is in Grace After Meals that we turn to and initiate this historical perspective, as we will now explain.

Grace After Meals - "*Birchas Hamazon*" - consists of four blessings. The first three are derived from the *Torah*; the fourth was composed later, after the destruction of the Second Temple. The first blessing thanks God for sustaining us by providing the world with food. The second contains an appreciation for the land of Israel and the bounty it provides. The third blessing gives thanks for Jerusalem and the Temple.

The concluding blessing is known as - "*Hatov v'Hameitiv*" - "Who is Good and Does Good". The *Talmud* (*Berachos* 48b) provides us with its historical background. Roman legions under the emperor Hadrian laid siege to the city of Betar in the land of Israel (its exact location is uncertain), in the course of a Jewish revolt there in the year 132 C.E. For three-and-a-half years Hadrian and his formidable army sustained its offensive, at last vanquishing the Jewish resistance and slaying its leader, the great *Bar-Kochba*. Although the exact number of Jews

בָּרֵךְ

who died is unknown, it is clear from the *Talmud* and *Midrash* that many thousands of corpses lay unburied for a long time (there is a tradition that it was seven years), as the Romans did not immediately authorize their interment. A miracle took place, and the unattended corpses did not rot. Only after Hadrian's death and his succession by Antoninus Pius did *Rabban Gamliel*, the head of the Great Academy in Yavne, secure permission to bury Betar's dead.

The Rabbis of that day instituted the blessing "Who is Good" to give thanks for the remains that didn't decompose, and "Who Does Good" because approval for their burial was finally granted. But why did the Rabbis incorporate this blessing into Grace After Meals? What possible relationship is there between the first three blessings and this fourth and last one?

The answer can best be introduced by asking yet another question. How can we continue to thank God for the land of Israel in Grace After Meals after having been exiled from it for almost 2000 years? The answer is: the miracle of Betar!

The very destruction of Betar contains a majestic augury for the Jewish nation in its exile. After the Second Temple's destruction (70 C.E.) the Jews continued to live in the Land; but with Bar-Kochba's defeat the exile was sealed. The miracle of the corpses conveyed a Heavenly sign: Yes, God said to us; you have sinned and I have punished, but be certain that I will never leave you, My chosen nation. I am with you, even in Exile, and will surely bring you back to the land of Israel.

It is this interpretation that brought the Rabbis to place the blessing of "Who Is Good and Does Good" in Grace After Meals directly after the two blessings that give thanks for the land of Israel - because the miracle of Betar entitles us to continue these thanks, even today.

Grace After Meals is thus a pivotal point in the Seder, the point at which we turn from thanking God for choosing us at the Exodus (entitling us to co-residence with His Presence in the land of Israel), to thanking Him for having affirmed that choice for all eternity (ensuring us that we will again see Israel and Jerusalem rebuilt after repatriation from our miserable exile.) The positioning of Grace After Meals in the Seder sequence thus becomes clear.

בָּרֵךְ

The third of the four cups is poured, over which we recite Grace After Meals.
(O.C. 479:1)

A SONG OF ASCENTS [TO JERUSALEM] WHEN THE ALMIGHTY WILL BRING THE EXILES BACK TO ZION, WE WILL HAVE BEEN LIKE THOSE IN A DREAM. OUR MOUTHS WILL BE FILLED WITH LAUGHTER AND OUR TONGUE WITH JOYOUS SONG. THEN IT WILL BE SAID AMONG THE NATIONS: "THE ALMIGHTY HAS DONE GREAT THINGS FOR THEM." THE ALMIGHTY HAS DONE GREAT THINGS FOR US, WE WERE GLADDENED. RESTORE OUR EXILES, O ETERNAL, AS SPRINGS THAT FLOW IN THE DESERT. THEY THAT SOW IN TEARS SHALL REAP IN JOY. HE THAT GOES FORTH WEEPING, BEARING PRECIOUS SEED, SHALL RETURN REJOICING, BEARING HIS SHEAVES OF GRAIN.

(Psalm CXXVI)

שִׁיר הַמַּעֲלוֹת, בְּשׁוּב יהוה אֶת שִׁיבַת צִיּוֹן, הָיִינוּ כְּחֹלְמִים: אָז יִמָּלֵא שְׂחוֹק פִּינוּ וּלְשׁוֹנֵנוּ רִנָּה, אָז יֹאמְרוּ בַגּוֹיִם, הִגְדִּיל יהוה לַעֲשׂוֹת עִם אֵלֶּה: הִגְדִּיל יהוה לַעֲשׂוֹת עִמָּנוּ, הָיִינוּ שְׂמֵחִים: שׁוּבָה יהוה אֶת שְׁבִיתֵנוּ, כַּאֲפִיקִים בַּנֶּגֶב: הַזֹּרְעִים בְּדִמְעָה בְּרִנָּה יִקְצֹרוּ: הָלוֹךְ יֵלֵךְ וּבָכֹה נֹשֵׂא מֶשֶׁךְ הַזָּרַע, בֹּא יָבֹא בְרִנָּה, נֹשֵׂא אֲלֻמֹּתָיו:

When three or more men (ages thirteen and older) have eaten together, the following introductory phrases precede Grace After Meals. When ten or more are present, the words in the parentheses are added.

The Leader Begins:

GENTLEMEN, LET US BLESS (THE ALMIGHTY).

רַבּוֹתַי נְבָרֵךְ

The Company Responds and then the Leader:

MAY THE NAME OF THE ALMIGHTY BE BLESSED FROM NOW TO ETERNITY.

יְהִי שֵׁם יהוה מְבוֹרָךְ מֵעַתָּה וְעַד עוֹלָם.

Leader:

WITH THE CONSENT OF THE MAS-

בִּרְשׁוּת מָרָנָן וְרַבָּנָן וְרַבּוֹתַי נְבָרֵךְ

TER OF THE HOUSE AND THOSE PRESENT, LET US BLESS HIM (THE ALMIGHTY) WHOSE FOOD WE HAVE EATEN.

(אֱלֹהֵינוּ) שֶׁאָכַלְנוּ מִשֶּׁלוֹ.

Company then Leader:

BLESSED IS HE (THE ALMIGHTY) WHOSE BOUNTY WE HAVE EATEN AND THROUGH WHOSE GOODNESS WE LIVE.

בָּרוּךְ (אֱלֹהֵינוּ) שֶׁאָכַלְנוּ מִשֶּׁלוֹ וּבְטוּבוֹ חָיִינוּ.

BLESSED ARE YOU ALMIGHTY, OUR GOD, KING OF THE UNIVERSE, WHO SUSTAINS THE WHOLE WORLD WITH HIS GOODNESS, WITH GRACE, WITH KINDNESS AND MERCY. HE GIVES FOOD TO ALL CREATURES, FOR HIS KINDNESS ENDURES FOREVER. AND THROUGH HIS ABUNDANT GOODNESS, WE HAVE NEVER BEEN LACKING, NOR SHOULD FOOD FOR US EVER BE LACKING, FOREVER AND EVER, FOR THE SAKE OF HIS GREAT NAME. FOR HE IS THE ALMIGHTY WHO PROVIDES FOR ALL, AND SUSTAINS ALL AND DOES GOOD TO ALL, AND PROVIDES FOOD FOR ALL HIS CREATURES WHOM HE CREATED. BLESSED ARE YOU ALMIGHTY, WHO SUSTAINS ALL.

בָּרוּךְ אַתָּה יהוה, אֱלֹהֵינוּ מֶלֶךְ הָעוֹלָם, הַזָּן אֶת הָעוֹלָם כֻּלּוֹ, בְּטוּבוֹ בְּחֵן בְּחֶסֶד וּבְרַחֲמִים. הוּא נוֹתֵן לֶחֶם לְכָל בָּשָׂר, כִּי לְעוֹלָם חַסְדּוֹ. וּבְטוּבוֹ הַגָּדוֹל, תָּמִיד לֹא חָסַר לָנוּ, וְאַל יֶחְסַר לָנוּ מָזוֹן לְעוֹלָם וָעֶד, בַּעֲבוּר שְׁמוֹ הַגָּדוֹל, כִּי הוּא אֵל זָן וּמְפַרְנֵס לַכֹּל, וּמֵטִיב לַכֹּל, וּמֵכִין מָזוֹן לְכָל בְּרִיּוֹתָיו אֲשֶׁר בָּרָא. בָּרוּךְ אַתָּה יהוה, הַזָּן אֶת הַכֹּל.

WE THANK YOU ALMIGHTY, OUR GOD, FOR HAVING GIVEN AS A HERITAGE TO OUR FOREFATHERS A LAND WHICH IS DESIRABLE, GOODLY AND AMPLE; AND FOR REMOVING US FROM THE LAND OF EGYPT,

נוֹדֶה לְךָ יהוה אֱלֹהֵינוּ, עַל שֶׁהִנְחַלְתָּ לַאֲבוֹתֵינוּ אֶרֶץ חֶמְדָּה טוֹבָה וּרְחָבָה, וְעַל שֶׁהוֹצֵאתָנוּ יהוה אֱלֹהֵינוּ מֵאֶרֶץ מִצְרַיִם, וּפְדִיתָנוּ מִבֵּית

ALMIGHTY, OUR GOD, AND REDEEMING US FROM THE HOUSE OF SLAVERY; AND FOR YOUR COVENANT WHICH YOU HAVE SEALED IN OUR FLESH; AND FOR YOUR TORAH WHICH YOU TAUGHT US, AND FOR YOUR LAWS WHICH YOU MADE KNOWN TO US; AND FOR THE LIFE OF GRACE AND KINDNESS WHICH YOU BESTOWED ON US. AND FOR THE FOOD WE EAT WHICH NOURISHES AND SUS-TAINS US CONTINUOUSLY, DAILY, IN EVERY TIME AND IN EVERY HOUR.

FOR EVERYTHING, ALMIGHTY, OUR GOD, WE THANK YOU AND BLESS YOU. MAY YOUR NAME FOREVER BE BLESSED IN THE MOUTHS OF ALL LIVING THINGS, AS IT IS WRITTEN: (Deuteronomy VIII:10) "AND YOU SHALL EAT AND BE SATISFIED AND YOU SHALL BLESS THE ALMIGHTY, YOUR GOD, FOR THE GOOD LAND HE HAS GIVEN YOU." BLESSED ARE YOU ALMIGHTY, FOR THE LAND AND THE SUSTENANCE.

HAVE MERCY ALMIGHTY, OUR GOD, ON ISRAEL YOUR PEOPLE, ON YOUR CITY JERUSALEM AND ZION, THE DWELLING PLACE OF YOUR GLORY. AND ON THE ROYAL HOUSE OF DAVID YOUR ANOINTED AND THE GREAT AND HOLY TEMPLE

עֲבָדִים, וְעַל בְּרִיתְךָ שֶׁחָתַמְתָּ בִּבְשָׂרֵנוּ, וְעַל תּוֹרָתְךָ שֶׁלִּמַּדְתָּנוּ, וְעַל חֻקֶּיךָ שֶׁהוֹדַעְתָּנוּ, וְעַל חַיִּים חֵן וָחֶסֶד שֶׁחוֹנַנְתָּנוּ, וְעַל אֲכִילַת מָזוֹן שָׁאַתָּה זָן וּמְפַרְנֵס אוֹתָנוּ תָּמִיד, בְּכָל יוֹם וּבְכָל עֵת וּבְכָל שָׁעָה.

וְעַל הַכֹּל יהוה אֱלֹהֵינוּ, אֲנַחְנוּ מוֹדִים לָךְ, וּמְבָרְכִים אוֹתָךְ, יִתְבָּרַךְ שִׁמְךָ בְּפִי כָּל חַי תָּמִיד לְעוֹלָם וָעֶד. כַּכָּתוּב, וְאָכַלְתָּ וְשָׂבָעְתָּ, וּבֵרַכְתָּ אֶת יהוה אֱלֹהֶיךָ עַל הָאָרֶץ הַטֹּבָה אֲשֶׁר נָתַן לָךְ. בָּרוּךְ אַתָּה יהוה, עַל הָאָרֶץ וְעַל הַמָּזוֹן.

רַחֶם נָא יהוה אֱלֹהֵינוּ, עַל יִשְׂרָאֵל עַמֶּךָ, וְעַל יְרוּשָׁלַיִם עִירֶךָ, וְעַל צִיּוֹן מִשְׁכַּן כְּבוֹדֶךָ, וְעַל מַלְכוּת בֵּית דָּוִד מְשִׁיחֶךָ, וְעַל הַבַּיִת הַגָּדוֹל וְהַקָּדוֹשׁ שֶׁנִּקְרָא שִׁמְךָ עָלָיו. אֱלֹהֵינוּ,

WHICH BEARS YOUR NAME.
OUR GOD, OUR FATHER, TEND
AND SUSTAIN US, SUPPORT
AND MAINTAIN US, AND
RELIEVE US. GRANT US RELIEF
ALMIGHTY, OUR GOD, SPEEDI-
LY FROM ALL OUR TROUBLES.
ALMIGHTY, OUR GOD, MAKE US
NOT DEPENDENT ON THE GIFTS
AND LOANS OF MORTALS, LET
US DEPEND ONLY ON YOUR
AMPLE AND OPEN HAND,
WHICH IS HOLY AND GENER-
OUS, SO THAT WE MAY NEVER
BE PUT TO SHAME OR HUMILI-
ATED.

אָבִינוּ, רְעֵנוּ, זוּנֵנוּ, פַּרְנְסֵנוּ,
וְכַלְכְּלֵנוּ, וְהַרְוִיחֵנוּ, וְהַרְוַח לָנוּ
יהוה אֱלֹהֵינוּ, מְהֵרָה מִכָּל
צָרוֹתֵינוּ. וְנָא אַל תַּצְרִיכֵנוּ,
יהוה אֱלֹהֵינוּ, לֹא לִידֵי מַתְּנַת
בָּשָׂר וָדָם, וְלֹא לִידֵי הַלְוָאָתָם,
כִּי אִם לְיָדְךָ הַמְּלֵאָה,
הַפְּתוּחָה, הַקְּדוֹשָׁה, וְהָרְחָבָה,
שֶׁלֹּא נֵבוֹשׁ וְלֹא נִכָּלֵם לְעוֹלָם
וָעֶד.

On Sabbath add:

BY YOUR GRACE STRENGTHEN US,
ALMIGHTY, OUR GOD, WITH YOUR COM-
MANDMENTS AND ESPECIALLY WITH THE
COMMANDMENT CONCERNING THE SEVENTH
DAY. FOR THIS DAY IS GREAT AND HOLY
BEFORE YOU, TO ABSTAIN FROM WORK AND
REST ON IT WITH LOVE ACCORDING TO YOUR
WILL. MAY IT BE YOUR WILL ALMIGHTY,
OUR GOD, TO GRANT US SUCH REPOSE THAT
THERE BE NO DISTRESS, SORROW AND SIGH-
ING ON OUR DAY OF REST. LET US SEE
ALMIGHTY, OUR GOD, YOUR CITY ZION CON-
SOLED, AND THE REBUILDING OF JERUSALEM
YOUR HOLY CITY, FOR YOU ARE THE MASTER
OF SALVATION AND CONSOLATION.

רְצֵה וְהַחֲלִיצֵנוּ, יהוה אֱלֹהֵינוּ,
בְּמִצְוֹתֶיךָ, וּבְמִצְוַת יוֹם הַשְּׁבִיעִי
הַשַּׁבָּת הַגָּדוֹל וְהַקָּדוֹשׁ הַזֶּה. כִּי יוֹם זֶה
גָּדוֹל וְקָדוֹשׁ הוּא לְפָנֶיךָ, לִשְׁבָּת בּוֹ
וְלָנוּחַ בּוֹ בְּאַהֲבָה, כְּמִצְוַת רְצוֹנֶךָ.
וּבִרְצוֹנְךָ הָנִיחַ לָנוּ, יהוה אֱלֹהֵינוּ,
שֶׁלֹּא תְהֵא צָרָה וְיָגוֹן וַאֲנָחָה בְּיוֹם
מְנוּחָתֵנוּ. וְהַרְאֵנוּ, יהוה אֱלֹהֵינוּ,
בְּנֶחָמַת צִיּוֹן עִירֶךָ, וּבְבִנְיַן יְרוּשָׁלַיִם
עִיר קָדְשֶׁךָ, כִּי אַתָּה הוּא בַּעַל
הַיְשׁוּעוֹת וּבַעַל הַנֶּחָמוֹת.

OUR GOD AND GOD OF OUR
FATHERS, MAY THERE ASCEND,
COME AND ARRIVE, BE SEEN,
ACCEPTED, AND HEARD,
RECALLED AND RECOLLECTED
OUR REMEMBRANCE AND REC-
OLLECTION, THE REMEM-
BRANCE OF OUR FATHERS, AND
THE MESSIAH, THE SON OF

אֱלֹהֵינוּ וֵאלֹהֵי אֲבוֹתֵינוּ,
יַעֲלֶה, וְיָבֹא, וְיַגִּיעַ, וְיֵרָאֶה,
וְיֵרָצֶה, וְיִשָּׁמַע, וְיִפָּקֵד, וְיִזָּכֵר,
זִכְרוֹנֵנוּ, וּפִקְדוֹנֵנוּ, וְזִכְרוֹן
אֲבוֹתֵינוּ, וְזִכְרוֹן מָשִׁיחַ בֶּן דָּוִד
עַבְדֶּךָ, וְזִכְרוֹן יְרוּשָׁלַיִם עִיר
קָדְשֶׁךָ, וְזִכְרוֹן כָּל עַמְּךָ בֵּית

DAVID, YOUR SERVANT; THE REMEMBRANCE OF JERUSALEM YOUR HOLY CITY AND ALL YOUR PEOPLE THE HOUSE OF ISRAEL. MAY THESE COME BEFORE YOU FOR DELIVER-ANCE, WELL BEING, GRACE, KINDNESS, COMPASSION, FOR LIFE AND FOR PEACE ON THIS DAY OF THE FESTIVAL OF MAT-ZOHS. REMEMBER US ALMIGHTY, OUR GOD, ON THIS DAY FOR OUR WELL BEING, CONSIDER US FOR BLESSING; SAVE US TO LIVE. IN THE MAT-TER OF SALVATION AND COM-PASSION SPARE US AND BE GRACIOUS TO US, BE MERCIFUL AND SAVE US. FOR OUR EYES ARE CONTINUALLY TOWARDS YOU, FOR YOU ARE THE ALMIGHTY KING WHO IS GRA-CIOUS AND COMPASSIONATE.

AND REBUILD JERUSALEM THE HOLY CITY, PROMPTLY IN OUR DAYS. BLESSED ARE YOU ALMIGHTY, WHO WILL REBUILD JERUSALEM IN HIS MERCY, AMEN.

BLESSED ARE YOU ALMIGHTY, OUR GOD, KING OF THE UNI-VERSE. ALMIGHTY, YOU ARE OUR FATHER, OUR KING, OUR MIGHTY ONE, OUR CREATOR, OUR REDEEMER, OUR MAKER, AND SANCTIFIER. SANCTIFIER OF JACOB, OUR SHEPHERD AND SHEPHERD OF ISRAEL, THE

יִשְׂרָאֵל, לְפָנֶיךָ, לִפְלֵיטָה, לְטוֹבָה, לְחֵן, וּלְחֶסֶד, וּלְרַחֲמִים, לְחַיִּים וּלְשָׁלוֹם, בְּיוֹם חַג הַמַּצּוֹת הַזֶּה. זָכְרֵנוּ, יהוה אֱלֹהֵינוּ בּוֹ לְטוֹבָה, וּפָקְדֵנוּ בוֹ לִבְרָכָה, וְהוֹשִׁיעֵנוּ בוֹ לְחַיִּים טוֹבִים. וּבִדְבַר יְשׁוּעָה וְרַחֲמִים, חוּס וְחָנֵּנוּ, וְרַחֵם עָלֵינוּ וְהוֹשִׁיעֵנוּ, כִּי אֵלֶיךָ עֵינֵינוּ, כִּי אֵל מֶלֶךְ חַנּוּן וְרַחוּם אָתָּה.

וּבְנֵה יְרוּשָׁלַיִם, עִיר הַקֹּדֶשׁ, בִּמְהֵרָה בְיָמֵינוּ. בָּרוּךְ אַתָּה יהוה, בּוֹנֵה בְרַחֲמָיו יְרוּשָׁלָיִם. אָמֵן.

בָּרוּךְ אַתָּה יהוה, אֱלֹהֵינוּ מֶלֶךְ הָעוֹלָם, הָאֵל אָבִינוּ, מַלְכֵּנוּ, אַדִּירֵנוּ, בּוֹרְאֵנוּ, גּוֹאֲלֵנוּ, יוֹצְרֵנוּ, קְדוֹשֵׁנוּ קְדוֹשׁ יַעֲקֹב, רוֹעֵנוּ רוֹעֵה יִשְׂרָאֵל. הַמֶּלֶךְ הַטּוֹב וְהַמֵּטִיב לַכֹּל, שֶׁבְּכָל יוֹם וָיוֹם הוּא הֵטִיב,

BENEFICENT KING, WHO DEALS BENEFICENTLY WITH ALL. DAILY HE HAS DONE, IS DOING AND WILL DO BENEFICENTLY TO US. HE HAS BESTOWED, DOES BESTOW AND WILL FOREVER BESTOW WITH GRACE, KINDNESS AND COMPASSION, RELIEF, HELP AND SUCCESS, BLESSING, DELIVERANCE, AND CONSOLATION, SUPPORT, MAINTENANCE AND COMPASSION, LIFE, PEACE AND ALL GOODNESS. MAY YOU NEVER DEPRIVE US OF ANY GOOD.

הוּא מֵטִיב, הוּא יֵיטִיב לָנוּ. הוּא גְמָלָנוּ, הוּא גוֹמְלֵנוּ, הוּא יִגְמְלֵנוּ, לָעַד, לְחֵן וּלְחֶסֶד וּלְרַחֲמִים וּלְרֶוַח, הַצָּלָה וְהַצְלָחָה, בְּרָכָה וִישׁוּעָה, נֶחָמָה, פַּרְנָסָה וְכַלְכָּלָה, וְרַחֲמִים וְחַיִּים וְשָׁלוֹם, וְכָל טוֹב, וּמִכָּל טוּב לְעוֹלָם אַל יְחַסְּרֵנוּ.

MAY THE ALL-MERCIFUL RULE OVER US FOREVER.

הָרַחֲמָן, הוּא יִמְלוֹךְ עָלֵינוּ לְעוֹלָם וָעֶד.

MAY THE ALL-MERCIFUL BE BLESSED IN THE HEAVENS AND ON EARTH.

הָרַחֲמָן, הוּא יִתְבָּרֵךְ בַּשָּׁמַיִם וּבָאָרֶץ.

MAY THE ALL-MERCIFUL BE PRAISED FOR ALL GENERATIONS AND GLORIFIED AMONG US FOREVER AND EVER, AND HONORED THROUGH US FOR ALL ETERNITY.

הָרַחֲמָן, הוּא יִשְׁתַּבַּח לְדוֹר דּוֹרִים, וְיִתְפָּאַר בָּנוּ לָעַד וּלְנֵצַח נְצָחִים, וְיִתְהַדַּר בָּנוּ לָעַד וּלְעוֹלְמֵי עוֹלָמִים.

MAY THE ALL-MERCIFUL SUPPORT US WITH AN HONORABLE LIVELIHOOD.

הָרַחֲמָן, הוּא יְפַרְנְסֵנוּ בְּכָבוֹד.

MAY THE ALL-MERCIFUL BREAK THE OPPRESSOR'S YOKE FROM OUR NECK AND LEAD US PROUDLY TO OUR LAND.

הָרַחֲמָן, הוּא יִשְׁבּוֹר עֻלֵּנוּ מֵעַל צַוָּארֵינוּ, וְהוּא יוֹלִיכֵנוּ קוֹמְמִיּוּת לְאַרְצֵנוּ.

MAY THE ALL-MERCIFUL SEND A PLENTIFUL BLESSING ON THIS HOUSEHOLD AND UPON

הָרַחֲמָן, הוּא יִשְׁלַח לָנוּ בְּרָכָה מְרֻבָּה בַּבַּיִת הַזֶּה, וְעַל שֻׁלְחָן

THIS TABLE AT WHICH WE HAVE EATEN.

MAY THE ALL-MERCIFUL SEND US THE PROPHET ELIJAH, WHO IS REMEMBERED FOR GOOD, BEARING GOOD TIDINGS OF DELIVERANCE AND CONSOLATION.

זֶה שֶׁאָכַלְנוּ עָלָיו.

הָרַחֲמָן, הוּא יִשְׁלַח לָנוּ אֶת אֵלִיָּהוּ הַנָּבִיא זָכוּר לַטּוֹב, וִיבַשֶּׂר לָנוּ בְּשׂוֹרוֹת טוֹבוֹת יְשׁוּעוֹת וְנֶחָמוֹת.

When eating at your parents' table or another host, recite:

MAY THE ALL-MERCIFUL BLESS (MY FATHER, MY TEACHER,) THE MASTER OF THIS HOUSE, AND (MY MOTHER, MY TEACHER,) THE MISTRESS OF THIS HOUSE; THEM, THEIR HOUSEHOLD, THEIR CHILDREN AND ALL THAT IS THEIRS,

הָרַחֲמָן, הוּא יְבָרֵךְ אֶת (אָבִי מוֹרִי), בַּעַל הַבַּיִת הַזֶּה, וְאֶת (אִמִּי מוֹרָתִי), בַּעֲלַת הַבַּיִת הַזֶּה, אוֹתָם וְאֶת בֵּיתָם וְאֶת זַרְעָם, וְאֶת כָּל אֲשֶׁר לָהֶם.

When eating at your own table, recite:

MAY THE ALL-MERCIFUL BLESS ME, MY SPOUSE, MY CHILDREN AND ALL THAT IS MINE,

הָרַחֲמָן, הוּא יְבָרֵךְ אוֹתִי וְאֶת אִשְׁתִּי וְאֶת זַרְעִי, וְאֶת כָּל אֲשֶׁר לִי.

All continue here:

OURS AND ALL THAT IS OURS - JUST AS OUR ANCESTORS ABRAHAM, ISAAC AND JACOB WERE BLESSED WITH EVERY AND ALL MANNER OF BLESSING, THUS MAY HE BLESS US, ALL TOGETHER WITH A COMPLETE BLESSING AND LET US SAY, AMEN.

אוֹתָנוּ וְאֶת כָּל אֲשֶׁר לָנוּ, כְּמוֹ שֶׁנִּתְבָּרְכוּ אֲבוֹתֵינוּ אַבְרָהָם יִצְחָק וְיַעֲקֹב, בַּכֹּל מִכֹּל כֹּל, כֵּן יְבָרֵךְ אוֹתָנוּ, כֻּלָּנוּ יַחַד, בִּבְרָכָה שְׁלֵמָה, וְנֹאמַר אָמֵן.

IN THE HIGH HEAVEN, MAY THEY PLEAD FOR THEM AND FOR US THE MERIT WHICH SHALL BRING ENDURING PEACE. MAY WE RECEIVE A BLESSING FROM THE ALMIGHTY AND RIGHTEOUSNESS FROM THE GOD OF OUR SALVATION; AND MAY WE FIND GRACE AND GOOD UNDER-

במָּרוֹם יְלַמְּדוּ עֲלֵיהֶם וְעָלֵינוּ זְכוּת, שֶׁתְּהֵא לְמִשְׁמֶרֶת שָׁלוֹם, וְנִשָּׂא בְרָכָה מֵאֵת יְהוָה, וּצְדָקָה מֵאֱלֹהֵי יִשְׁעֵנוּ, וְנִמְצָא חֵן וְשֵׂכֶל טוֹב, בְּעֵינֵי אֱלֹהִים וְאָדָם.

STANDING IN THE EYES OF THE ALMIGHTY AND OF MAN.

On the Sabbath add:

MAY THE ALL-MERCIFUL CAUSE US TO INHERIT THE DAY WHICH IS WHOLLY A SABBATH AND REST IN THE LIFE EVERLASTING.

הָרַחֲמָן, הוּא יַנְחִילֵנוּ יוֹם שֶׁכֻּלוֹ שַׁבָּת וּמְנוּחָה. לְחַיֵּי הָעוֹלָמִים:

Some add the words in parentheses on the two Seder nights:

MAY THE ALL-MERCIFUL CAUSE US TO INHERIT THE DAY WHICH IS ENTIRELY GOOD (THAT EVERLASTING DAY, THE DAY WHEN THE JUST WILL SIT WITH CROWNS ON THEIR HEAD, ENJOYING THE REFLECTION OF THE ALMIGHTY'S MAJESTY AND MAY OUR PORTION BE WITH THEM!)

הָרַחֲמָן, הוּא יַנְחִילֵנוּ יוֹם שֶׁכֻּלוֹ טוֹב. (יוֹם שֶׁכֻּלוֹ אָרוּךְ יוֹם שֶׁצַּדִּיקִים יוֹשְׁבִים וְעַטְרוֹתֵיהֶם בְּרָאשֵׁיהֶם וְנֶהֱנִים מִזִּיו הַשְּׁכִינָה וִיהִי חֶלְקֵנוּ עִמָּהֶם.)

MAY THE ALL-MERCIFUL MAKE US WORTHY TO BEHOLD THE DAYS OF THE MESSIAH AND THE LIFE IN THE WORLD TO COME.

הָרַחֲמָן, הוּא יְזַכֵּנוּ לִימוֹת הַמָּשִׁיחַ וּלְחַיֵּי הָעוֹלָם הַבָּא.

HE IS A TOWER OF SALVATION TO HIS KING, AND SHOWS KINDNESS TO HIS ANOINTED, TO DAVID AND TO HIS SEED, FOR EVERMORE. *(PSALM XVIII:51)* HE WHO MAKES PEACE IN HIS CELESTIAL PLACES, MAY HE MAKE PEACE FOR US AND FOR ALL ISRAEL, LET US SAY, AMEN.

מִגְדּוֹל יְשׁוּעוֹת מַלְכּוֹ, וְעֹשֶׂה חֶסֶד לִמְשִׁיחוֹ, לְדָוִד וּלְזַרְעוֹ עַד עוֹלָם. עֹשֶׂה שָׁלוֹם בִּמְרוֹמָיו, הוּא יַעֲשֶׂה שָׁלוֹם, עָלֵינוּ וְעַל כָּל יִשְׂרָאֵל, וְאִמְרוּ אָמֵן.

FEAR THE ALMIGHTY, YOU HIS HOLY ONES, FOR THEY THAT FEAR HIM SHALL SUFFER NO LACK *(PSALM XXXIV:10)*. YOUNG LIONS MAY BE LACKING AND ENDURE HUNGER, BUT THOSE THAT SEEK THE ALMIGHTY SHALL NOT WANT ANY GOOD. *(PSALM XXXIV:11)* GIVE THANKS TO THE ALMIGHTY, FOR HE IS

יְראוּ אֶת יהוה קְדוֹשָׁיו, כִּי אֵין מַחְסוֹר לִירֵאָיו. כְּפִירִים רָשׁוּ וְרָעֵבוּ, וְדֹרְשֵׁי יהוה לֹא יַחְסְרוּ כָל טוֹב. הוֹדוּ לַיהוה כִּי טוֹב, כִּי לְעוֹלָם חַסְדּוֹ. פּוֹתֵחַ אֶת יָדֶךָ, וּמַשְׂבִּיעַ לְכָל חַי רָצוֹן. בָּרוּךְ הַגֶּבֶר אֲשֶׁר יִבְטַח בַּיהוה, וְהָיָה יהוה מִבְטַחוֹ. נַעַר הָיִיתִי גַם

GOOD, HIS MERCY ENDURES FOREVER *(PSALM CXVIII:1)* YOU OPEN YOUR HAND AND SATISFY THE DESIRE OF EVERY LIVING CREATURE *(PSALM CXLV:16).* BLESSED IS THE MAN WHO WILL TRUST IN THE ALMIGHTY, AND THE ALMIGHTY WILL BE HIS TRUST. I HAVE BEEN YOUNG AND AM NOW OLD; YET I HAVE NOT SEEN THE RIGHTEOUS FORSAKEN NOR HIS CHILDREN BEGGING FOR BREAD *(PSALM XXXVII:24)* THE ALMIGHTY WILL GIVE STRENGTH TO HIS PEOPLE; THE ALMIGHTY WILL BLESS HIS PEOPLE WITH PEACE *(PSALM XXIX:11).*

זָקַנְתִּי, וְלֹא רָאִיתִי צַדִּיק נֶעֱזָב, וְזַרְעוֹ מְבַקֶּשׁ לָחֶם. יהוה עֹז לְעַמּוֹ יִתֵּן, יהוה יְבָרֵךְ אֶת עַמּוֹ בַשָּׁלוֹם.

We recite the following blessing and drink the third cup of wine while reclining. *(O.C. 479:1)*

BLESSED ARE YOU ALMIGHTY, OUR GOD, KING OF THE UNIVERSE, WHO CREATED THE FRUIT OF THE VINE.

בָּרוּךְ אַתָּה יהוה, אֱלֹהֵינוּ מֶלֶךְ הָעוֹלָם, בּוֹרֵא פְּרִי הַגָּפֶן.

After the last cup is poured, we open the front door and recite "Pour out your wrath..."

The Bible refers to this evening as ליל שימורים - *"It was a night of watching unto the Almighty for bringing them out of the land of Egypt, this same night is a night of watching unto the Almighty for all the children of Israel throughout their generations."* *(Exodus XII:42)* *We open the front door, assured of our safety, because this is a "night of watching". In the merit of this faith, the Messiah will come and cause the Almighty to pour His wrath upon those who deny Him.* *(Ramah 480:1)*

POUR OUT YOUR WRATH UPON THE NATIONS THAT DO NOT ACKNOWLEDGE YOU, AND ON THE KINGDOMS THAT CALL NOT ON YOUR NAME. FOR THEY HAVE DEVOURED JACOB, AND LAID WASTE HIS DWELLING. *(Psalm LXXIX:6).* POUR OUT YOUR FURY UPON THEM AND LET YOUR BURNING ANGER OVERTAKE THEM *(Psalm LXIX:25).* PURSUE THEM WITH ANGER AND ANNIHILATE THEM FROM UNDER THE HEAVENS OF THE LORD.

(Lamentations III:66).

שְׁפֹךְ חֲמָתְךָ אֶל הַגּוֹיִם אֲשֶׁר לֹא יְדָעוּךָ, וְעַל מַמְלָכוֹת אֲשֶׁר בְּשִׁמְךָ לֹא קָרָאוּ: כִּי אָכַל אֶת יַעֲקֹב, וְאֶת נָוֵהוּ הֵשַׁמּוּ: שְׁפָךְ עֲלֵיהֶם זַעֲמֶךָ, וַחֲרוֹן אַפְּךָ יַשִּׂיגֵם: תִּרְדֹּף בְּאַף וְתַשְׁמִידֵם, מִתַּחַת שְׁמֵי יהוה:

HALLEL

Recitation of Praise to the Almighty

Hallel's place in the Seder is evident: We were miraculously redeemed and must give praise.

Unlike other occasions on which we say *Hallel* (on all festivals), its recitation is split on Seder night: we say half of it before the meal, and the other half following it. Why?

The answer follows directly from our introduction to the Grace After Meals section. As with Grace After Meals, the dividing of *Hallel* bespeaks the two kinds of praise we are bidden to pronounce:

The first, for our personally experiencing the salvation of the Exodus ("In each generation a Jew is obligated to view himself as having gone out of Egypt...").

The second, for the bequeathment of eternal chosenness set in motion by the historic events of our Egyptian redemption.

Before the meal, while still engaged in *Maggid*, we say *Hallel* as newly freed slaves. After the meal, living in the contemporary present, we recite the second half of *Hallel* praising the Almighty for our permanent historic election as His chosen nation - sure to be redeemed from our miserable exile.

הלל

NOT FOR OUR SAKE, ALMIGHTY, NOT FOR OUR SAKE, BUT FOR YOUR NAME'S SAKE GIVE GLORY, FOR YOUR KINDNESS AND YOUR TRUTH. WHY SHOULD THE NATIONS SAY, WHERE THEN IS THEIR GOD? BUT OUR GOD IS IN THE HEAVENS, HE DOES WHATSOEVER HE DESIRES. THEIR IDOLS ARE SILVER AND GOLD, THE HANDIWORK OF HUMAN HANDS. THEY HAVE MOUTHS, BUT SPEAK NOT; THEY HAVE EYES, BUT THEY SEE NOT, THEY HAVE EARS, BUT HEAR NOT; THEY HAVE A NOSE BUT SMELL NOT. THEY HAVE HANDS, BUT THEY FEEL NOT, THEY HAVE FEET BUT THEY WALK NOT, THEY GIVE FORTH NO SOUND FROM THEIR THROAT. LIKE THEM SHALL BE THEIR MAKERS - EVERYONE THAT TRUSTS IN THEM. ISRAEL, TRUST IN THE ALMIGHTY, HE IS THEIR HELP AND THEIR SHIELD. HOUSE OF AARON, TRUST IN THE ALMIGHTY, HE IS THEIR HELP AND THEIR SHIELD. THEY THAT FEAR THE ALMIGHTY, TRUST IN THE ALMIGHTY; HE IS THEIR HELP AND THEIR SHIELD.

(Psalm CXV: 1-11)

לֹא לָנוּ, יהוה, לֹא לָנוּ, כִּי לְשִׁמְךָ תֵּן כָּבוֹד, עַל חַסְדְּךָ עַל אֲמִתֶּךָ: לָמָּה יֹאמְרוּ הַגּוֹיִם, אַיֵּה נָא אֱלֹהֵיהֶם: וֵאלֹהֵינוּ בַשָּׁמַיִם, כֹּל אֲשֶׁר חָפֵץ עָשָׂה: עֲצַבֵּיהֶם כֶּסֶף וְזָהָב, מַעֲשֵׂה יְדֵי אָדָם: פֶּה לָהֶם וְלֹא יְדַבֵּרוּ, עֵינַיִם לָהֶם וְלֹא יִרְאוּ: אָזְנַיִם לָהֶם וְלֹא יִשְׁמָעוּ, אַף לָהֶם וְלֹא יְרִיחוּן: יְדֵיהֶם וְלֹא יְמִישׁוּן, רַגְלֵיהֶם וְלֹא יְהַלֵּכוּ, לֹא יֶהְגּוּ בִּגְרוֹנָם: כְּמוֹהֶם יִהְיוּ עֹשֵׂיהֶם, כֹּל אֲשֶׁר בֹּטֵחַ בָּהֶם: יִשְׂרָאֵל בְּטַח בַּיהוה, עֶזְרָם וּמָגִנָּם הוּא: בֵּית אַהֲרֹן בִּטְחוּ בַיהוה, עֶזְרָם וּמָגִנָּם הוּא: יִרְאֵי יהוה בִּטְחוּ בַיהוה, עֶזְרָם וּמָגִנָּם הוּא:

THE ALMIGHTY HAS BEEN MINDFUL OF US. HE WILL BLESS, HE WILL BLESS THE HOUSE OF ISRAEL; HE WILL BLESS THE HOUSE OF AARON. HE WILL BLESS THOSE THAT FEAR THE ALMIGHTY, SMALL AND GREAT ALIKE. MAY THE ALMIGHTY INCREASE YOU, BOTH YOU AND YOUR CHILDREN. BLESSED ARE YOU OF THE ALMIGHTY, CREATOR OF HEAVEN AND EARTH. THE HEAVENS, ARE THE HEAVENS OF THE ALMIGHTY. BUT THE EARTH HE HAS GIVEN TO MANKIND. THE DEAD PRAISE NOT THE ALMIGHTY, NOR THOSE WHO DESCEND INTO SILENCE. BUT WE WILL BLESS THE ALMIGHTY FROM THIS TIME FORTH UNTIL EVERMORE. HALLELUYAH!

(Psalm CXV: 12-18)

יְהוה זְכָרָנוּ יְבָרֵךְ, יְבָרֵךְ אֶת בֵּית יִשְׂרָאֵל, יְבָרֵךְ אֶת בֵּית אַהֲרֹן: יְבָרֵךְ יִרְאֵי יהוה, הַקְּטַנִּים עִם הַגְּדֹלִים: יֹסֵף יהוה עֲלֵיכֶם, עֲלֵיכֶם וְעַל בְּנֵיכֶם: בְּרוּכִים אַתֶּם לַיהוה, עֹשֵׂה שָׁמַיִם וָאָרֶץ: הַשָּׁמַיִם שָׁמַיִם לַיהוה, וְהָאָרֶץ נָתַן לִבְנֵי אָדָם: לֹא הַמֵּתִים יְהַלְלוּ יָהּ, וְלֹא כָּל יֹרְדֵי דוּמָה: וַאֲנַחְנוּ נְבָרֵךְ יָהּ, מֵעַתָּה וְעַד עוֹלָם, הַלְלוּיָהּ:

I LOVE THE ALMIGHTY FOR HE HEARS MY VOICE AND MY SUPPLICATION. HE HAS INCLINED HIS EAR TO ME, I WILL CALL UPON HIM AS LONG AS I LIVE. THE PANGS OF DEATH HAVE ENCIRCLED ME AND THE ANGUISH OF THE GRAVE SEIZE ME; DISTRESS AND SORROW BEFALL ME. THEN I CALLED UPON THE NAME OF THE ALMIGHTY: "I BESEECH YOU, ALMIGHTY GOD, SAVE MY SOUL." THE ALMIGHTY IS GRA-

אָהַבְתִּי כִּי יִשְׁמַע יהוה, אֶת קוֹלִי תַּחֲנוּנָי: כִּי הִטָּה אָזְנוֹ לִי, וּבְיָמַי אֶקְרָא: אֲפָפוּנִי חֶבְלֵי מָוֶת, וּמְצָרֵי שְׁאוֹל מְצָאוּנִי, צָרָה וְיָגוֹן אֶמְצָא: וּבְשֵׁם יהוה אֶקְרָא, אָנָּה יהוה מַלְּטָה נַפְשִׁי: חַנּוּן יהוה וְצַדִּיק, וֵאלֹהֵינוּ מְרַחֵם: שֹׁמֵר פְּתָאִים יהוה, דַּלּוֹתִי וְלִי יְהוֹשִׁיעַ: שׁוּבִי נַפְשִׁי לִמְנוּחָיְכִי, כִּי יהוה גָּמַל עָלָיְכִי: כִּי חִלַּצְתָּ נַפְשִׁי מִמָּוֶת,

CIOUS AND JUST, OUR GOD IS MERCIFUL. THE ALMIGHTY PROTECTS THE SIMPLE, WHEN I WAS BROUGHT LOW THE ALMIGHTY SAVED ME. RETURN MY SOUL, TO YOUR REST, FOR THE ALMIGHTY HAS BEEN BOUNTIFUL WITH YOU. YOU, [THE ALMIGHTY], HAVE DELIVERED MY SOUL FROM DEATH, MY EYES FROM TEARS, MY FOOT FROM STUMBLING. I WILL WALK IN THE PRESENCE OF THE ALMIGHTY IN THE LAND OF THE LIVING. I KEPT MY FAITH [IN THE ALMIGHTY], ALTHOUGH I SAY I AM GREATLY AFFLICTED. IN MY HASTE I SAID, ALL MEN ARE DECEITFUL.

(Psalm CXVI: 1-11)

WHAT CAN I RENDER TO THE ALMIGHTY FOR ALL HIS BENEFACTIONS TO ME? I WILL RAISE THE CUP OF SALVATION, AND PROCLAIM THE NAME OF THE ALMIGHTY. MY VOWS TO THE ALMIGHTY I WILL PAY IN THE PRESENCE NOW OF HIS ENTIRE PEOPLE. PRECIOUS IN THE SIGHT OF THE ALMIGHTY IS THE DEATH OF HIS DEVOUT ONES. I BESEECH THE ALMIGHTY, TRULY I AM YOUR SERVANT: I AM YOUR SERVANT, THE SON OF YOUR HANDMAID; YOU HAVE LOOSENED MY BONDS. I WILL OFFER TO YOU THE SACRIFICE OF

אֶת עֵינִי מִן דִּמְעָה, אֶת רַגְלִי מִדֶּחִי: אֶתְהַלֵּךְ לִפְנֵי יהוה, בְּאַרְצוֹת הַחַיִּים: הֶאֱמַנְתִּי כִּי אֲדַבֵּר, אֲנִי עָנִיתִי מְאֹד: אֲנִי אָמַרְתִּי בְחָפְזִי, כָּל הָאָדָם כֹּזֵב:

מָה אָשִׁיב לַיהוה, כָּל תַּגְמוּלוֹהִי עָלָי: כּוֹס יְשׁוּעוֹת אֶשָּׂא, וּבְשֵׁם יהוה אֶקְרָא: נְדָרַי לַיהוה אֲשַׁלֵּם, נֶגְדָה נָא לְכָל עַמּוֹ: יָקָר בְּעֵינֵי יהוה, הַמָּוְתָה לַחֲסִידָיו: אָנָּה יהוה כִּי אֲנִי עַבְדֶּךָ, אֲנִי עַבְדְּךָ בֶּן אֲמָתֶךָ, פִּתַּחְתָּ לְמוֹסֵרָי: לְךָ אֶזְבַּח זֶבַח תּוֹדָה, וּבְשֵׁם יהוה אֶקְרָא: נְדָרַי לַיהוה אֲשַׁלֵּם, נֶגְדָה נָא לְכָל עַמּוֹ: בְּחַצְרוֹת בֵּית יהוה, בְּתוֹכֵכִי יְרוּשָׁלָיִם, הַלְלוּיָה:

THANKSGIVING, AND PRO-
CLAIM THE NAME OF THE
ALMIGHTY. MY VOWS TO THE
ALMIGHTY, I WILL PAY IN THE
PRESENCE NOW OF HIS ENTIRE
PEOPLE; IN THE COURTYARDS
OF THE ALMIGHTY'S HOUSE, IN
YOUR MIDST, O JERUSALEM,
HALLELUYAH!
(Psalm CXVI: 12-19)

PRAISE THE ALMIGHTY, ALL
NATIONS, LAUD HIM, ALL PEO-
PLES. FOR HIS KINDNESS IS
MIGHTY OVER US; THE
ALMIGHTY'S TRUTH ENDURES
FOREVER. HALLELUYAH!
(Psalm 117)

הַלְלוּ אֶת יהוה כָּל גּוֹיִם,
שַׁבְּחוּהוּ כָּל הָאֻמִּים: כִּי גָבַר
עָלֵינוּ חַסְדּוֹ, וֶאֱמֶת יהוה
לְעוֹלָם, הַלְלוּיָהּ:

GIVE THANKS TO THE
ALMIGHTY, FOR HE IS GOOD
FOR HIS KINDNESS IS ETERNAL

הוֹדוּ לַיהוה כִּי טוֹב,
כִּי לְעוֹלָם חַסְדּוֹ

LET ISRAEL NOW SAY,
FOR HIS KINDNESS IS ETERNAL

יֹאמַר נָא יִשְׂרָאֵל,
כִּי לְעוֹלָם חַסְדּוֹ

LET THE HOUSE OF AARON
NOW SAY
FOR HIS KINDNESS IS ETERNAL

יֹאמְרוּ נָא בֵית אַהֲרֹן,
כִּי לְעוֹלָם חַסְדּוֹ

LET THEM THAT FEAR THE
ALMIGHTY NOW SAY
FOR HIS KINDNESS IS ETERNAL
(Psalm 118: 1-4)

יֹאמְרוּ נָא יִרְאֵי יהוה,
כִּי לְעוֹלָם חַסְדּוֹ

FROM THE STRAITS OF MY DIS-
TRESS, I CALLED UPON THE
ALMIGHTY; THE ALMIGHTY
ANSWERED ME IN THE BROAD
PLACES. THE ALMIGHTY IS
WITH ME, I WILL NOT FEAR:
WHAT CAN MAN DO TO ME?

מִן הַמֵּצַר קָרָאתִי יָּהּ, עָנָנִי
בַמֶּרְחַב יָהּ: יהוה לִי לֹא
אִירָא, מַה יַּעֲשֶׂה לִי אָדָם:
יהוה לִי בְּעֹזְרָי, וַאֲנִי אֶרְאֶה
בְשֹׂנְאָי: טוֹב לַחֲסוֹת בַּיהוה,

THE ALMIGHTY IS FOR ME AS MY HELPER; THEREFORE I SHALL SEE [THE DEFEAT OF] THOSE THAT HATE ME. IT IS BETTER TO TAKE REFUGE IN THE ALMIGHTY THAN TO TRUST IN MAN. IT IS BETTER TO TAKE REFUGE IN THE ALMIGHTY THAN TO TRUST IN PRINCES. ALL NATIONS SURROUND ME: IN THE NAME OF THE ALMIGHTY I SURELY CUT THEM DOWN. THEY SURROUND ME, THEY UTTERLY SURROUND ME, IN THE NAME OF THE ALMIGHTY I SURELY CUT THEM DOWN. THEY SWARMED ABOUT ME LIKE BEES; THEY WERE EXTINGUISHED AS A FIRE OF THORNS: IN THE NAME OF THE ALMIGHTY I SURELY CUT THEM DOWN. YOU THRUST AT ME THAT I MIGHT FALL: BUT THE ALMIGHTY HELPED ME. THE ALMIGHTY IS MY STRENGTH AND SONG; HE HAS BECOME MY DELIVERANCE. THE VOICE OF EXULTING AND TRIUMPH RINGS IN THE TENTS OF THE RIGHTEOUS: THE RIGHT HAND OF THE ALMIGHTY DOES VALIANTLY. THE RIGHT HAND OF THE ALMIGHTY IS EXALTED: THE RIGHT HAND OF THE ALMIGHTY DOES VALIANTLY. I SHALL NOT DIE, BUT LIVE, AND RECOUNT THE WORKS OF THE ALMIGHTY. THE ALMIGHTY HAS SURELY CHASTISED ME: BUT HE HAS NOT GIVEN ME OVER TO DEATH. OPEN FOR ME THE GATES OF RIGHTEOUSNESS: I WILL ENTER THROUGH THEM. I WILL GIVE THANKS TO THE ALMIGHTY. THIS IS THE GATEWAY OF THE ALMIGHTY, THE RIGHTEOUS MAY ENTER IT.

מִבְּטֹחַ בָּאָדָם: טוֹב לַחֲסוֹת בַּיהוה, מִבְּטֹחַ בִּנְדִיבִים: כָּל גּוֹיִם סְבָבוּנִי, בְּשֵׁם יהוה כִּי אֲמִילַם: סַבּוּנִי גַם סְבָבוּנִי, בְּשֵׁם יהוה כִּי אֲמִילַם: סַבּוּנִי כִדְבֹרִים, דֹּעֲכוּ כְּאֵשׁ קוֹצִים, בְּשֵׁם יהוה כִּי אֲמִילַם: דָּחֹה דְחִיתַנִי לִנְפֹּל, וַיהוה עֲזָרָנִי: עָזִּי וְזִמְרָת יָה, וַיְהִי לִי לִישׁוּעָה: קוֹל רִנָּה וִישׁוּעָה בְּאָהֳלֵי צַדִּיקִים, יְמִין יהוה עֹשָׂה חָיִל: יְמִין יהוה רוֹמֵמָה, יְמִין יהוה עֹשָׂה חָיִל: לֹא אָמוּת כִּי אֶחְיֶה, וַאֲסַפֵּר מַעֲשֵׂי יָה: יַסֹּר יִסְּרַנִּי יָּה, וְלַמָּוֶת לֹא נְתָנָנִי: פִּתְחוּ לִי שַׁעֲרֵי צֶדֶק, אָבֹא בָם אוֹדֶה יָה: זֶה הַשַּׁעַר לַיהוה, צַדִּיקִים יָבֹאוּ בוֹ:

(Psalm CXVIII:5-20)

Each of the following four verses are recited twice:

I WILL THANK YOU, FOR YOU HAVE ANSWERED ME AND BECOME MY DELIVERANCE.

אוֹדְךָ כִּי עֲנִיתָנִי, וַתְּהִי לִי לִישׁוּעָה:

THE STONE WHICH THE BUILDERS REJECTED HAS BECOME THE CHIEF CORNERSTONE.

אֶבֶן מָאֲסוּ הַבּוֹנִים, הָיְתָה לְרֹאשׁ פִּנָּה:

THIS IS THE ALMIGHTY'S DOING IT IS MARVELOUS IN OUR EYES.

מֵאֵת יהוה הָיְתָה זֹּאת, הִיא נִפְלָאת בְּעֵינֵינוּ:

THIS IS THE DAY WHICH THE ALMIGHTY HAS APPOINTED, LET US BE GLAD AND REJOICE ON IT.

זֶה הַיּוֹם עָשָׂה יהוה, נָגִילָה וְנִשְׂמְחָה בוֹ:

WE IMPLORE YOU, ALMIGHTY, SAVE US NOW!

אָנָּא יהוה הוֹשִׁיעָה נָּא:

WE IMPLORE YOU, ALMIGHTY, SAVE US NOW!

אָנָּא יהוה הוֹשִׁיעָה נָּא:

WE IMPLORE YOU, ALMIGHTY, SEND US SUCCESS NOW!

אָנָּא יהוה הַצְלִיחָה נָּא:

WE IMPLORE YOU, ALMIGHTY, SEND US SUCCESS NOW!

אָנָּא יהוה הַצְלִיחָה נָּא:

Each of the following four verses are recited twice:

BLESSED BE HE WHO COMES IN THE NAME OF THE ALMIGHTY: WE BLESS YOU FROM THE HOUSE OF THE ALMIGHTY.

בָּרוּךְ הַבָּא בְּשֵׁם יהוה, בֵּרַכְנוּכֶם מִבֵּית יהוה:

THE ALMIGHTY IS GOD, HE HAS GIVEN US LIGHT: BRING THE FESTIVAL SACRIFICE BOUND WITH CORD, EVEN

אֵל יהוה וַיָּאֶר לָנוּ, אִסְרוּ חַג בַּעֲבֹתִים עַד קַרְנוֹת הַמִּזְבֵּחַ:

UNTO THE CORNERS OF THE ALTAR.

Yᴏᴜ ARE MY GOD, AND I WILL GIVE THANKS TO YOU: YOU ARE MY GOD, I WILL EXALT YOU.

Oᴏ GIVE THANKS TO THE ALMIGHTY, FOR HE IS GOOD: FOR HIS KINDNESS IS ETERNAL.

(Psalm CXVIII: 21-29)

Aʟʟ YOUR WORKS, ALMIGHTY, OUR GOD, SHALL PRAISE YOU; YOUR PIOUS ONES WITH THE RIGHTEOUS WHO PERFORM YOUR WILL. AND YOUR ENTIRE NATION, THE HOUSE OF ISRAEL, WITH JOYFUL SONG SHALL GIVE THANKS, BLESS, LAUD, GLORIFY, EXALT, REVERE, SANCTIFY AND ACKNOWLEDGE THE SOVEREIGNTY OF YOUR NAME, O OUR KING, FOR TO YOU IT IS GOOD TO RENDER THANKSGIVING AND PLEASANT TO SING PRAISE TO YOUR NAME. FOR YOU ARE ALMIGHTY GOD FROM EVER-LASTING TO EVERLASTING.

Oᴏ GIVE THANKS TO THE ALMIGHTY, FOR HE IS GOOD
FOR HIS KINDNESS IS ETERNAL

Oᴏ GIVE THANKS TO THE GOD OF GODS
FOR HIS KINDNESS IS ETERNAL

Oᴏ GIVE THANKS TO THE LORD OF LORDS
FOR HIS KINDNESS IS ETERNAL

אֵלִי אַתָּה וְאוֹדֶךָּ, אֱלֹהַי אֲרוֹמְמֶךָּ:

הוֹדוּ לַיהוה כִּי טוֹב, כִּי לְעוֹלָם חַסְדּוֹ:

יְהַלְלוּךָ יהוה אֱלֹהֵינוּ כָּל מַעֲשֶׂיךָ. וַחֲסִידֶיךָ צַדִּיקִים עוֹשֵׂי רְצוֹנֶךָ. וְכָל עַמְּךָ בֵּית יִשְׂרָאֵל, בְּרִנָּה יוֹדוּ וִיבָרְכוּ. וִישַׁבְּחוּ וִיפָאֲרוּ. וִירוֹמְמוּ וְיַעֲרִיצוּ. וְיַקְדִּישׁוּ וְיַמְלִיכוּ אֶת שִׁמְךָ מַלְכֵּנוּ. כִּי לְךָ טוֹב לְהוֹדוֹת וּלְשִׁמְךָ נָאֶה לְזַמֵּר. כִּי מֵעוֹלָם וְעַד עוֹלָם אַתָּה אֵל.

הוֹדוּ לַיהוה כִּי טוֹב,
כִּי לְעוֹלָם חַסְדּוֹ

הוֹדוּ לֵאלֹהֵי הָאֱלֹהִים,
כִּי לְעוֹלָם חַסְדּוֹ

הוֹדוּ לַאֲדֹנֵי הָאֲדֹנִים,
כִּי לְעוֹלָם חַסְדּוֹ

TO HIM WHO ALONE DOES
GREAT WONDERS
FOR HIS KINDNESS IS ETERNAL

לְעֹשֵׂה נִפְלָאוֹת גְּדֹלוֹת לְבַדּוֹ,
כִּי לְעוֹלָם חַסְדּוֹ

TO HIM THAT MADE THE HEAV-
ENS WITH WISDOM
FOR HIS KINDNESS IS ETERNAL

לְעוֹשֵׂה הַשָּׁמַיִם בִּתְבוּנָה,
כִּי לְעוֹלָם חַסְדּוֹ

TO HIM THAT SPREAD THE
EARTH ON THE WATERS
FOR HIS KINDNESS IS ETERNAL

לְרוֹקַע הָאָרֶץ עַל הַמָּיִם,
כִּי לְעוֹלָם חַסְדּוֹ

[TO HIM] THAT MADE THE GREAT
LIGHTS
FOR HIS KINDNESS IS ETERNAL

לְעֹשֵׂה אוֹרִים גְּדֹלִים,
כִּי לְעוֹלָם חַסְדּוֹ

THE SUN TO RULE BY DAY
FOR HIS KINDNESS IS ETERNAL

אֶת הַשֶּׁמֶשׁ לְמֶמְשֶׁלֶת בַּיּוֹם,
כִּי לְעוֹלָם חַסְדּוֹ

THE MOON AND STARS TO
RULE BY NIGHT
FOR HIS KINDNESS IS ETERNAL

אֶת הַיָּרֵחַ וְכוֹכָבִים
לְמֶמְשְׁלוֹת בַּלָּיְלָה,
כִּי לְעוֹלָם חַסְדּוֹ

TO HIM THAT SMOTE EGYPT
THROUGH THEIR FIRSTBORN
FOR HIS KINDNESS IS ETERNAL

לְמַכֵּה מִצְרַיִם בִּבְכוֹרֵיהֶם,
כִּי לְעוֹלָם חַסְדּוֹ

AND BROUGHT ISRAEL FORTH
FROM AMONG THEM
FOR HIS KINDNESS IS ETERNAL

וַיּוֹצֵא יִשְׂרָאֵל מִתּוֹכָם,
כִּי לְעוֹלָם חַסְדּוֹ

WITH A MIGHTY HAND AND
OUTSTRETCHED ARM
FOR HIS KINDNESS IS ETERNAL

בְּיָד חֲזָקָה וּבִזְרוֹעַ נְטוּיָה,
כִּי לְעוֹלָם חַסְדּוֹ

TO HIM THAT PARTED THE RED
SEA
FOR HIS KINDNESS IS ETERNAL

לְגֹזֵר יַם סוּף לִגְזָרִים,
כִּי לְעוֹלָם חַסְדּוֹ

AND MADE ISRAEL PASS
THROUGH THE MIDST OF IT
FOR HIS KINDNESS IS ETERNAL

וְהֶעֱבִיר יִשְׂרָאֵל בְּתוֹכוֹ,
כִּי לְעוֹלָם חַסְדּוֹ

AND THREW PHARAOH AND HIS
HOST INTO THE RED SEA
FOR HIS KINDNESS IS ETERNAL

וְנִעֵר פַּרְעֹה וְחֵילוֹ בְיַם סוּף,
כִּי לְעוֹלָם חַסְדּוֹ

TO HIM THAT LED HIS PEOPLE

לְמוֹלִיךְ עַמּוֹ בַּמִּדְבָּר,

THROUGH THE WILDERNESS
FOR HIS KINDNESS IS ETERNAL

TO HIM THAT STRUCK DOWN
GREAT KINGS
FOR HIS KINDNESS IS ETERNAL

AND SLEW MIGHTY KINGS
FOR HIS KINDNESS IS ETERNAL

SICHON, KING OF THE
EMORITES
FOR HIS KINDNESS IS ETERNAL

AND OG, KING OF BASHAN
FOR HIS KINDNESS IS ETERNAL

AND GAVE THEIR LAND FOR AN
INHERITANCE
FOR HIS KINDNESS IS ETERNAL

AN INHERITANCE TO ISRAEL
HIS SERVANT
FOR HIS KINDNESS IS ETERNAL

REMEMBERED US IN OUR
LOWLINESS
FOR HIS KINDNESS IS ETERNAL

AND REDEEMED US FROM OUR
OPPRESSORS
FOR HIS KINDNESS IS ETERNAL

WHO GIVES FOOD TO ALL
CREATURES
FOR HIS KINDNESS IS ETERNAL

*GIVE THANKS TO GOD OF THE
HEAVENS*
FOR HIS KINDNESS IS ETERNAL
(Psalm CXXXVI)

THE SOUL OF EVERY LIVING
BEING SHALL BLESS YOUR
NAME ALMIGHTY, OUR GOD,
AND THE SPIRIT OF ALL FLESH

כִּי לְעוֹלָם חַסְדּוֹ

לְמַכֵּה מְלָכִים גְּדֹלִים,
כִּי לְעוֹלָם חַסְדּוֹ

וַיַּהֲרֹג מְלָכִים אַדִּירִים,
כִּי לְעוֹלָם חַסְדּוֹ
לְסִיחוֹן מֶלֶךְ הָאֱמֹרִי,
כִּי לְעוֹלָם חַסְדּוֹ

וּלְעוֹג מֶלֶךְ הַבָּשָׁן,
כִּי לְעוֹלָם חַסְדּוֹ
וְנָתַן אַרְצָם לְנַחֲלָה,
כִּי לְעוֹלָם חַסְדּוֹ

נַחֲלָה לְיִשְׂרָאֵל עַבְדּוֹ,
כִּי לְעוֹלָם חַסְדּוֹ

שֶׁבְּשִׁפְלֵנוּ זָכַר לָנוּ,
כִּי לְעוֹלָם חַסְדּוֹ

וַיִּפְרְקֵנוּ מִצָּרֵינוּ,
כִּי לְעוֹלָם חַסְדּוֹ

נֹתֵן לֶחֶם לְכָל בָּשָׂר,
כִּי לְעוֹלָם חַסְדּוֹ

הוֹדוּ לְאֵל הַשָּׁמָיִם,
כִּי לְעוֹלָם חַסְדּוֹ:

נִשְׁמַת כָּל חַי. תְּבָרֵךְ אֶת
שִׁמְךָ יהוה אֱלֹהֵינוּ, וְרוּחַ כָּל
בָּשָׂר תְּפָאֵר וּתְרוֹמֵם זִכְרְךָ

SHALL EVER GLORIFY AND EXALT YOUR REMEMBRANCE, OUR KING. FROM EVERLASTING TO EVERLASTING YOU ARE THE ALMIGHTY. BESIDE YOU WE HAVE NO KING, WHO REDEEMS AND SAVES, SETS FREE AND DELIVERS, SUPPORTS AND PITIES IN ALL TIMES OF TROUBLE AND DISTRESS. WE HAVE NO KING BUT YOU. YOU ARE ALMIGHTY OF THE FIRST AND THE LAST, THE GOD OF ALL CREATURES, THE MASTER OF ALL GENERATIONS. YOU ARE ADORED WITH ALL MANNER OF PRAISE; WHO GOVERNS THE UNIVERSE WITH KINDNESS AND ITS CREATURES WITH MERCY. THE ETERNAL NEITHER SLUMBERS NOR SLEEPS, BUT ROUSES THE SLEEPERS AND AWAKENS THOSE WHO SLUMBER, HE CAUSES THE MUTE TO SPEAK; LOOSENS THE BOUND AND SUPPORTS THE FALLEN AND RAISES UP THOSE WHO ARE BOWED DOWN. TO YOU ALONE DO WE GIVE THANKS. WERE OUR MOUTHS FILLED WITH MELODIOUS SONGS, AS THE FULLNESS OF THE SEA, OUR TONGUES WITH EXULTATION AS THE RAGING WAVES, AND OUR LIPS WITH PRAISE, LIKE THE EXPANSES OF THE FIRMAMENT, OUR EYES SHINING LIKE THE SUN AND MOON, AND OUR HANDS

מַלְכֵּנוּ תָּמִיד. מִן הָעוֹלָם וְעַד הָעוֹלָם אַתָּה אֵל, וּמִבַּלְעָדֶיךָ אֵין לָנוּ מֶלֶךְ גּוֹאֵל וּמוֹשִׁיעַ, פּוֹדֶה וּמַצִּיל וּמְפַרְנֵס וּמְרַחֵם בְּכָל עֵת צָרָה וְצוּקָה, אֵין לָנוּ מֶלֶךְ אֶלָּא אָתָּה: אֱלֹהֵי הָרִאשׁוֹנִים וְהָאַחֲרוֹנִים. אֱלוֹהַ כָּל בְּרִיּוֹת, אֲדוֹן כָּל תּוֹלָדוֹת: הַמְהֻלָּל בְּרוֹב הַתִּשְׁבָּחוֹת. הַמְנַהֵג עוֹלָמוֹ בְּחֶסֶד, וּבְרִיּוֹתָיו בְּרַחֲמִים. וַיהוה לֹא יָנוּם וְלֹא יִישָׁן, הַמְעוֹרֵר יְשֵׁנִים, וְהַמֵּקִיץ נִרְדָּמִים. וְהַמֵּשִׂיחַ אִלְּמִים. וְהַמַּתִּיר אֲסוּרִים. וְהַסּוֹמֵךְ נוֹפְלִים. וְהַזּוֹקֵף כְּפוּפִים. לְךָ לְבַדְּךָ אֲנַחְנוּ מוֹדִים: אִלּוּ פִינוּ מָלֵא שִׁירָה כַּיָּם, וּלְשׁוֹנֵנוּ רִנָּה כַּהֲמוֹן גַּלָּיו. וְשִׂפְתוֹתֵינוּ שֶׁבַח כְּמֶרְחֲבֵי רָקִיעַ. וְעֵינֵינוּ מְאִירוֹת כַּשֶּׁמֶשׁ וְכַיָּרֵחַ. וְיָדֵינוּ פְרוּשׂוֹת כְּנִשְׁרֵי שָׁמָיִם. וְרַגְלֵינוּ קַלּוֹת כָּאַיָּלוֹת. אֵין אֲנַחְנוּ מַסְפִּיקִים לְהוֹדוֹת לְךָ, יהוה אֱלֹהֵינוּ וֵאלֹהֵי אֲבוֹתֵינוּ, וּלְבָרֵךְ אֶת שְׁמֶךָ, עַל אַחַת מֵאֶלֶף אֶלֶף אַלְפֵי אֲלָפִים וְרִבֵּי רְבָבוֹת פְּעָמִים, הַטּוֹבוֹת שֶׁעָשִׂיתָ עִם אֲבוֹתֵינוּ, וְעִמָּנוּ: מִמִּצְרַיִם גְּאַלְתָּנוּ, יהוה

SPREAD OUT AS FLYING EAGLES HEAVENWARD, AND OUR FEET SWIFT AS HINDS; OUR EFFORTS COULD NOT RENDER SUFFICIENT THANKS TO YOU ALMIGHTY, OUR GOD, AND GOD OF OUR FATHERS, AND TO BLESS YOUR NAME FOR EVEN ONE OF THE THOUSAND, THOUSANDS OF THOUSANDS, AND MYRIAD MYRIAD FAVORS WHICH YOU HAVE CONFERRED ON OUR ANCESTORS AND US. FROM EGYPT DID YOU REDEEM US, ALMIGHTY, OUR GOD. FROM THE HOUSE OF SLAVERY; IN TIME OF FAMINE YOU DID SUSTAIN US; AND IN PLENTY YOU DID MAINTAIN US. FROM THE SWORD YOU DID DELIVER US, FROM PESTILENCE YOU DID SAVE US, AND FROM DISEASE AND RAGING SICKNESS YOU DID SPARE US. UNTIL NOW, YOUR MERCIES HAVE SUPPORTED US AND YOUR KINDNESS HAS NOT ABANDONED US. O ALMIGHTY, OUR GOD, FORSAKE US NOT IN THE FUTURE. THEREFORE, THE LIMBS WHICH YOU HAVE FORMED WITHIN US, THE SPIRIT AND SOUL WHICH YOU HAVE BREATHED INTO OUR NOSTRILS, THE TONGUE YOU PLACED IN OUR MOUTH, BEHOLD, THEY THANK, BLESS, LAUD, GLORIFY, EXALT, REVERE, HALLOW, AND

אֱלֹהֵינוּ, וּמִבֵּית עֲבָדִים פְּדִיתָנוּ. בְּרָעָב זַנְתָּנוּ, וּבְשָׂבָע כִּלְכַּלְתָּנוּ, מֵחֶרֶב הִצַּלְתָּנוּ, וּמִדֶּבֶר מִלַּטְתָּנוּ, וּמֵחֳלָיִם רָעִים וְנֶאֱמָנִים דִּלִּיתָנוּ: עַד הֵנָּה עֲזָרוּנוּ רַחֲמֶיךָ, וְלֹא עֲזָבוּנוּ חֲסָדֶיךָ, וְאַל תִּטְּשֵׁנוּ יהוה אֱלֹהֵינוּ לָנֶצַח: עַל כֵּן אֵבָרִים שֶׁפִּלַּגְתָּ בָּנוּ, וְרוּחַ וּנְשָׁמָה שֶׁנָּפַחְתָּ בְּאַפֵּינוּ, וְלָשׁוֹן אֲשֶׁר שַׂמְתָּ בְּפִינוּ: הֵן הֵם יוֹדוּ וִיבָרְכוּ, וִישַׁבְּחוּ וִיפָאֲרוּ, וִירוֹמְמוּ וְיַעֲרִיצוּ, וְיַקְדִּישׁוּ וְיַמְלִיכוּ אֶת שִׁמְךָ מַלְכֵּנוּ: כִּי כָל פֶּה לְךָ יוֹדֶה, וְכָל לָשׁוֹן לְךָ תִשָּׁבַע. וְכָל בֶּרֶךְ לְךָ תִכְרַע. וְכָל קוֹמָה לְפָנֶיךָ תִשְׁתַּחֲוֶה. וְכָל לְבָבוֹת יִירָאוּךָ. וְכָל קֶרֶב וּכְלָיוֹת יְזַמְּרוּ לִשְׁמֶךָ. כַּדָּבָר שֶׁכָּתוּב, כָּל עַצְמוֹתַי תֹּאמַרְנָה יהוה מִי כָמוֹךָ: מַצִּיל עָנִי מֵחָזָק מִמֶּנּוּ, וְעָנִי וְאֶבְיוֹן מִגֹּזְלוֹ. מִי יִדְמֶה לָּךְ, וּמִי יִשְׁוֶה לָּךְ, וּמִי יַעֲרָךְ לָךְ. הָאֵל הַגָּדוֹל, הַגִּבּוֹר וְהַנּוֹרָא, אֵל עֶלְיוֹן, קוֹנֵה שָׁמַיִם וָאָרֶץ: נְהַלֶּלְךָ, וּנְשַׁבֵּחֲךָ וּנְפָאֶרְךָ וּנְבָרֵךְ אֶת שֵׁם קָדְשֶׁךָ: כָּאָמוּר: לְדָוִד, בָּרְכִי נַפְשִׁי אֶת יהוה, וְכָל קְרָבַי אֶת שֵׁם קָדְשׁוֹ:

ACKNOWLEDGE YOUR SOVEREIGN NAME, OUR KING. FOR EVERY MOUTH SHALL OFFER THANKS TO YOU AND EVERY TONGUE SHALL SWEAR ALLEGIANCE TO YOU, EVERY KNEE SHALL BEND TO YOU AND EVERY UPRIGHT BEING SHALL PROSTATE BEFORE YOU. EVERY HEART SHALL FEAR YOU AND OUR INNERMOST BEING SHALL SING PRAISES TO YOUR NAME, AS IT IS WRITTEN, *(Psalm XXXV:10)* "ALL MY BONES SHALL SAY, O ALMIGHTY, WHO IS LIKE YOU: WHO DELIVERS THE WEAK FROM HIM THAT IS TOO STRONG FOR HIM AND THE POOR AND NEEDY FROM HE THAT SEEKS TO ROB HIM. WHO IS LIKE YOU? WHO IS EQUAL TO YOU? WHO CAN BE COMPARED TO YOU? GREAT, MIGHTY AND AWE INSPIRING GOD, MOST SUPREME GOD, MASTER OF HEAVEN AND EARTH. WE WILL PRAISE, LAUD, GLORIFY AND BLESS YOUR HOLY NAME AS IT IS SAID : *(Psalm CIII:1)* "A PSALM BY DAVID BLESS THE ETERNAL, O MY SOUL, AND ALL THAT IS WITHIN ME, BLESS HIS HOLY NAME"

YOU ARE THE ALMIGHTY IN THE VASTNESS OF YOUR POWER, AND GREAT BY YOUR GLORIOUS NAME. MIGHTY FOREVER AND REVERED IN YOUR AWE INSPIRING DEEDS, THE KING WHO SITS ON THE HIGH AND LOFTY THRONE.

הָאֵל, בְּתַעֲצֻמוֹת עֻזֶּךָ. הַגָּדוֹל, בִּכְבוֹד שְׁמֶךָ. הַגִּבּוֹר, לָנֶצַח, וְהַנּוֹרָא, בְּנוֹרְאוֹתֶיךָ: הַמֶּלֶךְ, הַיּוֹשֵׁב עַל כִּסֵּא, רָם וְנִשָּׂא:

HE WHO ABIDES FOREVER, EXALTED AND HOLY IS YOUR NAME.   IT   IS   WRITTEN: "REJOICE IN THE ALMIGHTY, YOU RIGHTEOUS, IT IS FITTING FOR THE UPRIGHT TO SPEAK HIS PRAISE.

שׁוֹכֵן עַד, מָרוֹם וְקָדוֹשׁ שְׁמוֹ. וְכָתוּב, רַנְּנוּ צַדִּיקִים בַּיהוה, לַיְשָׁרִים נָאוָה תְהִלָּה.

BY THE MOUTH OF THE UPRIGHT YOU ARE PRAISED;

בְּפִי יְשָׁרִים תִּתְהַלָּל.

BY THE UTTERANCES OF THE RIGHTEOUS YOU ARE BLESSED;

וּבְדִבְרֵי צַדִּיקִים תִּתְבָּרַךְ.

BY THE TONGUE OF THE PIOUS YOU ARE EXALTED;

AND AMONG THE HOLY YOU ARE SANCTIFIED.

IN THE ASSEMBLIES OF THE MULTITUDES OF YOUR PEOPLE, THE HOUSE OF ISRAEL, WITH RINGING SONG SHALL YOUR NAME, OUR KING, BE GLORIFIED IN EVERY GENERATION. FOR IT IS THE DUTY OF ALL CREATURES TOWARD YOU, ALMIGHTY, OUR GOD, GOD OF OUR FATHERS, TO THANK AND PRAISE, LAUD AND GLORIFY, EXALT AND MAGNIFY, BLESS, EXTOL AND ADORE, AND SING PRAISES EVEN BEYOND ALL THE EXPRESSIONS OF SONGS OF PRAISE BY DAVID, SON OF JESSE, YOUR ANOINTED SERVANT.

PRAISED BE YOUR NAME FOREVER, OUR KING, ALMIGHTY, THE GREAT AND HOLY MONARCH IN THE HEAVENS AND ON EARTH. FOR TO YOU ALMIGHTY, OUR GOD, GOD OF OUR FATHERS, IT IS PLEASANT AND FITTING TO RENDER SONG AND LAUDING, PRAISE AND HYMNS, EXPRESSING YOUR DOMINION AND RULE, ETERNITY, GRANDEUR, VICTORY, TRIUMPH AND RENOWN, SANCTITY, MAJESTY, BLESSINGS AND

וּבִלְשׁוֹן חֲסִידִים תִּתְרוֹמָם.

וּבְקֶרֶב קְדוֹשִׁים תִּתְקַדָּשׁ:

וּבְמַקְהֲלוֹת רִבְבוֹת עַמְּךָ בֵּית יִשְׂרָאֵל. בְּרִנָּה יִתְפָּאַר שִׁמְךָ מַלְכֵּנוּ, בְּכָל דּוֹר וָדוֹר. שֶׁכֵּן חוֹבַת כָּל הַיְצוּרִים, לְפָנֶיךָ יהוה אֱלֹהֵינוּ, וֵאלֹהֵי אֲבוֹתֵינוּ, לְהוֹדוֹת לְהַלֵּל לְשַׁבֵּחַ לְפָאֵר לְרוֹמֵם לְהַדֵּר לְבָרֵךְ לְעַלֵּה וּלְקַלֵּס, עַל כָּל דִּבְרֵי שִׁירוֹת וְתִשְׁבָּחוֹת דָּוִד בֶּן יִשַׁי עַבְדְּךָ מְשִׁיחֶךָ:

וְיִשְׁתַּבַּח שִׁמְךָ לָעַד מַלְכֵּנוּ, הָאֵל הַמֶּלֶךְ הַגָּדוֹל וְהַקָּדוֹשׁ, בַּשָּׁמַיִם וּבָאָרֶץ. כִּי לְךָ נָאֶה יהוה אֱלֹהֵינוּ וֵאלֹהֵי אֲבוֹתֵינוּ, שִׁיר וּשְׁבָחָה, הַלֵּל וְזִמְרָה, עֹז וּמֶמְשָׁלָה, נֶצַח, גְּדֻלָּה וּגְבוּרָה, תְּהִלָּה וְתִפְאֶרֶת קְדֻשָּׁה וּמַלְכוּת: בְּרָכוֹת וְהוֹדָאוֹת מֵעַתָּה וְעַד עוֹלָם. בָּרוּךְ אַתָּה יהוה אֵל מֶלֶךְ גָּדוֹל בַּתִּשְׁבָּחוֹת אֵל הַהוֹדָאוֹת אֲדוֹן

THANKSGIVINGS, FROM NOW AND FOREVER. BLESSED ARE YOU ALMIGHTY GOD, GREAT KING, EXALTED THROUGH PRAISES, KING OF THANKSGIVINGS, LORD OF WONDERS, WHO CHOOSES SONGS OF PRAISE, ALMIGHTY KING, LIFE OF ALL WORLDS.

הַנִּפְלָאוֹת הַבּוֹחֵר בְּשִׁירֵי זִמְרָה מֶלֶךְ אֵל חֵי הָעוֹלָמִים.

We recite the following blessing and drink the fourth cup of wine while reclining. (O.C. 480:1)

BLESSED ARE YOU ALMIGHTY, OUR GOD, KING OF THE UNIVERSE, WHO CREATES THE FRUIT OF THE VINE.

בָּרוּךְ אַתָּה יהוה, אֱלֹהֵינוּ מֶלֶךְ הָעוֹלָם, בּוֹרֵא פְּרִי הַגָּפֶן.

After drinking the fourth cup, the concluding blessing is recited, (on the Sabbath include the passages in parentheses).

BLESSED ARE YOU ALMIGHTY, OUR GOD, KING OF THE UNIVERSE, FOR THE VINE AND THE FRUIT OF THE VINE FOR THE PRODUCE OF THE FIELD, FOR THE DESIRABLE, GOOD AND SPACIOUS LAND WHICH YOU WERE PLEASED TO GRANT OUR FATHERS AS A HERITAGE. THAT THEY MAY EAT OF ITS FRUIT AND BE SATISFIED WITH ITS GOOD GIFTS. HAVE MERCY, ALMIGHTY GOD, ON ISRAEL YOUR PEOPLE, ON JERUSALEM YOUR CITY, ON ZION THE ABODE OF YOUR

בָּרוּךְ אַתָּה יהוה, אֱלֹהֵינוּ מֶלֶךְ הָעוֹלָם, עַל הַגֶּפֶן וְעַל פְּרִי הַגֶּפֶן, וְעַל תְּנוּבַת הַשָּׂדֶה, וְעַל אֶרֶץ חֶמְדָּה טוֹבָה וּרְחָבָה, שֶׁרָצִיתָ וְהִנְחַלְתָּ לַאֲבוֹתֵינוּ, לֶאֱכוֹל מִפִּרְיָהּ וְלִשְׂבּוֹעַ מִטּוּבָהּ. רַחֶם נָא יהוה אֱלֹהֵינוּ, עַל יִשְׂרָאֵל עַמֶּךָ, וְעַל יְרוּשָׁלַיִם עִירֶךָ, וְעַל צִיּוֹן מִשְׁכַּן כְּבוֹדֶךָ, וְעַל מִזְבְּחֶךָ, וְעַל הֵיכָלֶךָ, וּבְנֵה יְרוּשָׁלַיִם, עִיר הַקֹּדֶשׁ,

MAJESTY, ON YOUR ALTAR AND YOUR TEMPLE. REBUILD THE HOLY CITY OF JERUSALEM SPEEDILY IN OUR DAYS. BRING US THERE AND GLADDEN US WITH ITS RESTORATION; MAY WE EAT OF ITS FRUIT AND BE SATIS-FIED WITH ITS GOOD GIFTS; MAY WE BLESS YOU FOR IT IN HOLINESS AND PURITY (FAVOR US AND MAY IT BE YOUR WILL TO FORTIFY US ON THIS DAY OF SAB-BATH). MAKE US JOYFUL ON THIS FESTIVAL OF MATZOHS. FOR YOU ALMIGHTY ARE GOOD AND BENEFICENT TO ALL; WE THANK YOU FOR OUR LAND AND THE FRUIT OF THE VINE. BLESSED ARE YOU ALMIGHTY, FOR THE LAND AND THE FRUIT - OF THE VINE.

בִּמְהֵרָה בְיָמֵינוּ, וְהַעֲלֵנוּ לְתוֹכָהּ, וְשַׂמְּחֵנוּ בְּבִנְיָנָהּ, וְנֹאכַל מִפִּרְיָהּ, וְנִשְׂבַּע מִטּוּבָהּ, וּנְבָרֶכְךָ עָלֶיהָ בִּקְדוּשָׁה וּבְטָהֳרָה: (וּרְצֵה וְהַחֲלִיצֵנוּ בְּיוֹם הַשַּׁבָּת הַזֶּה) וְשַׂמְּחֵנוּ בְּיוֹם חַג הַמַּצּוֹת הַזֶּה, כִּי אַתָּה יהוה טוֹב וּמֵטִיב לַכֹּל, וְנוֹדֶה לְךָ עַל הָאָרֶץ וְעַל פְּרִי הַגָּפֶן. בָּרוּךְ אַתָּה יהוה עַל הָאָרֶץ וְעַל פְּרִי הַגָּפֶן:

NIRTZA

Acceptance of the Seder service by the Almighty

Because we were indeed chosen for eternity, we know our exile is but temporary and will be relieved by the coming of the Messiah, when we will be reunited with the Divine Presence in the land of Israel. This concluding section of the Haggadah looks forward to that great day.

נִרְצָה

THE PASSOVER SEDER HAS NOW BEEN CONCLUDED ACCORDING TO ITS RULES, PERFORMING ALL THE LAWS AND STATUTES OF THE FEAST. AS WE HAVE BEEN DEEMED WORTHY TO PREPARE IT NOW, GRANT ALSO THAT WE MAY BE WORTHY TO FULFILL IT. YOU, O PURE ONE, WHO DWELLS ON HIGH, RAISE UP YOUR INNUMERABLE PEOPLE. O HASTEN TO LEAD US TO THE PLANTS OF YOUR VINEYARD ONCE MORE REDEEMED, TO ZION WITH JOYFUL SONG.

חֲסַל סִדּוּר פֶּסַח כְּהִלְכָתוֹ. כְּכָל מִשְׁפָּטוֹ וְחֻקָּתוֹ. כַּאֲשֶׁר זָכִינוּ לְסַדֵּר אוֹתוֹ. כֵּן נִזְכֶּה לַעֲשׂוֹתוֹ. זָךְ שׁוֹכֵן מְעוֹנָה. קוֹמֵם קְהַל עֲדַת מִי מָנָה. בְּקָרוֹב נַהֵל נִטְעֵי כַנָּה. פְּדוּיִם לְצִיּוֹן בְּרִנָּה:

NEXT YEAR IN JERUSALEM

לְשָׁנָה הַבָּאָה בִּירוּשָׁלָיִם.

The following is recited on the first seder night only:

AND IT CAME TO PASS AT MIDNIGHT

וּבְכֵן וַיְהִי בַּחֲצִי הַלַּיְלָה:

OF YORE, YOU PERFORMED MANY WONDERS BY **NIGHT**

אָז רוֹב נִסִּים הִפְלֵאתָ בַּלַּיְלָה.

AT THE BEGINNING OF THE FIRST WATCH THIS **NIGHT**

בְּרֹאשׁ אַשְׁמוֹרֶת זֶה הַלַּיְלָה

YOU BROUGHT ABRAHAM, THE TRUE CONVERT, TO TRIUMPH WHEN FOR HIM WAS DIVIDED THE **NIGHT**

גֵּר צֶדֶק נִצַּחְתּוֹ כְּנֶחֱלַק לוֹ לַיְלָה:

לְשָׁנָה הַבָּאָה בִּירוּשָׁלָיִם

AND IT CAME TO PASS AT MIDNIGHT

וַיְהִי בַּחֲצִי הַלַּיְלָה:

YOU JUDGED THE KING OF GERAR [WITH DEATH] IN A DREAM BY **NIGHT**

דַּנְתָּ מֶלֶךְ גְּרָר בַּחֲלוֹם הַלַּיְלָה.

YOU TERRIFIED [LABAN] THE ARAMEAN IN THE DARK OF **NIGHT**

הִפְחַדְתָּ אֲרַמִּי בְּאֶמֶשׁ לַיְלָה.

ISRAEL WRESTLED THE ANGEL AND PREVAILED BY **NIGHT**

וַיָּשַׂר יִשְׂרָאֵל לְמַלְאָךְ וַיּוּכַל לוֹ לַיְלָה:

AND IT CAME TO PASS AT MIDNIGHT

וַיְהִי בַּחֲצִי הַלַּיְלָה:

THE EGYPTIAN FIRSTBORN YOU CRUSHED THIS **NIGHT**

זֶרַע בְּכוֹרֵי פַּתְרוֹס מָחַצְתָּ בַּחֲצִי הַלַּיְלָה.

THEIR HOST THEY FOUND NOT, WHEN ARISING AT **NIGHT**

חֵילָם לֹא מָצְאוּ בְּקוּמָם בַּלַּיְלָה.

THE PRINCE'S [SISERA] ARMY YOU SWEPT AWAY BY THE STARS OF THE **NIGHT**

טִיסַת נְגִיד חֲרֹשֶׁת סִלִּיתָ בְּכוֹכְבֵי לַיְלָה:

AND IT CAME TO PASS AT MIDNIGIIT

וַיְהִי בַּחֲצִי הַלַּיְלָה:

[SANCHEREB], THE BLASPHEMER, BESIEGED YOUR ABODE, BUT YOU FRUSTRATED HIM WITH ROTTEN CORPSES THIS **NIGHT**

יָעַץ מְחָרֵף לְנוֹפֵף אִוּוּי, הוֹבַשְׁתָּ פְגָרָיו בַּלַּיְלָה.

BEL [BABYLONIA] AND HIS HEA- THEN IDOL WERE OVER- THROWN IN THE DARKNESS OF **NIGHT**

כָּרַע בֵּל וּמַצָּבוֹ בְּאִישׁוֹן לַיְלָה.

TO THE BELOVED MAN [DANIEL] WAS REVEALED MYSTERIOUS

לְאִישׁ חֲמוּדוֹת נִגְלָה רָז

VISIONS AT **NIGHT**	חֲזוֹת **לַיְלָה:**
AND IT CAME TO PASS AT MIDNIGHT	וַיְהִי בַּחֲצִי הַלַּיְלָה:

HE [BELSHAZZAR] WHO MADE HIMSELF DRUNK FROM THE HOLY VESSELS, WAS SLAIN THAT
NIGHT

מִשְׁתַּכֵּר בִּכְלֵי קוֹדֶשׁ נֶהֱרַג בּוֹ **בַּלַּיְלָה.**

[DANIEL], SAVED FROM THE LION'S DEN WHEN HE INTERPRETED THE TERRORS OF THE
NIGHT

נוֹשַׁע מִבּוֹר אֲרָיוֹת פּוֹתֵר בְּעֶתּוֹתֵי **לַיְלָה.**

THE AGAGI [HAMAN] WROTE HIS EDICTS OF HATE TO EXTERMINATE THE JEWS AT
NIGHT

שִׂנְאָה נָטַר אֲגָגִי וְכָתַב סְפָרִים **בַּלַּיְלָה:**

AND IT CAME TO PASS AT MIDNIGHT

וַיְהִי בַּחֲצִי הַלַּיְלָה:

YOU TRIUMPHED OVER HIM [AHASUERUS] BY DISTURBING HIS ROYAL SLEEP AT
NIGHT

עוֹרַרְתָּ נִצְחֲךָ עָלָיו בְּנֶדֶד שְׁנַת **לַיְלָה.**

TRAMPLE THE WINE PRESS FOR THOSE WHO ASK THE WATCHMAN HOW LONG THE
NIGHT

פּוּרָה תִדְרוֹךְ לְשׁוֹמֵר מַה **מִלַּיְלָה.**

[THE ALMIGHTY], WATCHMAN OF ISRAEL, CRIES OUT, THE MORNING HAS COME AFTER THE
NIGHT

צָרַח כַּשּׁוֹמֵר וְשָׂח אָתָא בוֹקֶר וְגַם **לַיְלָה:**

AND IT CAME TO PASS AT MIDNIGHT

וַיְהִי בַּחֲצִי הַלַּיְלָה:

HASTEN THE DAY OF REDEMPTION, WHICH IS NEITHER DAY NOR
NIGHT

קָרֵב יוֹם אֲשֶׁר הוּא לֹא יוֹם וְלֹא **לַיְלָה.**

MAKE KNOWN, MOST HIGH, THAT YOURS IS THE DAY AND THE
NIGHT

רָם הוֹדַע כִּי לְךָ הַיּוֹם אַף לְךָ הַלָּיְלָה.

APPOINT WATCHMEN FOR YOUR CITY [JERUSALEM] ALL DAY AND ALL
NIGHT

שׁוֹמְרִים הַפְקֵד לְעִירְךָ כָּל הַיּוֹם וְכָל הַלָּיְלָה.

ILLUMINATE AS THE DAY THE DARKNESS OF OUR
NIGHT

תָּאִיר כְּאוֹר יוֹם חֶשְׁכַת לַיְלָה.

AND IT CAME TO PASS AT MIDNIGHT

וַיְהִי בַּחֲצִי הַלָּיְלָה:

The following is recited on the second seder night only:

YOU SHALL SAY, THIS IS THE PASSOVER SACRIFICE

וּבְכֵן וַאֲמַרְתֶּם זֶבַח פֶּסַח:

YOUR MIGHTY DEEDS YOU DID POWERFULLY DISPLAY ON
PASSOVER

אֹמֶץ גְּבוּרוֹתֶיךָ הִפְלֵאתָ בַּפֶּסַח.

SUPREME OF ALL THE FEASTS DID YOU EXALT
PASSOVER

בְּרֹאשׁ כָּל מוֹעֲדוֹת נִשֵּׂאתָ פֶּסַח.

YOU REVEALED TO THE ORIENTAL [ABRAHAM] THE MIRACLES PERFORMED AT MIDNIGHT ON
PASSOVER

גִּלִּיתָ לְאֶזְרָחִי חֲצוֹת לֵיל פֶּסַח:

YOU SHALL SAY, THIS IS THE PASSOVER SACRIFICE

וַאֲמַרְתֶּם זֶבַח פֶּסַח:

YOU VISITED HIS [ABRAHAM'S] DOOR DURING THE HEAT OF THE DAY ON
PASSOVER

דְּלָתָיו דָּפַקְתָּ כְּחוֹם הַיּוֹם בַּפֶּסַח.

HE ENTERTAINED THE ANGELS WITH MATZOHS ON
PASSOVER

הִסְעִיד נוֹצְצִים עֻגוֹת מַצּוֹת בַּפֶּסַח.

TO THE HERD HE RAN AND PRE-PARED A CALF, SYMBOLIC OF THE SACRIFICE OF **PASSOVER**

וְאֶל הַבָּקָר רָץ זֵכֶר לְשׁוֹר עָרַךְ **פֶּסַח:**

YOU SHALL SAY, THIS IS THE PASSOVER SACRIFICE

וַאֲמַרְתֶּם זֶבַח פֶּסַח:

THE SODOMITES PROVOKED THE ALMIGHTY, AND WERE CONSUMED BY FIRE ON **PASSOVER**

זוֹעֲמוּ סְדוֹמִים וְלוֹהֲטוּ בָּאֵשׁ **בְּפֶּסַח.**

LOT WAS SPARED AND HE BAKED MATZOHS AT THE TIME OF **PASSOVER**

חֻלַּץ לוֹט מֵהֶם וּמַצּוֹת אָפָה בְּקֵץ **פֶּסַח.**

YOU SWEPT CLEAN THE LAND OF MOPH AND NOPH [EGYPT] WHEN YOU PASSED THROUGH ON **PASSOVER**

טֵאטֵאתָ אַדְמַת מוֹף וְנוֹף בְּעָבְרְךָ **בְּפֶּסַח:**

YOU SHALL SAY, THIS IS THE PASSOVER SACRIFICE

וַאֲמַרְתֶּם זֶבַח פֶּסַח:

ALMIGHTY, YOU SMOTE EVERY FIRSTBORN ON THE NIGHT OF **PASSOVER**

יָהּ רֹאשׁ כָּל אוֹן מָחַצְתָּ בְּלֵיל שִׁמּוּר **פֶּסַח.**

YET YOU PASSED OVER YOUR FIRSTBORN [ISRAEL] MARKED WITH THE BLOOD OF THE SAC-RIFICE OF **PASSOVER**

כַּבִּיר, עַל בֵּן בְּכוֹר פָּסַחְתָּ בְּדַם **פֶּסַח.**

YOU PERMITTED NO DESTROY-ER TO ENTER WITHIN MY [ISRAEL'S] DOORS, ON *PASSOVER*

לְבִלְתִּי תֵת מַשְׁחִית לָבֹא בִּפְתָחַי **בְּפֶּסַח:**

AND YOU SHALL SAY, THIS IS THE PASSOVER SACRIFICE

וַאֲמַרְתֶּם זֶבַח פֶּסַח:

THE WALLED CITY [JERICHO] WAS BELEAGUERED AND

מְסֻגֶּרֶת סֻגָּרָה בְּעִתּוֹתֵי **פֶּסַח.**

BESIEGED ON **PASSOVER**
MIDIAN WAS DESTROYED BY THE CAKE OF BARLEY, FROM THE OFFERING OF AN OMER, ON **PASSOVER**

נִשְׁמְדָה מִדְיָן בִּצְלִיל שְׂעוֹרֵי עוֹמֶר **פֶּסַח.**

THE MIGHTY PUL AND LUD [ASSYRIA] WAS DESTROYED WITH BURNING AND CONFLAGRATION ON **PASSOVER**

שׂוֹרְפוּ מִשְׁמַנֵּי פּוּל וְלוּד בִּיקַד יְקוֹד **פֶּסַח:**

AND YOU SHALL SAY, THIS IS THE PASSOVER SACRIFICE

וַאֲמַרְתֶּם זֶבַח פֶּסַח:

He [SANCHEREB] REMAINED IN NOB BUT FOR THE APPROACH OF **PASSOVER**

עוֹד הַיּוֹם בְּנוֹב לַעֲמוֹד עַד גָּעָה עוֹנַת **פֶּסַח.**

THE HAND WROTE THE DECREE OF EXTERMINATION AGAINST TZUL [BABYLONIA], ON **PASSOVER**

פַּס יָד כָּתְבָה לְקַעֲקֵעַ צוּל **בְּפֶּסַח.**

THE WATCH WAS SET AND THE TABLE ROYALLY SPREAD ON **PASSOVER**

צָפֹה הַצָּפִית עָרוֹךְ הַשֻּׁלְחָן **בְּפֶּסַח:**

YOU SHALL SAY, THIS IS THE PASSOVER SACRIFICE

וַאֲמַרְתֶּם זֶבַח פֶּסַח:

Hadassah [ESTHER] ASSEMBLED THE CONGREGATION TO FAST THREE DAYS ON **PASSOVER**

קָהָל כִּנְּסָה הֲדַסָּה לְשַׁלֵּשׁ צוֹם **בְּפֶּסַח:**

THE HEAD OF THE WICKED HOUSE [HAMAN] YOU CAUSED TO BE HANGED ON THE GALLOWS FIFTY CUBITS HIGH ON **PASSOVER**

רֹאשׁ מִבֵּית רָשָׁע מָחַצְתָּ בְּעֵץ חֲמִשִּׁים **בְּפֶּסַח.**

THE DOUBLE PUNISHMENT IN A MOMENT YOU WILL BRING ON UTZ [EDOM] ON **PASSOVER**

שְׁתֵּי אֵלֶּה רֶגַע תָּבִיא לְעוּצִית **בְּפֶּסַח.**

YOUR HAND WILL THEN SHOW ITSELF OMNIPOTENT, YOUR RIGHT ARM EXALTED, AS ON THE NIGHT WHEN THE FESTIVAL OF PASSOVER WAS SANCTIFIED

YOU SHALL SAY, THIS IS THE PASSOVER SACRIFICE

תָּעֹז יָדְךָ וְתָרוּם יְמִינֶךָ כְּלֵיל הִתְקַדֵּשׁ חַג **פֶּסַח:**

וַאֲמַרְתֶּם זֶבַח פֶּסַח:

TO HIM PRAISE IS BECOMING TO HIM IT IS EVER DUE

כִּי לוֹ נָאֶה כִּי לוֹ יָאֶה

MIGHTY IN HIS MAJESTY, PERFECTLY DISTINGUISHED, HIS LEGIONS OF ANGELS SING TO HIM:

TO YOU AND YOU ALONE, TO YOU, YES YOU INDEED, TO YOU, ONLY YOU, TO YOU, ALMIGHTY, IS THE SOVEREIGNTY. TO HIM PRAISE IS BECOMING: TO HIM IT IS EVER DUE.

אַדִּיר בִּמְלוּכָה. בָּחוּר כַּהֲלָכָה. גְּדוּדָיו יֹאמְרוּ לוֹ. לְךָ וּלְךָ. לְךָ כִּי לְךָ. לְךָ אַף לְךָ. לְךָ יְהוה הַמַּמְלָכָה: כִּי לוֹ נָאֶה. כִּי לוֹ יָאֶה:

PREEMINENT IN HIS ROYALTY, GLORIOUS INDEED, HIS FAITHFUL SAY TO HIM:

TO YOU AND YOU ALONE, TO YOU, YES YOU INDEED, TO YOU, ONLY YOU, TO YOU, ALMIGHTY, IS THE SOVEREIGNTY. TO HIM PRAISE IS BECOMING: TO HIM IT IS EVER DUE.

דָּגוּל בִּמְלוּכָה. הָדוּר כַּהֲלָכָה. וָתִיקָיו יֹאמְרוּ לוֹ. לְךָ וּלְךָ. לְךָ כִּי לְךָ. לְךָ אַף לְךָ. לְךָ יְהוה הַמַּמְלָכָה: כִּי לוֹ נָאֶה. כִּי לוֹ יָאֶה:

PURE IN HIS KINGSHIP, ABSOLUTELY POWERFUL, HIS ATTENDANTS SAY TO HIM:

TO YOU AND YOU ALONE, TO YOU, YES YOU INDEED, TO YOU,

זַכַּאי בִּמְלוּכָה. חָסִין כַּהֲלָכָה. טַפְסְרָיו יֹאמְרוּ לוֹ. לְךָ וּלְךָ. לְךָ כִּי לְךָ. לְךָ אַף לְךָ. לְךָ יְהוה

ONLY YOU, TO YOU, ALMIGHTY, IS THE SOVEREIGNTY. TO HIM PRAISE IS BECOMING: TO HIM IT IS EVER DUE.

UNIQUE IN HIS DOMINION, TRULY OMNIPOTENT, HIS DISCIPLES SAY TO HIM:

TO YOU AND YOU ALONE, TO YOU, YES YOU INDEED, TO YOU, ONLY YOU, TO YOU, ALMIGHTY, IS THE SOVEREIGNTY. TO HIM PRAISE IS BECOMING: TO HIM IT IS EVER DUE.

FOREMOST IN HIS RULE, MOST REVERED, THE HOSTS SURROUNDING HIM SAY:

TO YOU AND YOU ALONE, TO YOU, YES YOU INDEED, TO YOU, ONLY YOU, TO YOU, ALMIGHTY, IS THE SOVEREIGNTY. TO HIM PRAISE IS BECOMING: TO HIM IT IS EVER DUE.

HUMBLE IN HIS RULE, WHO PERFECTLY REDEEMS, HIS RIGHTEOUS SAY TO HIM:

TO YOU AND YOU ALONE, TO YOU, YES YOU INDEED, TO YOU, ONLY YOU, TO YOU, ALMIGHTY, IS THE SOVEREIGNTY. TO HIM PRAISE IS BECOMING: TO HIM IT IS EVER DUE.

MOST HOLY IN HIS KINGDOM, VERILY MERCIFUL, HIS SHINANIM SAY TO HIM:

TO YOU AND YOU ALONE, TO YOU, YES YOU INDEED, TO YOU,

הַמַּמְלָכָה: כִּי לוֹ נָאֶה. כִּי לוֹ יָאֶה:

כַּבִּיר בִּמְלוּכָה. **יָ**חִיד **לְ**מוּדָיו יֹאמְרוּ כַּהֲלָכָה. לוֹ. לְךָ וּלְךָ. לְךָ כִּי לְךָ. לְךָ אַף לְךָ. לְךָ יְהֹוָה הַמַּמְלָכָה: כִּי לוֹ נָאֶה. כִּי לוֹ יָאֶה:

נוֹרָא בִּמְלוּכָה. **מ**וֹשֵׁל **ס**בִיבָיו יֹאמְרוּ כַּהֲלָכָה. לוֹ. לְךָ וּלְךָ. לְךָ כִּי לְךָ. לְךָ אַף לְךָ. לְךָ יְהֹוָה הַמַּמְלָכָה: כִּי לוֹ נָאֶה. כִּי לוֹ יָאֶה:

פּוֹדֶה בִּמְלוּכָה. **עָ**נִיו **צ**דִּיקָיו יֹאמְרוּ כַּהֲלָכָה. לוֹ. לְךָ וּלְךָ. לְךָ כִּי לְךָ. לְךָ אַף לְךָ. לְךָ יְהֹוָה הַמַּמְלָכָה: כִּי לוֹ נָאֶה. כִּי לוֹ יָאֶה:

רַחוּם בִּמְלוּכָה. **קָ**דוֹשׁ **שׁ**נְאַנָּיו יֹאמְרוּ כַּהֲלָכָה. לוֹ. לְךָ וּלְךָ. לְךָ כִּי לְךָ. לְךָ אַף לְךָ. לְךָ יְהֹוָה

ONLY YOU, TO YOU, ALMIGHTY, IS THE SOVEREIGNTY. TO HIM PRAISE IS BECOMING: TO HIM IT IS EVER DUE.

הַמַּמְלָכָה: כִּי לוֹ נָאֶה. כִּי
לוֹ יָאֶה:

ALMIGHTY IN HIS MONARCHY, HE SUPPORTS PERFECTLY, HIS WHOLE ONES SAY TO HIM:

TO YOU AND YOU ALONE, TO YOU, YES YOU INDEED, TO YOU, ONLY YOU, TO YOU, ALMIGHTY, IS THE SOVEREIGNTY. TO HIM PRAISE IS BECOMING: TO HIM IT IS EVER DUE.

תַּקִּיף בִּמְלוּכָה. תּוֹמֵךְ
כַּהֲלָכָה. תְּמִימָיו יֹאמְרוּ
לוֹ. לְךָ וּלְךָ. לְךָ כִּי לְךָ. לְךָ
אַף לְךָ. לְךָ יהוה
הַמַּמְלָכָה: כִּי לוֹ נָאֶה. כִּי
לוֹ יָאֶה:

HE WHO IS MOST MIGHTY:

אַדִּיר הוּא

MAY HE WHO IS MOST MIGHTY SOON REBUILD HIS HOUSE; SPEEDILY, SPEEDILY, PROMPTLY IN OUR DAYS; ALMIGHTY REBUILD, O ALMIGHTY REBUILD, REBUILD YOUR HOUSE IN GOOD TIME.

אַדִּיר הוּא. יִבְנֶה בֵּיתוֹ
בְּקָרוֹב. בִּמְהֵרָה, בִּמְהֵרָה,
בְּיָמֵינוּ, בְּקָרוֹב. אֵל, בְּנֵה,
אֵל, בְּנֵה. בְּנֵה בֵּיתְךָ
בְּקָרוֹב:

MAY HE WHO IS THE SUPREME, THE GREATEST, PRE-EMINENT, SOON REBUILD HIS HOUSE; SPEEDILY, SPEEDILY, PROMPTLY IN OUR DAYS; ALMIGHTY REBUILD, O ALMIGHTY REBUILD, REBUILD YOUR HOUSE IN GOOD TIME.

בָּחוּר הוּא. גָּדוֹל הוּא.
דָּגוּל הוּא. יִבְנֶה בֵּיתוֹ
בְּקָרוֹב. בִּמְהֵרָה, בִּמְהֵרָה,
בְּיָמֵינוּ, בְּקָרוֹב. אֵל, בְּנֵה,
אֵל, בְּנֵה. בְּנֵה בֵּיתְךָ
בְּקָרוֹב:

MAY HE WHO IS ALL-GLORIOUS AND FAITHFUL, REFINED AND RIGHTEOUS; SOON REBUILD HIS HOUSE; SPEEDILY, SPEEDILY, PROMPTLY IN OUR

הָדוּר הוּא. וָתִיק הוּא.
זַכַּאי הוּא. חָסִיד הוּא.
יִבְנֶה בֵּיתוֹ בְּקָרוֹב.

DAYS; ALMIGHTY REBUILD, O ALMIGHTY REBUILD, REBUILD YOUR HOUSE IN GOOD TIME.

בִּמְהֵרָה, בִּמְהֵרָה, בְּיָמֵינוּ, בְּקָרוֹב. אֵל, בְּנֵה, אֵל, בְּנֵה. בְּנֵה בֵיתְךָ בְּקָרוֹב:

MAY HE WHO IS PURE, SINGULAR, POWERFUL AND ALL-WISE, MAJESTIC, AWESOME, SUBLIME, AND MIGHTY; REDEEMER AND RIGHTEOUS, SOON REBUILD HIS HOUSE; SPEEDILY, SPEEDILY, PROMPTLY IN OUR DAYS; ALMIGHTY, REBUILD, O ALMIGHTY REBUILD, REBUILD YOUR HOUSE IN GOOD TIME.

טָהוֹר הוּא. **יָ**חִיד הוּא. **כַּ**בִּיר הוּא. **לָ**מוּד הוּא. **מֶ**לֶךְ הוּא. **נוֹ**רָא הוּא. **סַ**גִּיב הוּא. **עִ**זּוּז הוּא. **פּוֹ**דֶה הוּא. **צַ**דִּיק הוּא. יִבְנֶה בֵיתוֹ בְּקָרוֹב: בִּמְהֵרָה, בִּמְהֵרָה, בְּיָמֵינוּ, בְּקָרוֹב. אֵל, בְּנֵה, אֵל, בְּנֵה. בְּנֵה בֵיתְךָ בְּקָרוֹב:

MAY HE WHO IS MOST HOLY AND MERCIFUL, THE ALMIGHTY AND OMNIPOTENT, SOON REBUILD HIS HOUSE; SPEEDILY, SPEEDILY, PROMPTLY IN OUR DAYS; ALMIGHTY REBUILD, O ALMIGHTY REBUILD, REBUILD YOUR HOUSE IN GOOD TIME.

קָדוֹשׁ הוּא **רַ**חוּם הוּא. **שַׁ**דַּי הוּא. **תַּ**קִּיף הוּא. יִבְנֶה בֵיתוֹ בְּקָרוֹב. בִּמְהֵרָה בִּמְהֵרָה בְּיָמֵינוּ בְּקָרוֹב. אֵל בְּנֵה אֵל בְּנֵה. בְּנֵה בֵיתְךָ בְּקָרוֹב:

WHO KNOWS ONE?

אֶחָד מִי יוֹדֵעַ.

I KNOW ONE: ONE IS THE ALMIGHTY IN THE HEAVENS AND ON EARTH.

אֶחָד אֲנִי יוֹדֵעַ. אֶחָד אֱלֹהֵינוּ שֶׁבַּשָּׁמַיִם וּבָאָרֶץ:

WHO KNOWS TWO?

שְׁנַיִם מִי יוֹדֵעַ.

I KNOW TWO: TWO ARE THE TABLETS OF THE COVENANT,

שְׁנַיִם אֲנִי יוֹדֵעַ. שְׁנֵי לֻחוֹת

ONE IS THE ALMIGHTY IN THE HEAVENS AND ON EARTH.

WHO KNOWS THREE?

I KNOW THREE: THREE ARE PATRIARCHS, TWO ARE THE TABLETS OF THE COVENANT AND ONE IS THE ALMIGHTY IN THE HEAVENS AND ON EARTH.

WHO KNOWS FOUR?

I KNOW FOUR: FOUR ARE THE MATRIARCHS, THREE ARE THE PATRIARCHS, TWO ARE THE TABLETS OF THE COVENANT, ONE IS THE ALMIGHTY IN THE HEAVENS AND ON EARTH.

WHO KNOWS FIVE?

I KNOW FIVE: FIVE ARE THE BOOKS OF THE TORAH, FOUR ARE THE MATRIARCHS, THREE ARE THE PATRIARCHS, TWO ARE THE TABLETS OF THE COVENANT, ONE IS THE ALMIGHTY IN THE HEAVENS AND ON EARTH.

WHO KNOWS SIX?

I KNOW SIX: SIX ARE THE ORDERS OF THE MISHNAH, FIVE ARE THE BOOKS OF THE TORAH, FOUR ARE THE MATRIARCHS, THREE ARE THE PATRIARCHS, TWO ARE THE TABLETS OF THE COVENANT, ONE IS THE ALMIGHTY IN THE HEAVENS AND ON EARTH.

הַבְּרִית. אֶחָד אֱלֹהֵינוּ שֶׁבַּשָּׁמַיִם וּבָאָרֶץ.

שְׁלֹשָׁה מִי יוֹדֵעַ. שְׁלֹשָׁה אֲנִי יוֹדֵעַ. שְׁלֹשָׁה אָבוֹת. שְׁנֵי לֻחוֹת הַבְּרִית. אֶחָד אֱלֹהֵינוּ שֶׁבַּשָּׁמַיִם וּבָאָרֶץ.

אַרְבַּע מִי יוֹדֵעַ. אַרְבַּע אֲנִי יוֹדֵעַ. אַרְבַּע אִמָהוֹת. שְׁלֹשָׁה אָבוֹת. שְׁנֵי לֻחוֹת הַבְּרִית. אֶחָד אֱלֹהֵינוּ שֶׁבַּשָּׁמַיִם וּבָאָרֶץ.

חֲמִשָּׁה מִי יוֹדֵעַ. חֲמִשָּׁה אֲנִי יוֹדֵעַ. חֲמִשָּׁה חוּמְשֵׁי תוֹרָה. אַרְבַּע אִמָהוֹת. שְׁלֹשָׁה אָבוֹת. שְׁנֵי לֻחוֹת הַבְּרִית. אֶחָד אֱלֹהֵינוּ שֶׁבַּשָּׁמַיִם וּבָאָרֶץ.

שִׁשָׁה מִי יוֹדֵעַ. שִׁשָׁה אֲנִי יוֹדֵעַ. שִׁשָׁה סִדְרֵי מִשְׁנָה. חֲמִשָּׁה חוּמְשֵׁי תוֹרָה. אַרְבַּע אִמָהוֹת. שְׁלֹשָׁה אָבוֹת. שְׁנֵי לֻחוֹת הַבְּרִית. אֶחָד אֱלֹהֵינוּ שֶׁבַּשָּׁמַיִם וּבָאָרֶץ.

WHO KNOWS SEVEN?

I KNOW SEVEN: SEVEN ARE THE DAYS OF THE WEEK, SIX ARE THE ORDERS OF THE MISHNAH, FIVE ARE THE BOOKS OF THE TORAH, FOUR ARE THE MATRIARCHS, THREE ARE THE PATRIARCHS, TWO ARE THE TABLETS OF THE COVENANT, ONE IS THE ALMIGHTY IN THE HEAVENS AND ON EARTH.

WHO KNOWS EIGHT?

I KNOW EIGHT: EIGHT ARE THE DAYS TILL BRIS MILAH, SEVEN ARE THE DAYS OF THE WEEK, SIX ARE THE ORDERS OF THE MISHNAH, FIVE ARE THE BOOKS OF THE TORAH, FOUR ARE THE MATRIARCHS, THREE ARE THE PATRIARCHS, TWO ARE THE TABLETS OF THE COVENANT, ONE IS THE ALMIGHTY IN THE HEAVENS AND ON EARTH.

WHO KNOWS NINE?

I KNOW NINE: NINE ARE THE MONTHS PRECEDING CHILDBIRTH, EIGHT ARE THE DAYS TILL BRIS MILAH, SEVEN ARE THE DAYS OF THE WEEK, SIX ARE THE ORDERS OF THE MISHNAH, FIVE ARE THE BOOKS OF THE TORAH, FOUR ARE THE MATRIARCHS, THREE ARE THE PATRIARCHS, TWO ARE THE TABLETS OF THE COVENANT, ONE IS THE ALMIGHTY IN THE

שִׁבְעָה מִי יוֹדֵעַ.

שִׁבְעָה אֲנִי יוֹדֵעַ. שִׁבְעָה יְמֵי שַׁבַּתָּא. שִׁשָּׁה סִדְרֵי מִשְׁנָה. חֲמִשָּׁה חוּמְשֵׁי תוֹרָה. אַרְבַּע אִמָּהוֹת. שְׁלֹשָׁה אָבוֹת. שְׁנֵי לֻחוֹת הַבְּרִית. אֶחָד אֱלֹהֵינוּ שֶׁבַּשָּׁמַיִם וּבָאָרֶץ.

שְׁמוֹנָה מִי יוֹדֵעַ.

שְׁמוֹנָה אֲנִי יוֹדֵעַ. שְׁמוֹנָה יְמֵי מִילָה. שִׁבְעָה יְמֵי שַׁבַּתָּא. שִׁשָּׁה סִדְרֵי מִשְׁנָה. חֲמִשָּׁה חוּמְשֵׁי תוֹרָה. אַרְבַּע אִמָּהוֹת. שְׁלֹשָׁה אָבוֹת. שְׁנֵי לֻחוֹת הַבְּרִית. אֶחָד אֱלֹהֵינוּ שֶׁבַּשָּׁמַיִם וּבָאָרֶץ.

תִּשְׁעָה מִי יוֹדֵעַ.

תִּשְׁעָה אֲנִי יוֹדֵעַ. תִּשְׁעָה יַרְחֵי לֵידָה. שְׁמוֹנָה יְמֵי מִילָה. שִׁבְעָה יְמֵי שַׁבַּתָּא. שִׁשָּׁה סִדְרֵי מִשְׁנָה. חֲמִשָּׁה חוּמְשֵׁי תוֹרָה. אַרְבַּע אִמָּהוֹת. שְׁלֹשָׁה אָבוֹת. שְׁנֵי לֻחוֹת הַבְּרִית. אֶחָד אֱלֹהֵינוּ שֶׁבַּשָּׁמַיִם וּבָאָרֶץ.

HEAVENS AND ON EARTH.

WHO KNOWS TEN?

I KNOW TEN: TEN ARE THE TEN COMMANDMENTS, NINE ARE THE MONTHS PRECEDING CHILDBIRTH, EIGHT ARE THE DAYS TILL BRIS MILAH, SEVEN ARE THE DAYS OF THE WEEK, SIX ARE THE ORDERS OF THE MISHNAH, FIVE ARE THE BOOKS OF THE TORAH, FOUR ARE THE MATRIARCHS, THREE ARE THE PATRIARCHS, TWO ARE THE TABLETS OF THE COVENANT, ONE IS THE ALMIGHTY IN THE HEAVENS AND ON EARTH.

WHO KNOWS ELEVEN?

I KNOW ELEVEN: ELEVEN ARE THE STARS [IN JOSEPH'S DREAM], TEN ARE THE TEN COMMAND-MENTS, NINE ARE THE MONTHS PRECEDING CHILDBIRTH, EIGHT ARE THE DAYS TILL BRIS MILAH, SEVEN ARE THE DAYS OF THE WEEK, SIX ARE THE ORDERS OF THE MISHNAH, FIVE ARE THE BOOKS OF THE TORAH, FOUR ARE THE MATRI-ARCHS, THREE ARE THE PATRI-ARCHS, TWO ARE THE TABLETS OF THE COVENANT, ONE IS THE ALMIGHTY IN THE HEAVENS AND ON EARTH.

WHO KNOWS TWELVE?

I KNOW TWELVE: TWELVE ARE THE TRIBES [OF ISRAEL], ELEVEN

עֲשָׂרָה מִי יוֹדֵעַ. עֲשָׂרָה אֲנִי יוֹדֵעַ. עֲשָׂרָה דִבְּרַיָא. תִּשְׁעָה יַרְחֵי לֵידָה. שְׁמוֹנָה יְמֵי מִילָה. שִׁבְעָה יְמֵי שַׁבַּתָּא. שִׁשָּׁה סִדְרֵי מִשְׁנָה. חֲמִשָּׁה חוּמְשֵׁי תוֹרָה. אַרְבַּע אִמָּהוֹת. שְׁלֹשָׁה אָבוֹת. שְׁנֵי לֻחוֹת הַבְּרִית. אֶחָד אֱלֹהֵינוּ שֶׁבַּשָּׁמַיִם וּבָאָרֶץ.

אַחַד עָשָׂר מִי יוֹדֵעַ. אַחַד עָשָׂר אֲנִי יוֹדֵעַ. אַחַד עָשָׂר כּוֹכְבַיָּא. עֲשָׂרָה דִבְּרַיָא. תִּשְׁעָה יַרְחֵי לֵידָה. שְׁמוֹנָה יְמֵי מִילָה. שִׁבְעָה יְמֵי שַׁבַּתָּא. שִׁשָּׁה סִדְרֵי מִשְׁנָה. חֲמִשָּׁה חוּמְשֵׁי תוֹרָה. אַרְבַּע אִמָּהוֹת. שְׁלֹשָׁה אָבוֹת. שְׁנֵי לֻחוֹת הַבְּרִית. אֶחָד אֱלֹהֵינוּ שֶׁבַּשָּׁמַיִם וּבָאָרֶץ.

שְׁנֵים עָשָׂר מִי יוֹדֵעַ. שְׁנֵים עָשָׂר אֲנִי יוֹדֵעַ. שְׁנֵים

ARE THE STARS [IN JOSEPH'S DREAM], TEN ARE THE TEN COMMANDMENTS, NINE ARE THE MONTHS PRECEDING CHILDBIRTH, EIGHT ARE THE DAYS TILL BRIS MILAH, SEVEN ARE THE DAYS OF THE WEEK, SIX ARE THE ORDERS OF THE MISHNAH, FIVE ARE THE BOOKS OF THE TORAH, FOUR ARE THE MATRIARCHS, THREE ARE THE PATRIARCHS, TWO ARE THE TABLETS OF THE COVENANT, ONE IS THE ALMIGHTY IN THE HEAVENS AND ON EARTH.

עָשָׂר שִׁבְטַיָּא. אַחַד עָשָׂר כּוֹכְבַיָּא. עֲשָׂרָה דִבְּרַיָּא. תִּשְׁעָה יַרְחֵי לֵידָה. שְׁמוֹנָה יְמֵי מִילָה. שִׁבְעָה יְמֵי שַׁבַּתָּא. שִׁשָּׁה סִדְרֵי מִשְׁנָה. חֲמִשָּׁה חוּמְשֵׁי תוֹרָה. אַרְבַּע אִמָּהוֹת. שְׁלֹשָׁה אָבוֹת. שְׁנֵי לֻחוֹת הַבְּרִית. אֶחָד אֱלֹהֵינוּ שֶׁבַּשָּׁמַיִם וּבָאָרֶץ.

WHO KNOWS THIRTEEN?

I KNOW THIRTEEN: THIRTEEN ARE THE DIVINE ATTRIBUTES [OF THE ALMIGHTY], TWELVE ARE THE TRIBES [OF ISRAEL], ELEVEN ARE THE STARS [IN JOSEPH'S DREAM], TEN ARE THE TEN COMMANDMENTS, NINE ARE THE MONTHS PRECEDING CHILDBIRTH, EIGHT ARE THE DAYS TILL BRIS MILAH, SEVEN ARE THE DAYS OF THE WEEK, SIX ARE THE ORDERS OF THE MISHNAH, FIVE ARE THE BOOKS OF THE TORAH, FOUR ARE THE MATRIARCHS, THREE ARE THE PATRIARCHS, TWO ARE THE TABLETS OF THE COVENANT, ONE IS THE ALMIGHTY IN THE HEAVENS AND ON EARTH.

שְׁלֹשָׁה עָשָׂר מִי יוֹדֵעַ. שְׁלֹשָׁה עָשָׂר אֲנִי יוֹדֵעַ. שְׁלֹשָׁה עָשָׂר מִדַּיָּא. שְׁנֵים עָשָׂר שִׁבְטַיָּא. אַחַד עָשָׂר כּוֹכְבַיָּא. עֲשָׂרָה דִבְּרַיָּא. תִּשְׁעָה יַרְחֵי לֵידָה. שְׁמוֹנָה יְמֵי מִילָה. שִׁבְעָה יְמֵי שַׁבַּתָּא. שִׁשָּׁה סִדְרֵי מִשְׁנָה. חֲמִשָּׁה חוּמְשֵׁי תוֹרָה. אַרְבַּע אִמָּהוֹת. שְׁלֹשָׁה אָבוֹת. שְׁנֵי לֻחוֹת הַבְּרִית. אֶחָד אֱלֹהֵינוּ שֶׁבַּשָּׁמַיִם וּבָאָרֶץ.

ONE KID, ONE KID WHICH FATHER BOUGHT FOR TWO ZUZIM.

ONE KID, ONE KID.

AND THE CAT CAME AND ATE THE KID, WHICH FATHER BOUGHT FOR TWO ZUZIM.

ONE KID, ONE KID.

AND THE DOG CAME AND BIT THE CAT, THAT ATE THE KID, WHICH FATHER BOUGHT FOR TWO ZUZIM.

ONE KID, ONE KID.

AND THE STICK CAME AND HIT THE DOG, THAT BIT THE CAT, THAT ATE THE KID, WHICH FATHER BOUGHT FOR TWO ZUZIM.

ONE KID, ONE KID.

AND THE FIRE CAME AND BURNED THE STICK, THAT HIT THE DOG, THAT BIT THE CAT, THAT ATE THE KID, WHICH FATHER BOUGHT FOR TWO ZUZIM.

ONE KID, ONE KID.

AND THE WATER CAME AND EXTINGUISHED THE FIRE, THAT BURNED THE STICK, THAT HIT THE DOG, THAT BIT THE CAT, THAT ATE THE KID, WHICH FATHER BOUGHT FOR TWO ZUZIM.

ONE KID, ONE KID.

חַד גַּדְיָא. חַד גַּדְיָא.

דְּזַבִּין אַבָּא בִּתְרֵי זוּזֵי, חַד גַּדְיָא. חַד גַּדְיָא:

וְאָתָא שׁוּנְרָא, וְאָכְלָה לְגַדְיָא. דְּזַבִּין אַבָּא בִּתְרֵי זוּזֵי. חַד גַּדְיָא. חַד גַּדְיָא:

וְאָתָא כַלְבָּא, וְנָשַׁךְ לְשׁוּנְרָא. דְּאָכְלָה לְגַדְיָא. דְּזַבִּין אַבָּא בִּתְרֵי זוּזֵי. חַד גַּדְיָא. חַד גַּדְיָא:

וְאָתָא חוּטְרָא, וְהִכָּה לְכַלְבָּא. דְּנָשַׁךְ לְשׁוּנְרָא. דְּאָכְלָה לְגַדְיָא. דְּזַבִּין אַבָּא בִּתְרֵי זוּזֵי. חַד גַּדְיָא. חַד גַּדְיָא:

וְאָתָא נוּרָא, וְשָׂרַף לְחוּטְרָא. דְּהִכָּה לְכַלְבָּא. דְּנָשַׁךְ לְשׁוּנְרָא. דְּאָכְלָה לְגַדְיָא. דְּזַבִּין אַבָּא בִּתְרֵי זוּזֵי. חַד גַּדְיָא. חַד גַּדְיָא:

וְאָתָא מַיָּא, וְכָבָה לְנוּרָא. דְּשָׂרַף לְחוּטְרָא. דְּהִכָּה לְכַלְבָּא. דְּנָשַׁךְ לְשׁוּנְרָא. דְּאָכְלָה לְגַדְיָא. דְּזַבִּין אַבָּא בִּתְרֵי זוּזֵי. חַד גַּדְיָא. חַד גַּדְיָא:

AND THE OX CAME AND DRANK THE WATER, THAT EXTINGUISHED THE FIRE, THAT BURNED THE STICK, THAT HIT THE DOG, THAT BIT THE CAT, THAT ATE THE KID, WHICH FATHER BOUGHT FOR TWO ZUZIM.

ONE KID, ONE KID.

וְאָתָא תוֹרָא, וְשָׁתָא לְמַיָא. דְּכָבָה לְנוּרָא. דְּשָׂרַף לְחוּטְרָא. דְּהִכָּה לְכַלְבָּא. דְּנָשַׁךְ לְשׁוּנְרָא. דְּאָכְלָה לְגַדְיָא. דְּזַבִּין אַבָּא בִּתְרֵי זוּזֵי. חַד גַּדְיָא. חַד גַּדְיָא:

AND THE SLAUGHTERER CAME AND KILLED THE OX, THAT DRANK THE WATER, THAT EXTINGUISHED THE FIRE, THAT BURNED THE STICK, THAT HIT THE DOG, THAT BIT THE CAT, THAT ATE THE KID, WHICH FATHER BOUGHT FOR TWO ZUZIM.

ONE KID, ONE KID.

וְאָתָא הַשּׁוֹחֵט, וְשָׁחַט לְתוֹרָא. דְּשָׁתָא לְמַיָא. דְּכָבָה לְנוּרָא. דְּשָׂרַף לְחוּטְרָא. דְּהִכָּה לְכַלְבָּא. דְּנָשַׁךְ לְשׁוּנְרָא. דְּאָכְלָה לְגַדְיָא. דְּזַבִּין אַבָּא בִּתְרֵי זוּזֵי. חַד גַּדְיָא. חַד גַּדְיָא:

AND THE ANGEL OF DEATH CAME AND SLEW THE SLAUGH-TERER, THAT KILLED THE OX, THAT DRANK THE WATER, THAT EXTINGUISHED THE FIRE, THAT BURNED THE STICK, THAT HIT THE DOG, THAT BIT THE CAT, THAT ATE THE KID, WHICH FATHER BOUGHT FOR TWO ZUZIM.

ONE KID, ONE KID.

וְאָתָא מַלְאָךְ הַמָּוֶת, וְשָׁחַט לְשׁוֹחֵט. דְּשָׁחַט לְתוֹרָא. דְּשָׁתָא לְמַיָא. דְּכָבָה לְנוּרָא. דְּשָׂרַף לְחוּטְרָא. דְּהִכָּה לְכַלְבָּא. דְּנָשַׁךְ לְשׁוּנְרָא. דְּאָכְלָה לְגַדְיָא. דְּזַבִּין אַבָּא בִּתְרֵי זוּזֵי. חַד גַּדְיָא. חַד גַּדְיָא:

AND THE HOLY ONE, BLESSED IS HE, DESTROYED THE ANGEL OF DEATH, THAT SLEW THE SLAUGHTERER, THAT KILLED THE OX, THAT DRANK THE WATER, THAT EXTINGUISHED

וְאָתָא הַקָּדוֹשׁ בָּרוּךְ הוּא. וְשָׁחַט לְמַלְאָךְ הַמָּוֶת. דְּשָׁחַט לְשׁוֹחֵט. דְּשָׁחַט לְתוֹרָא. דְּשָׁתָא לְמַיָא.

THE FIRE, THAT BURNED THE STICK, THAT HIT THE DOG, THAT BIT THE CAT, THAT ATE THE KID, WHICH FATHER BOUGHT FOR TWO ZUZIM.

ONE KID, ONE KID.

דְּכָבָה לְנוּרָא. דְּשָׂרַף לְחוּטְרָא. דְּהִכָּה לְכַלְבָּא. דְּנָשַׁךְ לְשׁוּנְרָא. דְּאָכְלָה לְגַדְיָא. דְּזַבִּין אַבָּא בִּתְרֵי זוּזֵי. חַד גַּדְיָא. חַד גַּדְיָא:

APPENDICES

APPENDIX A

Time Lines of the Exodus

We are instructed by the Haggadah: every Jew *"...is obligated to view himself as having gone out of Egypt."* We are thus directed to make the Exodus a part of our personal history and life experience.

The time lines that follow are constructed to enable the reader to quickly and efficently gain an historical perspective of the Exodus, thus helping internalize the Seder's message.

Birth of the Jewish Nation in the Context of History

History was born in the first millisecond after Creation and is the sum total of God and man's interaction. Through the proper study of history we gain deep insights into ourselves and the Divine.

The time line below, the first of four presented, offers a basic perspective of all history from Creation, locating the birth of the Jewish Nation in the Divine scheme.

What is striking is not how distant and removed we are from Adam and Eve, Abraham and Moses, David and Solomon, and Maimonides, but how close we are to all these historic figures.

The dates listed are found either explicitly in the Bible and Talmud or are well documented by classical Jewish historians.

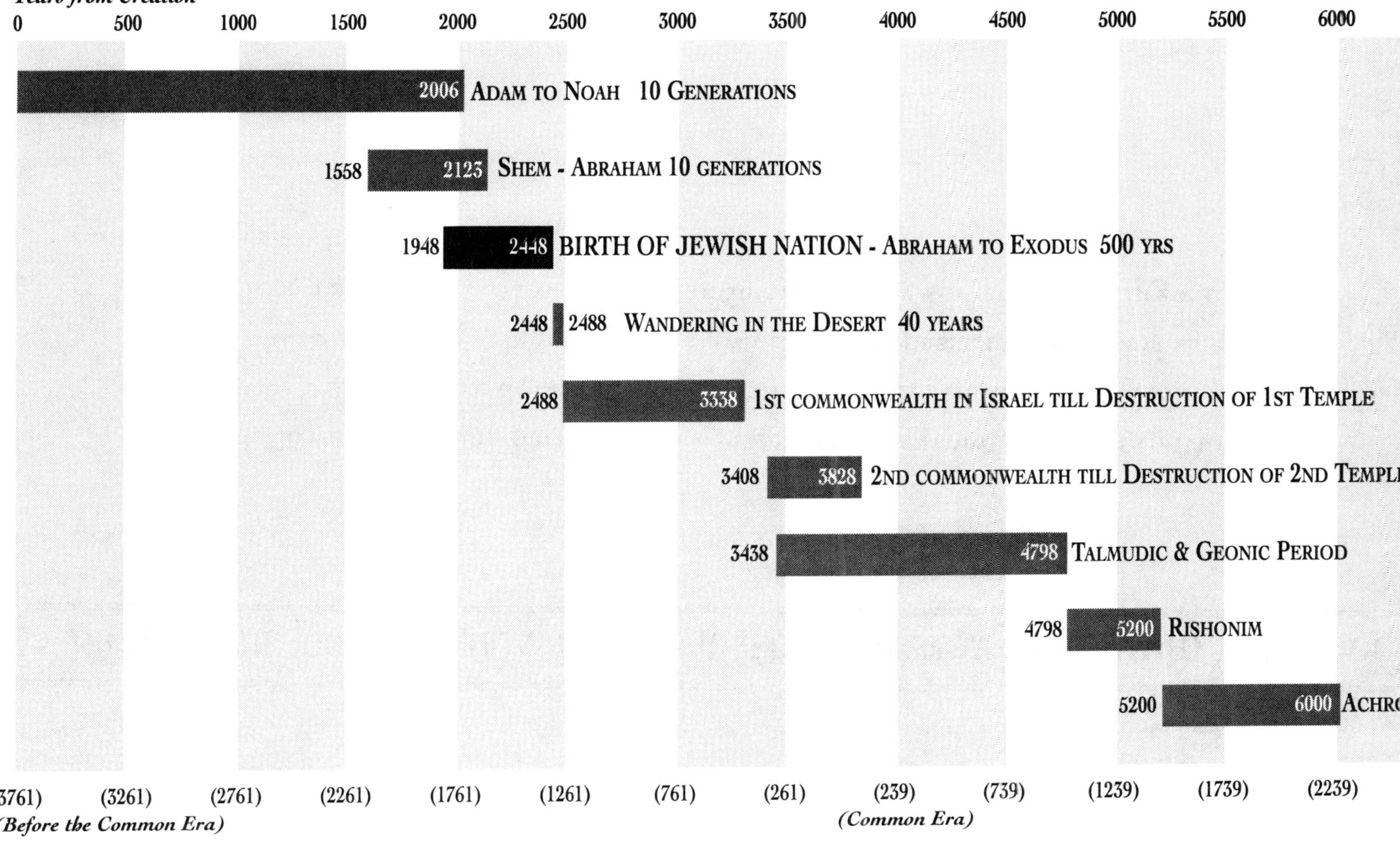

Years from Creation
0   500   1000   1500   2000   2500   3000   3500   4000   4500   5000   5500   6000
2006   ADAM TO NOAH   10 GENERATIONS
1558   2123   SHEM - ABRAHAM 10 generations
1948   2448   BIRTH OF JEWISH NATION - ABRAHAM TO EXODUS   500 YRS
2448   2488   WANDERING IN THE DESERT   40 YEARS
2488   3338   1ST COMMONWEALTH IN ISRAEL TILL DESTRUCTION OF 1ST TEMPLE
3408   3828   2ND COMMONWEALTH TILL DESTRUCTION OF 2ND TEMPLE
3438   4798   TALMUDIC & GEONIC PERIOD
4798   5200   RISHONIM
5200   6000   ACHRONIM
(3761)   (3261)   (2761)   (2261)   (1761)   (1261)   (761)   (261)   (239)   (739)   (1239)   (1739)   (2239)
(Before the Common Era)
(Common Era)

Birth of the Jewish Nation: Five Hundred Years from Abraham to the Exodus

The following time line details the seven generations from Abraham to Moses.
Moses was a mature adult of thirty when his father Amram died. Amram, in turn, was seventy-one when Levi, (his grandfather), passed away. Levi knew both Jacob and Isaac. Moses' father intimately knew someone who grew up with the patriarchs!

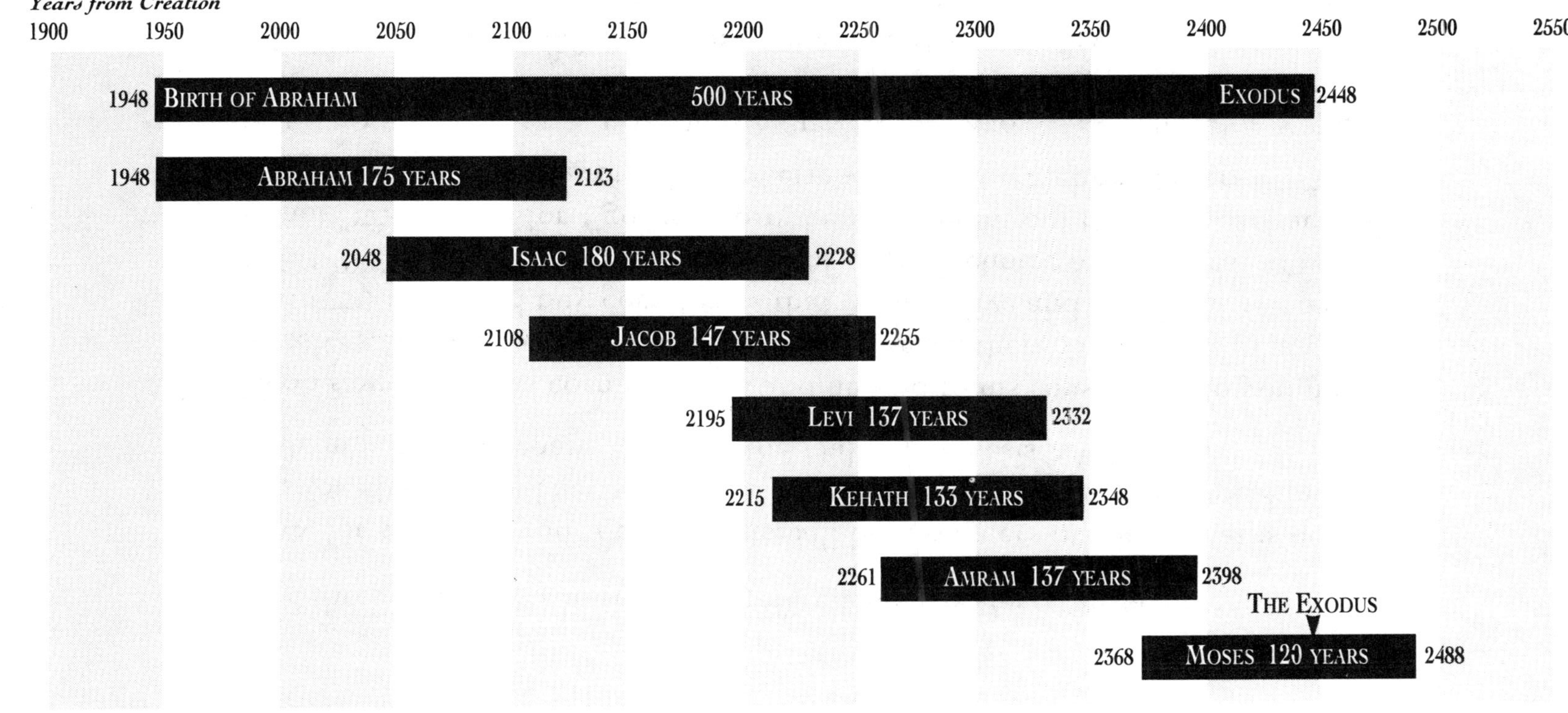

Years from Creation
1900 1950 2000 2050 2100 2150 2200 2250 2300 2350 2400 2450 2500 2550
1948 Birth of Abraham 500 Years Exodus 2448
1948 Abraham 175 years 2123
2048 Isaac 180 years 2228
2108 Jacob 147 years 2255
2195 Levi 137 years 2332
2215 Kehath 133 years 2348
2261 Amram 137 years 2398
The Exodus
2368 Moses 120 years 2488
(1861) (1811) (1761) (1711) (1661) (1611) (1561) (1511) (1461) (1361) (1311) (1261) (1211)
(Before the Common Era)

THE EGYPTIAN EXPERIENCE: THE THREE TIME SPANS MENTIONED IN THE BIBLE

We find three time spans in the Bible referencing the Jews' enslavement in Egypt:

1. "Know for sure that your descendants will be foreigners in a land that is not theirs for 400 years. They will be enslaved and oppressed". (God speaking to Abraham in the Covenant Between the Halves, Genesis XV:13)

2. "Jacob saw there was corn in Egypt and he said to his sons, 'why do you make yourselves an enigma?' And he said, 'I have heard there is corn in Egypt go down (רדו) there and buy corn for us that we may live and not die.' " (Genesis XLII: 1-2) The Rabbinic interpretation of Jacob's choice of the word "רדו" (r'du) and not "לכו" (l'chu) for "go" is to prophetically point out the 210 years actually spent by the Jews in Egypt - the numeric value of the Hebrew letters ר-ד-ו is 210.

3. "And the Israelites' time of dwelling in Egypt was 430 years." (Exodus XII:40)

The Rabbis point out: 430 years corresponds to the years from the Covenant Between the Halves to the Exodus, 400 years span the birth of Isaac through the Exodus, and 210 years is the actual time spent by the Israelites in Egypt.

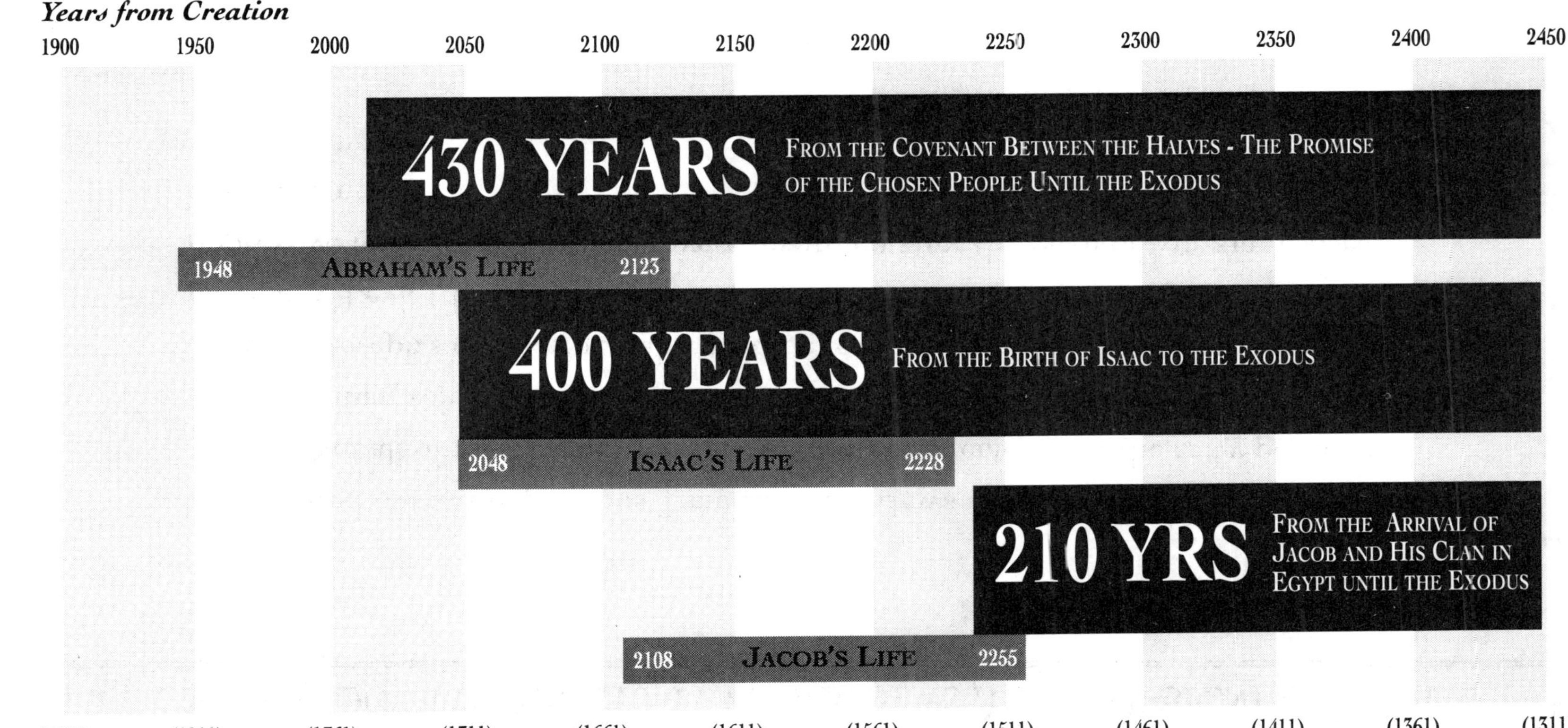

Years from Creation
1900   1950   2000   2050   2100   2150   2200   2250   2300   2350   2400   2450
430 YEARS   FROM THE COVENANT BETWEEN THE HALVES - THE PROMISE OF THE CHOSEN PEOPLE UNTIL THE EXODUS
1948   ABRAHAM'S LIFE   2123
400 YEARS   FROM THE BIRTH OF ISAAC TO THE EXODUS
2048   ISAAC'S LIFE   2228
210 YRS   FROM THE ARRIVAL OF JACOB AND HIS CLAN IN EGYPT UNTIL THE EXODUS
2108   JACOB'S LIFE   2255
(1861)   (1811)   (1761)   (1711)   (1661)   (1611)   (1561)   (1511)   (1461)   (1411)   (1361)   (1311)
(Before the Common Era)

A Breakdown of the 210 Years the Jews Actually Spent in Egypt

As pointed out in the previous Time Line, the Jews actually spent only 210 years in Egypt. Not all of these years were marked by enslavement. In the early period of their Egyptian sojourn, they were treated well and prospered economically.

After Joseph's death, Pharoah's attitude toward the Jews changed and with the passing of Levi, (the last of Joseph's brothers), the enslavement began. The most oppressive forms of enslavement were instituted after the birth of Miriam, Moses' older sister.

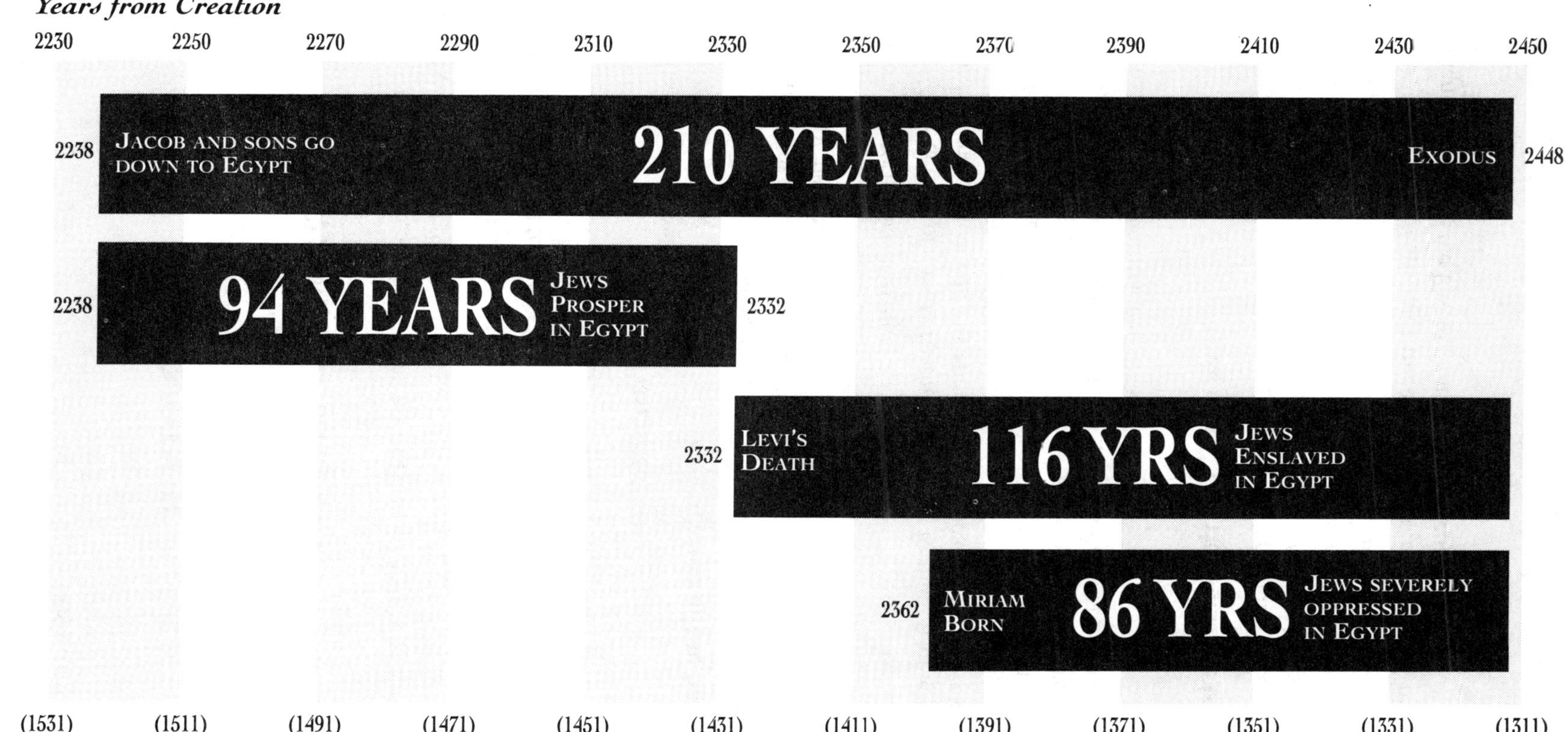

Years from Creation
2230   2250   2270   2290   2310   2330   2350   2370   2390   2410   2430   2450
2238   JACOB AND SONS GO DOWN TO EGYPT   210 YEARS   EXODUS   2448
2238   94 YEARS   JEWS PROSPER IN EGYPT   2332
2332   LEVI'S DEATH   116 YRS   JEWS ENSLAVED IN EGYPT
2362   MIRIAM BORN   86 YRS   JEWS SEVERELY OPPRESSED IN EGYPT
(1531)   (1511)   (1491)   (1471)   (1451)   (1431)   (1411)   (1391)   (1371)   (1351)   (1331)   (1311)
(Before the Common Era)

APPENDIX B

The Mitzvos of Passover

All the Biblical commandments of Passover can be grouped into one of two main categories:

1   Those pertaining to the **Pascal lamb** and

2   those related to *chometz* and *Matzoh*.

1 - The Pascal lamb

Preparation of the Sacrifice

The *Torah* commands us to ritually slaughter a goat or sheep in the afternoon of the 14th day of the lunar month Nissan. The slaughtering can only be performed in the courtyard of the Holy Temple in Jerusalem. (Today, in the absence of the Temple, we are of course unable to perform this *mitzvah*.)

The details of this *mitzvah* include the formation of groups in which each member shares a portion of the Pascal lamb, as well as the special duties of Kohanim throughout the process. If any group member owns *chometz* at the time of the slaughtering it invalidates the Pascal lamb. The animal's innards are removed and placed upon the Temple altar, where they burn overnight. The animal itself must be roasted; any other means of preparation invalidates it.

How and When the Sacrifice is Eaten

Once night falls and the Passover seder commences, we are directed to eat the Pascal lamb, together with *Matzoh* and *Marror*. The law further instructs us to eat the required minimum of an olive-sized portion at the end of the Seder meal, after we are already sated.

The *Torah* enumerates three negative commandments regarding the manner in which the Pascal lamb is to be eaten:

❑ It is forbidden to break any of its bones.

❑ It cannot be taken out of the place which has been designated for its eating, (a fixed, group-chosen location within the walls of Jerusalem).

❑ None of the meat may be left over till morning; whatever has not been consumed must be burned.

As previously stated, since the Holy Temple is no longer standing, we are unable to fulfill the *mitzvahs* requiring animal sacrifice. Therefore, none of the above commandments are performed today. However, several elements of our seder ritual were designed to recall the Pascal lamb.

For those not able to fulfill the requirements of the Pascal lamb in Nissan, the *Torah* prescribed "*Pesach Sheni*", a "second" opportunity to perform the *mitzvah* a month later, on the 15th of Iyar.

Who Eats the Sacrifice?

The commandment of the Pascal lamb is incumbent on both men and women. It is one of two positive commandments which, if violated, incur the severe punishment of kareis (see "The Premise").

There are four categories of people to whom we are not permitted to give any of the Pascal lamb. They are:

❑ A "*ben Neichor*", a Jew who has forsaken his religion for idol worship.

❑ A **partial convert**, someone who has completed part of the conversion process but not all of it, as well as

❑ A "*toshav*", a non-Jewish resident of the land of Israel who has abandoned idol worship.

❑ An "*Orail*", any Jew who has not been circumcised.

2 - Chometz and Matzoh

Chometz

The other major category of *mitzvahs* on Passover pertains to *chometz* and *Matzoh*, leavened and unleavened grain products. There are, in fact, six *mitzvahs* in the *Torah* concerning *chometz*, and one relating to Matzoh.

Removal of all *chometz* from our [*halachic*] possession prior to midday on the 14th of Nissan, the day before Passover, via destruction by fire and/or verbal renouncement of ownership.

Midday of the 14th of Nissan also marks the hour after which it is forbidden to eat *chometz*. For all of Passover proper as well, there is a [separate] prohibition to eat *chometz*.

Not only is *chometz* per se prohibited, but any food mixed with *chometz* is likewise forbidden.

The *Torah* forbids "having" or "seeing" *chometz* in one's possession during the entire holiday. Although the prohibitions against "having" or "seeing" are stated as distinct *mitzvahs*, they are, in reality, warnings against the same violation - the possession of *chometz*. The effect of the multiple phrasing is to double the transgression.

Matzoh

The eating of the *halachically*-specified amount of *Matzoh* on the night of the 15th of Nissan (Seder night) constitutes the fulfillment of a positive commandment, the only one regarding *Matzoh*.

The commandment to retell the Exodus saga is listed by Maimonides as part of the laws of *chometz* and *Matzoh*. This requires some explanation: what indeed does "retelling" have to do with *chometz* and *Matzoh*?

The answer can be gleaned from the words of the *Torah* and *Talmud*. The *Torah* tells us "... seven days you shall eat *Matzohs*, 'lechem oni', because you went forth from the land of Egypt in haste..." (*Deuteronomy XVI:3*) The *Torah* refers to *Matzoh* as "*lechem oni*". But what does *lechem oni* mean? The *Talmud* tells us (Tractate *Pesachim* 36a): "Shmuel said: '*Lechem oni*', [is] bread over which we answer many things." In other words, it is in the presence of *Matzoh* that we are instructed to retell the story of the Exodus. We thus understand Maimonides' pairing the mitzvahs of "retelling" and *Matzoh*.

APPENDIX C

Glossary of Hebrew Terms

Aaron: Older brother of Moses, who assisted in bringing the Divine plagues upon Egypt, served as High Priest during the Israelites' forty years in the desert and was universally beloved for bringing peace between all Jews. (2365-2488 from Creation; 1396-1273 B.C.E.)

Abraham: First of the Jewish nation's patriarchs. Most famous for recognizing God's existence and inculcating that understanding in others. (1948-2123 from Creation; 1813-1638 B.C.E.)

Afikomen: The piece of Matzoh broken off from the middle Matzoh during the Seder. This matzoh is in remembrance of the Pascal lamb eaten in Temple times at the end of the Passover meal. It is customary for children to take the afikomen and hide it until a gift is promised for its return. This is intended to arouse the children's interest and keep them alert till the conclusion of the Seder meal when the afikomen is eaten.

Al Achilas Matzoh: The Hebrew phrase meaning "Concerning the eating of Matzoh", which is the text of the blessing over matzoh.

Al HaMichya: An abridged form of grace which is recited after meals not including bread but rather one of the seven species enumerated in the Torah: wheat, barley, grapes, figs, pomegranates, olives and dates (Deuteronomy VIII:8). It's text is a summary of the first three paragraphs of Birchas HaMazon.

Amorite: A member of the ancient kingdom of Amor, in the land of Canaan (Israel).

Aramaic: Semitic language the Jews acquired after their captivity in Babylonia. The Babylonian Talmud is written in a mixture of Hebrew and Aramaic.

Aruch HaShulchan: A late 19th Century codification of Jewish Law authored by Rabbi Yechiel Michel HaLevi Epstein, Rabbi of the city of Navardhok.

Asher G'alanu: The blessing recited at the conclusion of Maggid.

Ashkenaz (pl.im): The name originally identified with Germany and its Jewry, but later applied to all of Europe. Ashkenaz is contrasted with Sepharad, the Hebrew name for Spain, a term which later encompassed all the Mediterranean and Middle Eastern countries and their Jewish populations.

Avodim Hayinu: The answer the Haggadah gives to the "Four Questions" (Ma

Nishtanah).

Babylonia: Ancient civilization in the fertile crescent (between the Tigris and Euphrates rivers). After the destruction of the first Temple the Jews were exiled to Babylonia (3338 from Creation; 423 B.C.E.). They remained there as a community until approximately the year 1000 C.E.

Bar-Kochba: Leader of the Jewish insurrection against Rome in the Second Century, C.E. Died when the Romans massacred the city of Betar (135 C.E.).

Bar/Bat mitzvah (Aramaic-Hebrew, "son/daughter of the commandment"): A boy or girl who has reached his or her majority (13 years and a day for a boy and 12 years and a day for a girl). The occasion is frequently marked by a celebration. However, the festivity is not to be mistaken with the confirmation of status, which is determined solely by age and biological maturity.

Bedikas Chometz (Hebrew, "search for chometz"): A formal search in the evening of the 14th of Nissan to rid the house of any chometz.

Beis HaMedrash: The Hebrew phrase for "house of Torah study".

Berachos The Hebrew term for "blessings": There are three categories of berachos:

> 1) Those preceding the performance of any Biblical or Rabbinic commandment.
> 2) Praise and thanks in recognition of God's controlling hand in all events, for example, when coming upon a site where a miracle was performed for Israel, giving praise upon seeing the wonders of nature, or expressing appreciation for material possessions such as acquiring a new house or suit of clothing.
> 3) Those performed before enjoying worldly pleasures. One must express gratitude and recognition to God, e.g., before eating, drinking, smelling fragrant scents, etc.

There are only two Biblically required blessings: after eating bread and before studying Torah. The specific text of all blessings however, are rabbinic, having their root in the work of the Great Assembly (circa 3338-3538 from Creation; 423-223 B.C.E.).

Bible: In Jewish law, a specific reference to the Five Books of Moses (Torah). In popular usage, it refers to all 24 books canonized by the sages, which include the Torah, Prophets and Writings.

Biblical Law: Law emanating from the Five Books of Moses or the oral tradition transmitted to Moses by God.

Bikurim (Hebrew, "first fruits"): The annual offering of first fruits harvested in the land of Israel and brought to the Holy Temple, as mentioned in Deuteronomy XXVI:1-11.

Birchas HaMitzvah (Hebrew, "the blessing over the commandment"): Refers to the blessing which precedes the performance of positive commandments.

Birchas HaMazon (Hebrew, "the blessing over meals"): Refers to the grace recited after eating a meal that includes bread. It is based on the Biblical command: "When you eat and are satisfied, you shall bless the Almighty your God for the good land He has given you." (Deuteronomy VIII:10)

Birchas ho'Daah: The Hebrew phrase for "a blessing of thanks" to the Almighty.

Biur: Hebrew term for the "ridding of chometz" from a Jew's possession.

Bo: Third Biblical weekly portion in the Book of Exodus.

Borei P'ri ho'Adama (Hebrew, "creates the fruit of the ground"): The text of the blessing recited prior to eating vegetables.

Canaanite: A member of one of the ancient kingdoms inhabiting the land of Canaan (Israel).

Chag HaMatzos (Hebrew, "Festival of Matzos"): The name of Passover as identified in the Torah.

Chagiga: A sacrifice brought in Temple times on the occasions of the three Festivals.

Charoses: A mixture of wine, apples and nuts eaten on Passover, the consistency of which should resemble mortar, symbolic of the verse *"... the Egyptians embittered their lives with hard labor, with mortar and bricks...". (Exodus I:14)*

Chaye Odom: Codifier of Jewish law in Lithuania in the late 18th - early 19th Century.

Chazeres: Romaine lettuce.

Chometz (Hebrew, "leavening"): Grain products which have (halachically) fermented. Leavening agents and leavened products are subject to rules prohibiting their use and possession during Passover.

Chometz U'Matzoh: (Hebrew, "leavening and matzoh").

Commandments: A reference to the 613 Biblical laws (mitzvos) of the Torah and all rabbinic decrees. Laws are to be differentiated from customs (minhagim).

Covenant Between the Halves: The most famous biblical covenant between God and Abraham (2018 from Creation: 1743 B.C.E.). Explained fully in this Haggadah commentary.

Creation: The original formation of the universe by God, ex nihilo, as described in Genesis, taking place in the year 3761 B.C.E.

Daily Prayer Service: A Jew is obligated to pray three times daily: in the morning, afternoon and evening. The text comprising these prayers and the laws associated with them constitute the daily prayer service.

Deuteronomy: The fifth of the Five Books of Moses. Literally the "second law" from the Greek "deuteros," second, and "nomos," law, in which the commandments are reviewed.

Diaspora: Areas of the world in which Jews were disperesed after their exile from the land of Israel.

Divine Presence: Jewish tradition teaches that God is everywhere. There are specific times and places where His presence is more discernible, such as during worship, Torah study and in the Holy Temple. (See Shechinah.)

Elijah (Hebrew, "Eliyahu"): Jewish prophet described by the Bible as having gone up to heaven and not dying. He is often referred to in Jewish literature as the promised precursor to the Messiah. According to tradition, Eliyahu will settle all controversies and disputes in Jewish law in the Messianic Age.

Esau: Older twin son of Isaac and Rebecca (the second patriarch and matriarch), and older brother of Jacob, known for his murderousness. (2108-2255 from Creation; (1653-1506 B.C.E.)

Exodus: The second book of the Torah, which tells of the formation of Israel as a people. It describes the oppressive slavery in Egypt and the miraculous liberation of the Israelites.

Gaon: Title applied to heads of the two major Babylonian academies at Sura and Pumbedisa. Thereafter the title has been used to describe any outstanding Talmudic scholar.

Genesis: From the Greek word meaning birth, a reference to the creation of the world through God's will. Also refers to the first of the Five Books of Moses, which describes the creation of the universe.

Girgashite: A member of the ancient kingdom of Girgash in the land of Canaan (Israel).

HaMotzi: (Hebrew, "who brings forth" [bread from the earth]): The blessing made prior to the eating of a meal with bread.

Haftorah (Hebrew, "conclusion"): A section from the Prophets recited after the reading of the Torah portion on the Sabbath and Festivals.

Haggadah: The traditional text used to conduct the Passover night service.

Halacha: The entire body of Torah law.

Hallel (Hebrew, "praise"): Psalms 113-118 which are recited on Rosh Chodesh (the new month) and the Festivals.

Hashem (Hebrew, "the name"): A reference to God.

Hatov v'HaMeitiv: The fourth blessing in Grace After Meals, composed after the miracle in Betar.

Hillel: Great sage of the Talmud.

Hittite: A member of an ancient kingdom in the land of Canaan (Israel).

Holy Temple: The sanctuary in Jerusalem on Mount Moriah. Two were built in ancient times, the first by King Solomon, the second by Ezra the Scribe.

Ikor: Hebrew, for "primary", or "most important".

Isaac: Abraham's son and the second of the patriarchs, (2048-2228, from Creation; 1713-1533 B.C.E.).

Israelite: Descendants of the Patriarchs; a Jew.

Jacob: Younger of the twin sons born to Isaac and Rebecca; his sons became the twelve tribes of Israel (2108-2255 from Creation; 1653-1506 B.C.E.).

Joseph: Jacob's eleventh son and the matriarch Rachel's firstborn. Sold by his brothers, after a fraternal dispute, to a band of Ishmaelites. After being brought to Egypt he rose from slave to viceroy. Following a reconciliation with his brothers, he requested that the entire family, including his father Jacob, come to Egypt (2199-2309 from Creation; 1562-1452 B.C.E.).

Judges: The book of Judges, deriving its name from its Hebrew equivalent - *shoftim*. For a period of 230 years twelve judges led the Jews, beginning with the death of Joshua and continuing until the coronation of King Saul. Their lives and times are described throughout the book's 21 chapters.

K'rias Sh'ma (Hebrew, "reciting" - "hear"): Hear O Israel - referring to the chief affirmation of faith declared by Jews twice daily, consisting of three paragraphs from the Torah. The first sentence consists of six words that proclaim the Oneness of the Almighty.

Kabbala: The term kabbala denotes "received tradition", and is used to describe the mystical teachings of Judaism.

Kadesh: The name of the Haggadah section containing Kiddush.

Kadmonite: A member of an ancient kingdom in the land of Canaan (Israel).

Kareis (Hebrew, "cut off"): The Divine punishment of excision from the Jewish community.

Kiddush (Hebrew, "sanctification"): Before the evening and morning meals on the Sabbath and Festivals, Kiddush is recited over wine.

Kings of Israel: The Jewish rulers of the kingdoms of Judah and Israel. This period in Jewish history began with the anointment of King Saul by the prophet

Samuel and ended with the destruction of the first Temple. We have been assured prophetically that one of King David's descendants will again rule as the Messiah.

Kohanim (Hebrew, "priest"): Descendants of Aaron who performed the Temple service in Jerusalem.

Laban: Older brother of the matriarch Rebecca, noted in the Bible for his scheming and deceit.

Land of Israel: The geographic area, whose boundaries are specified in the Bible, promised by God to Abraham and his descendants.

Lechem Oni: Hebrew appelation ("Bread of Affliction") used to describe Matzoh.

Leviticus: The third of the Five Books of Moses, containing the laws and regulations relating to priests and Levites.

Luzzato, Moshe Chaim: (b. 1707 Italy - d. 1746 Israel) Brilliant sage and saint who is best known for his ethical work, *Mesilas Yesharim*. Also known as *Ramchal*.

Magen Avraham: Rabbi Avraham Gombiner b. 1634 - d. Kalish, Poland, 1682, great commentator on the Code of Jewish Law.

Maggid: (Hebrew, "tell") The section of the Passover night seder service through which we fulfill the commandment of recounting the story of the Exodus.

Maharil: Rabbi Yaakov Moelin, b. Mainz, Germany 1365 - d. Worms, Germany 1427, one the most widely accepted medieval codifiers of Jewish law.

Maimonides: b. 1135 Spain - 1204 Egypt, preeminent codifier of Jewish law principally via his monumental work, *Mishneh Torah*. Also referred to as *Rambam*.

Malbim: Rabbi Meir Leib ben Yechiel Michel (1809-1879), great Biblical commentator from Romania.

Manna: The miraculous food which literally rained from heaven and sustained the Israelites during their 40 years in the desert following their exodus from Egypt.

Marror: Any one of five bitter herbs mentioned in the Talmud and eaten at the Passover seder in fulfillment of the commandment.

Matriarchs: The four mothers of the Jewish people: Sarah, Rebecca, Rachel and Leah.

Matzoh (Hebrew, "unleavened bread"): Dough baked before it has a chance to ferment and rise. The Torah commands us to eat matzo on Passover. Jewish law dictates that the entire process of making the matzos used on Passover take no longer than eighteen minutes.

Mechiltah: Earliest known commentary on the Book of Exodus.

Meiri: Great medieval Talmudic commentator from Provence (1249-1306).

MeTargeim: Commentator who translated the Old French words found in *Rashi* and *Tosafos*.

Midrash: The body of oral law which analyzes and expounds the meaning and interpretation of verses in the Torah, Prophets and Writings.

Minchas Chinuch: 19th Century commentary on the Sefer HaChinuch by Rabbi Joseph ben Moshe Babad (1800-1874).

Mishnah Berurah: Codification of Jewish law by Rabbi Yisroel Meir Kagan (the "Chofetz Chaim"), 1838-1933.

Mishnah: Codification of oral law redacted by Rabbi Judah The Prince, circa 200 CE.

Mitzvah pl. mitzvos (Hebrew, "commandment/s"):   Obligation, of either Biblical or rabbinic origin.

Moses: Son of Amram and Yocheved, born in the seventh generation from Abraham. The greatest Jewish leader, he was chosen by God to lead the Jews from Egypt and transmit the Torah to them. (2368-2488 from Creation; 1393-1273 B.C.E.).

Mount Sinai: The mountain on which the Torah was given.

Nachor: Brother of Abraham.

Nissan: First month of the Jewish year, the month in which Passover is observed

Numbers: The fourth of the Five Books of Moses, in which a census of the Jewish people was taken.

Orech Chaim O.C.(see Tur, Shulchan Aruch): Section of Jewish Law that considers daily rituals.

P'shat: Hebrew for "plain sense", the straightforward interpretation.

Parsha: Hebrew for "chapter", applied particularly to chapters of the Torah.

Parshas B'chukosai: Final section in the Book of Leviticus.

Pas Habo'ah b'Kissnin: Bread-like foods so processed (e.g. sweetened or made falt and crisp) that they are no longer eligible for the blessing of HaMotzi.

Pascal lamb: The sacrifice brought in the afternoon before Passover and eaten at the Seder. It can only be offered when the Holy Temple in Jerusalem stands.

Patriarchs (Hebrew word "Avos"): The three forefathers who laid the foundations of Israel as described in the Bible: Abraham, Isaac and Jacob.

Perezite: A member of an ancient kingdom in the land of Canaan (Israel).

Pharaoh: Ruler of Egypt.

Rabban Gamliel: Great Talmudic sage.

Rabbis: The transmitters of the tradition from Sinai.

Rabeinu Yerucham : Great medieval Talmudic scholar, b. France 1280 - d. Spain 1350.

Rashi: (Rabbi Shlomo Yitzchaki b. France 1040 - d. Troyes 1105) perhaps the greatest commentator on the Bible and Talmud renowned for his clear and terse writing. His exposition on the Chumash is the most popular and widely used.

Rava: Great Talmudic sage.

Rephaim: A member of an ancient Kingdom in the land of Canaan (Israel).

Ritva: Great commentator on the Talmud and halachist, Seville, Spain circa 1320.

Rosh Chodesh: (Hebrew, new moon) The new moon marking the beginning of each Hebrew month.

Sabbath: Seventh day of the week. The day following the six day of Creation, on which God rested. Sabbath observance is one of the cornerstones of the Jewish faith.

Sages of the Talmud: Referring to the sages mentioned in the Mishnah or Talmud.

Sanhedrin HaGadol (Hebrew, "great court"): The Supreme Court of Jewish law consisted of 71 members whose function was to interpret Biblical laws (halachos). The lesser courts (Sanhedrin Ketana) consisted of 23 members, tried capital cases, a court of three judged civil matters.

Seder: (Hebrew, order, arrangement) on Passover night the seder service commemorates the Exodus of the Jewish people from Egypt.

Sefer HaChinuch: Medieval Jewish work on the commandments (13th Century Spain).

Seraph: Form of Angel. The Seraph ranks high in the hierarchy of Angels.

Sh'La HaKadosh: Rabbi Yeshayah Horowitz, b. Prague, Bohemia circa 1560 - d. Tiberias, Israel 1630, great kabbalist and halachist.

Shechinah: The Divine Presence, manifested in this world.

Shulchan Aruch: (Hebrew, "prepared table") by Rabbi Joseph Karo (b. 1488 -

d. 1575) codification of the observances of traditional Judaism, it is generally printed together with the glosses of Rabbi Moses Isserles (b. 1525 - d. 1572) known as the Ramah. The arrangement of the Shulchan Aruch consists of four parts: 1) Orech Chayim - (O.C.) concerning behavior in the home and synagogue; 2) Yoreh Deah - laws regarding the forbidden and permitted; 3) Even HaEzer - marriage and family matters; 4) Chosen Mishpat - civil laws.

Song of Songs: A book in the Writings, written by King Solomon. According to our sages, a parable for the relationship between God and his beloved Jewish nation. Referred to by the Talmud as the "Holy of Holies".

Succos (Hebrew, "huts"): Festival commemorating the protection the Almighty afforded the Jews during their wanderings in the wilderness.

Tahara (Hebrew, "purity"): Referring to ritual purity.

Talis: A large talis is a four-cornered, fringed garment worn for morning prayers. A small talis is worn throughout the day.

Talmud ic/ist: An elaboration of the oral law found in the Mishnah. The term is used synonymously with Gemara.

Tanaa pl. im (Aramaic, "to teach"): applied to the sages mentioned in the Mishnah. Typical of the Tanaaim are the five rabbis mentioned in the Passover Haggadah discussing the Exodus: Rabbis Eliezer, Yehoshua, Elazar ben Azaryah, Akiva and Tarfon.

Taz: Rabbi David HaLevi, b. Ludmir, Poland 1586 - d. Lemberg (Lvov), Poland 1667, preeminent commentator on the Shulchan Aruch.

Temple: The Holy Temple in Jerusalem. The first Temple was built by King Solomon and stood for 410 years (2928 to 3338). The second temple was built by Ezra and Nechemia and stood for 420 years (3408 to 3828).

Terach: Father of Abraham.

Terumah: The portion of the harvest given to the priests.

Torah: Refers to the Five Books of Moses, both the written text and the oral tradition. The five books of the Torah are: Genesis (בראשית), Exodus (שמות), Leviticus (ויקרא), Numbers (במדבר) and Deuteronomy (דברים). The Torah scroll contains all five books of the Torah.

Toras Kohanim: Midrashic interpretation of Leviticus.

Tosafos: One of the preeminent *Talmudic* commentaries composed by various scholarly schools of Germany and France in the 12th through 14th centuries.

Tractate: A book of the Talmud.

Tractate Berachos: The first tractate of the Talmud, which discusses blessings and the Prayer service.

Tractate Pesachim: The tractate of the Talmud which discusses all the laws of Passover.

Tractate Sanhedrin: The tractate of the Talmud which discusses the Jewish court system.

Tumah (Hebrew "defilement"): Referring to ritual defilement.

Ur Casdim: Birthplace of Abraham, in what is now Iraq.

Writings: Third section of the Bible containing: Psalms, Proverbs, Job, the Five Megilloth, Daniel, Ezra, Nehemiah, Chronicles I and II.

Yarmulke: A Yiddish term for "skullcap".

Yebusite: A member of an ancient kingdom in the land of Canaan (Israel).

Yechaveh Daas: Responsa by Rabbi Ovadiah Yosef, former Sephardic Chief Rabbi of Israel.

Yerek: (Hebrew, "vegetable").

Yom Tov /pl. im: (Hebrew, good day): Applies to the Jewish festivals (Passover, Shavuous, Rosh HaShana, Yom Kippur, Succos, Shemini Atzeres) which are dedicated to joy. "You shall rejoice at your festival together with your son and daughter, your male and female servants, as well as the stranger, the orphan and the widow." *Deuteronomy XVI:14*)

Z'chira (Hebrew, "remembering"): refers to the daily obligation to remember the Exodus.

Z'man Cheiruseinu (Hebrew, "Time of our Freedom"): A reference to Passover.

About the Illustrator:

Jeremy Rosenstein is a brilliant young artist raised in Minneapolis. He graduated from the University of Wisconsin at Madison and Parsons School of Design. Jeremy lives in New York City and does freelance work.

"Working on a Haggadah was a moving experience for me, indeed a labor of love. I was able to utilize some of my warmest and fondest childhood memories of our family seder as inspiration for the drawings. I hope my illustrations will inspire the reader and enhance their Passover seder."

A List of the Illustrations:

•　The Cover introduces figures at a traditional seder table from various periods, representing an historical link of Jews throughout the ages.

In the upper left corner and going clockwise, a 16th century Italian Jew wears a "Jew's hat", the contemporary Jew wears glasses, the ancient Jew in embroidered clothing, the streimel of the chassid, an Ethiopian Falasha and a Moroccan Jew in a red Fez.

•　The seder plate and the correct placement of the various symbolic foods. Page 30

•　"Sanctification over wine" Page 34

•　Ritual washing of the hands. Page 40

•　The karpas vegetable dipped in salt water. Page 43

•　The breaking of the middle matzoh. Page 45

•　"Why is this night different". A depiction of the Haggadah's medium of question and answer (שואל ומשיב); the child asks the parent and in turn, the parent answers. Page 51

•　"We were slaves to Pharoah in Egypt". Page 55

•　"They spent the entire night recounting the story of the Exodus". The five rabbis who discussed the Exodus all night in Bnei Brak are shown in animated conversation. Page 59

Note: If the faces seem difficult to understand, the illustrator has used a technique where the face is presented as both a profile and frontal view. The reader will be helped to see this by alternately covering each half of the face.

•　"The *Torah* speaks of four types of children". Our Haggadah's commentary presents the four sons as four aspects of every child's personality, thus the four sons are illustrated as four faces on one child. Page 65

•　"Jacob and his sons went down to Egypt". The central figure is our forefather Jacob as he and his descendants go down to Egypt. Page 81

•　"Many have risen up against us to destroy us in each and every generation but the Holy One, blessed is He, saves us from their hand". Note the various threatening symbols: the spread eagle in the upper right (depicting the insignia of the Roman legions and more recently, the Nazis), a burning pyre and barbed wire. Each represents the many enemies who sought to destroy us, but the

Almighty has always saved us. Page 86

•   "The Egyptians did evil to us". The illustration is of Pharoah who conspired against the Jews in order to subjugate them. Page 90

•   "We cried out to the Almighty, God of our fathers". Throughout history, Jews have raised up their arms and cried out to their Father in Heaven Who answers their prayers. Page 92

•   The ten plagues are divided on the pages according to Rabbi Yehudah's abbreviations.

    • Blood: all the waters in Egypt turned to blood.

    • Frogs: the Midrash states that from one giant frog came forth a multitude of others.

    • Vermin: – Page 104

    • Wild Beasts

    • Pestilence (afflicted only animals)

    • Boils – Page 105

    • Hail

    • Locust

    • Darkness

    • Slaying of the Firstborn – Page 106

•   "He split the Red Sea for us". The Israelites walking through the Red Sea dry shod. Page 110

•   The Almighty commanded Moses to raise his staff and split the sea. Page 111

•   "You shall tell your son on that day". In each generation the parent is required to transmit to the next generation the understanding that we are the Almighty's nation, chosen to keep His holy Torah. Page 125

•   "Therefore it is our duty to thank, praise and laud...". We raise our wine cups until after the conclusion of the Asher G'alanu blessing. Page 129

•   We dip the bitter herb in charoses. Page 145

•   The Hillel sandwich Page 147

•   The festive meal is eaten. Page 149

•   The child brings the afikomen to the table in anticipation of the promised reward that will accompany its return. Page 151

•   "Next year in Jerusalem". This is the eternal hope of every Jew. The Almighty will bring about the final redemption of the Jewish people and we will live in peace and security, able to serve the Almighty with the Temple rebuilt in Jerusalem. Page 182